T0195903

S. D. MICHAEL

THE BEAUTY
of my
SHADOW

A Story of Strength

authorHOUSE®

AuthorHouse™ LLC
1663 Liberty Drive
Bloomington, IN 47403
www.authorhouse.com
Phone: 1-800-839-8640

Cover design: Andi Aspa

AUTHOR'S NOTE: In order to maintain their anonymity in some instances I have changed the names of individuals. I may also have changed some identifying characteristics and details. I have recreated events and conversations from my memories based on my own experience and opinion of those memories. It is in no way a present-time assessment of the character of those mentioned.

Published by AuthorHouse 10/08/2014

ISBN: 978-1-4969-4514-3 (sc)

Library of Congress Control Number: 2014917899

This book is printed on acid-free paper.

Carry out a random act of kindness, with no expectation of reward, safe in the knowledge that one day someone might do the same for you.

—Princess Diana (1961-1997)

Contents

The Soundtrack:
A Note from the Author

I would never have opened up to talk about a challenging experience in my life unless I could do so in a way that would help others. I decided to have a pianist perform and created the CD *Songs for Everyone* to help raise money for the advancement of education.[1] The music CD can be listened to from the first page as a soundtrack with my memoir. The tempo of the music was chosen for relaxation and you will learn in my story why. The CD is being sold by An Aid to Help Foundation, my family's non-profit. We hope the money we raise by sharing my story will provide encouragement and resources to educators, students, parents and families on ways to learn or teach others to make responsible choices in life. A percentage of author royalties from the sale of this book are donated to charity. See inside for details. Donated royalties are net of commissions. If you feel inspired to donate to our non-profit you can do so at www.anaid.org.

I decided to have the graphic designer use the sheet music of one of the songs from the CD for the cover of this book, so that it fits in with the music theme. It is the classical piece from 1888 called "Gymnopédie No. 1" by French composer and pianist Erik Satie. On the cover, it is angled downwards, almost as if to encourage the reader to turn the page and draw you into my journey.

This music helped me heal and you will learn about this in my memoir. I hope it can help you as well in your own life, if for nothing more than to listen to once and enjoy.

You may listen to samples and purchase a copy of the CD at www.anaid.org. The CD will be available as well in mp3 format and links to where it can be purchased are on the website. Or you may also purchase a copy of the CD by Mail. Send a cheque or money order of $20 in Canadian or US dollars to the address below. Please make cheques payable to An Aid to Help Foundation. Do not send cash or gifts.

Thank you for your support.

"Samantha writes simply and compellingly, drawing you into her story until you are more participant than observer. Her transformation from car accident victim and head injury patient to spiritual being is moving, at times shocking and a testament to the healing power of belief. Coupled with the moving "soundtrack" that she has prepared, the book becomes so much more than a story of sickness and recovery—it becomes an instrument of healing in itself."

—Marc Engfield, MD

www.drengfield.com

An Aid to Help Foundation
5-499 Terry Fox Drive
P.O. Box 91017
Kanata, Ontario
K2T 1H7 CANADA
info@anaid.org

Foreword

It was just after eleven o'clock on August 20, 1991. I had finished my morning patients and was listening to my telephone messages. Suddenly I heard my sister-in-law's anxious voice telling me that my eighteen-year-old niece had been in a serious car accident and was being transferred via helicopter from cottage country to Sunnybrook Hospital, in Toronto. My brother's family rarely phoned me, especially at 6:30 in the morning. My niece must have been severely injured to require transfer to a big hospital.

My office was located close to the hospital where she had been taken. I had three more patients booked that afternoon for psychotherapy. I was worried and had to see for myself what was going on. I needed to support my family so I quickly cancelled my appointments. I would have been totally preoccupied and of no help to any of my patients.

I called the hospital and learned that my niece had been admitted to the surgical intensive care unit (ICU). I eventually got through to one of the attending physicians to be told that she had a severe closed-head injury, was unconscious, unresponsive to stimuli, had significant oedema (swelling) and was going into surgery for repair of multiple facial cuts, fractures to bones all over her head, including the orbits that harbour the eyes and for the insertion of a "Richmond bolt", something I had never heard of before.

In such situations it helps to be in the medical field, although sometimes it is a drawback because, as physicians, we are too aware of possible complications, poor prognosis, botched surgeries and more.

When I saw my niece in the hospital, my heart sank. Here was this beautiful young woman comatose in a hospital bed, her body tanned and seemingly totally intact. Then my eyes rested on her head and face and tears welled up. What a horrible sight! Her features were completely distorted from excessive soft tissue swelling. I saw numerous facial abrasions, with lots of stitches down her right cheek and chin as well as on her forehead and eyelid. Her right ear was bruised and a metal bolt had been inserted on the right side, at the top of her head to monitor intracranial pressure. She was on a respirator, had a catheter in her bladder, a feeding tube in her nose and an intravenous (IV) in her arm. Cerebrospinal fluid was leaking from her nose and right ear. Her pupils were not reactive to light and slightly unequal and this was a worrisome sign.

What a severe accident this must have been. How did this happen? She had her whole life ahead of her and was about to go to university in a couple of weeks. What will the future hold for her?

~

In this book, Samantha recounts the story of her courageous journey of recovery. It has been a long, arduous path with many ups and downs towards the eventual adjustment to living with the deficits that almost always remain with individuals who suffer traumatic injuries of such magnitude.

Her journey has also had a significant, prolonged impact on all our family members. Her accident and its aftermath touched everyone in different ways for which each of us used various coping skills. My brother, Samantha's dad, was most affected and we had many long-distance calls during this time. My sister-in-law handled it with her usual calm demeanour and positive attitude, although on occasion she too had serious down times. As for me, at the time of the accident, I started a notebook and recorded events in a regular manner with details about progress and set-backs. I would read her hospital charts, talk with the doctors frequently and did my best to help interpret the specialists' lingo for my family.

I have been truly amazed at Samantha's strength, creativity, perseverance, industry and resilience. What she has achieved in regaining her independence and enhancing her desire to help others in meaningful ways is astonishing. She is an example to all who are recovering from trauma, illness or injuries—or simply those who are interested in improving their lives. My niece pulled through amazingly well thanks to her own strength of will as well as having excellent professional assistance. To this day, I am incredibly proud of her and extremely grateful that we did not lose her.

Gisele Microys, MD
Ottawa, Ontario

1
The Party

The loud voices at the front door penetrate the noise of the house party. It is after midnight and Sofia and Jason are arguing. As the host of this party in 2008, I am concerned and stand with the guests who have gathered to watch them fight.

Sofia's voice slurs as she demands that Jason gives her the car keys. They were at one time boyfriend and girlfriend, so they know each other well.

"Try to stop me," Sofia says.

Jason's jaw tightens.

"Spend the night here with Samantha or get a sober ride home with us," he says.

Sofia stumbles towards him. Her long brown hair flies everywhere while she clumsily attempts to grab for the keys. Jason pulls his hand back, causing her to fall against the door. She shows a devilish smile while squinting her dark brown eyes at him.

"Listen asshole," she says. "Give me my fucking keys!"

I met Sofia and Jason at a local Latin and ballroom dance school where I have been taking lessons for the past few years. This is the first time we have socialized outside the studio. I look at the people watching the fight and see Sofia's roommate, Julie, who came with her to the party.

"What's going on?" I ask.

"Jason is trying to stop her from taking off in her car. She behaves this way a lot when she drinks." Julie pauses, looks at her friend and then says, "She's a stubborn drunk."

"On the invite, I told her she could sleep here if she needed to," I say.

Julie shakes her head, showing a mixed expression of concern and objection. "We brought two cars for this reason. We thought one of us has a ride home and the other can stay," she says. "Now she wants to go home. Sometimes she's unstoppable when she gets like this but she has never hurt anyone."

"She easily could though," I say. I am surprised to hear her say what she just did.

At this point, Sofia, who is in her thirties and well built, shoves Jason in another grab for her keys. I decide to intervene.

"Sofia, you are not getting the keys," I say. "Someone will take you home but you're not driving."

"Don't worry, she won't be getting behind the wheel," Jason assures me.

Sofia shoves him again. He stands, unmoveable in front of the door. She reaches behind him, laughing as he stops each try. The two of them have obviously played this game before.

A commercial on television comes to mind where a guy says to a drunk something like, "Hey buddy, give me your keys". Then the drunk passively hands the keys over. But that is an advertisement, not real life. Sofia is nowhere near as compliant.

"What do you want me to do, Jason?" I ask.

When Sofia realizes Jason and I are talking about her, she becomes even more agitated.

"You're both stupid," she says loudly, reaching for the keys again. Frustrated that she cannot get them, she whips her head around to stare right at me. Anger flaming in her eyes, she stiffens her fist and arm.

"You give me the fucking keys. Now!" she yells as her eyes dart back and forth from my eyes to my right cheek. "Or else I'm going to hit you both in the fucking head!"

Her eyes are glued to my cheek. I know she is checking out my facial scar. I am thirty-five years old now but the accident that left me with this scar when I was a teenager is still fresh in my mind. Instinctively, my fingertips brush the scar's smooth, lumpy bumps. I step back. Jason notices my reaction and seems to want to protect me.

"I'll handle her," he says to me. "She won't hurt you."

The threat of getting punched in the head startles me and I go sit on the stairs. I am no longer focused on Sofia. What is happening for me emotionally now has my attention. I know anger. I know frustration. But this is different. This is life and death.

"When I was eighteen," I say to no one in particular, "a drunk driver screwed up the life I had. I'm lucky to be alive. I suffered a terrible head injury. Sofia's too drunk to care if she hurts others. She wants to get home, whatever the cost. The twenty-one-year-old, who almost killed me, said she couldn't understand why she wasn't more responsible with our lives the night I was hurt."

I never talk about this anymore. I have tried to forget what happened but it is hard. I will always remember the injury and the terrible aftermath. The endless rehabilitation I needed because of the permanent damage inflicted on my body and mind was a nightmare. This drunken woman's threat just now, to punch me in the head, touched a tender nerve and I feel a door inside me opening to some long buried memories.

"Someone who is about to behave irresponsibly is hard to stop or else I wouldn't have gotten cut up as badly as I did," I say. "I don't even need to get in a car with Sofia to feel threatened."

A sudden impulse has me get up and go to my den. As I walk, my breath is rapid, with a pounding heart. My eyes stay glued to Sofia, with every step I take. I want to tell her off because she could hurt someone but I stop myself. I have never felt this way before.

In the dark room, I reach for something on a bookshelf. It is a small picture frame I had moved for the party. I do not know why I moved it. I seem to do this a lot with this frame. It holds a memory that makes me unhappy sometimes. I hold the object close to me as I walk back to the stairs, so that nobody can see what it is. At the door, Jason and Sofia are still fighting. Sitting down, I look sentimentally at what I hold in my lap.

"In the children's rehabilitation hospital after that drunk driver almost killed me, one of the nicest people visited me. She later died in a car accident that happened for a few reasons," I say to my friend from dance sitting beside me. "Drunk driving—was the biggest one."

My eyes shoot to the door. I glare at Sofia and am quiet for a moment.

"This signature is Princess Diana's. When I met her, she signed a Recovery Book I kept for rehabilitation. This is the only thing I have left of that book. Her accident, which happened six years after I met her, was similar to mine in some ways."

The conversation on the stairs comes to an abrupt end. I do not want to say anything more. The argument at the front door gets louder. As I hold the piece of my Recovery Book I cannot take my eyes off the pen inscribed name—*Diana*.[2]

At that time I thought it was only for my mom. She held onto it up until Princess Diana died. After her death in 1997, I realized it was important to me to have it back and I did not know why. Sofia's attempt at wanting to drink and drive now triggered this memory for me. Sure there were more factors involved but ultimately it was a drunk driver that destroyed Princess Diana's life.

After I was hurt, some of the rehabilitation professionals helping encouraged me to keep a Recovery Book. In this book, people wrote their best wishes. It was meant as support, to assist me in coping with what had happened to me as a result of the injuries. I had to adjust to having my life being consumed by my medical needs. The rehabilitation from that car accident was like a job, where I had a schedule to keep. This was necessary because of how severely hurt I had been.

As I sit on the stairs, my need to share my experience tonight surprises me. I do not understand why I opened up about it. It is unusual for me to talk about what I went through.

I am immersed in my thoughts. Suddenly, the argument stops and I look up to the door. Sofia and Jason are now talking privately. Jason glances over and makes eye contact with me. He then walks towards me. I quickly turn my Recovery Book upside down on my lap, so he cannot see what I am holding.

"I'm driving her home," he says, sounding relieved.

"Thank you for stopping her," I say.

He gives me a sympathetic smile as he leaves. Julie and another friend grab a ride downtown with them as well. Sofia's car stays parked on the street.

Standing up, I go to the den and gently lay Princess Diana's framed signature, face down, again on the bookshelf. Behind me I can hear the dance music from the party. Around thirty guests came tonight. My home's open layout makes it easy to spread out and mingle. Joining them, I do not talk with anyone about the fight that just happened at the door. The majority of guests did not even notice. Everyone seems to be having a good time.

Phil, Heather's boyfriend, tries to get me to dance. I brush him off with a smile. I am having a hard time taking my mind off Sofia's threat to hit me in the head. To dance will not help me.

"I'll watch you guys," I say.

"But it's your party!" Phil says.

I am no longer in a good mood. I did not drink anything tonight. A glass of wine would probably make me forget what just happened but I do not want anything.

2
A Morning Visitor

At ten in the morning the doorbell rings. This surprises me on a weekend, especially after last night's late party. In my pyjamas, I open the door. Sofia is standing on the porch with a huge smile on her face.

"Jason dropped me off to get my car," she says.

She walks in my house, without me asking her to enter. My dog, Mya, a two-year-old beagle, greets her with excitement.[3]

Her tail wags non-stop and she submissively rolls over to have her stomach rubbed by Sofia. At a loss what to say to Sofia, I sit down on the stairs. Finally, Mya's greeting comes to an end.

Sofia starts to laugh as she talks about her behaviour the night before. I interrupt her.

"Are you hung over?"

"No. I never get hangovers," she says proudly.

Does she expect me to applaud her for this? I note that she is not apologizing for threatening to hit me in the head. She probably does not remember. The silence between us could be cut with a knife.

"Sofia," I say. "I have a scar."

This morning, I am not wearing any cover-up make-up as I normally do and the red marks on my face are definitely visible.

"I always wanted to ask you how you got it!" she says, almost playfully.

My dark brown eyes pierce through her. I pause for a moment, to remember how she looked at it last night.

"As a teenager, a drunk driver caused an accident in which I was almost killed. After one month in the hospital, I walked out with this," I say, pointing to my right cheek.

Almost as if to remind myself that I really have a scar, a part of me wants to look now at my face in a mirror. Sofia's eyes widen as she looks at my scar.

"Oh wow," she says. "I've always been curious about what happened to you."

I pause, thinking of what to say next.

"I had to be taken by helicopter to a Toronto hospital because of how badly hurt I was. I needed specialized care," I say.

As I imagine the helicopter ride, I shudder as my breath and heart rate speed up. The sound or thought of one makes me anxious still to this day. Even though, at the time I was unconscious, my body still remembers the pain I had been in.

"By the time they got me to the hospital, I was in a coma. X-rays showed my eye sockets were completely smashed. I also had bones broken through the bridge of my nose, along with my cheekbones, chin and jaw."

Sofia stares at me with her mouth open as I point to all the injuries, starting with my eyes and then naming one by one the bones which had been broken.

"Oh my goodness," she says.

She seems to think I am done with my list of injuries. But I am not.

"Bones got cracked from my temple through my ear and the base of my skull," I say. "My facial cuts were superficial in comparison. From the neck up I had been injured badly."

Sofia starts to ask questions about what happened to me but I stop the conversation from sharing more detail. My purpose for telling her about my injury is not to get her sympathy. I want my experience somehow to change her and snap her out of ever again drinking and driving like she wanted to do last night.

"I still need to undergo treatment to this day and this will never stop," I say. "Sure, I rebuilt myself a new life but this took many years of hard work. I will always have problems I did not experience before. I've learned the hard way how fragile my mind and body are. Everything from my concentration to memory was damaged from the head injury. I don't talk about this to people because those injuries are invisible compared to my scar. But I think you should know what happened to me."

Sofia is quiet. Unable to look me in the eye, she seems to understand how upset I am.

"This is my scar without make-up on," I say pausing. I let her again see the marks on my cheek. This time she does not seem as comfortable to look at it. "To put this behind me was hard. Over the last decade, I've seen that driver many times since then. She works on TV and every time I see Deborah, I'm reminded of what happened. It's like seeing a ghost. I even changed my name from Doris to Samantha, to try to move on from the bad memories."

It is awkward for me to say my old name.

"Oh my goodness, are you serious?" she asks.

I am hoping Sofia will be able to relate to my story. I sense however that I need to be more straightforward.

"A criminal record becomes a permanent part of your life," I say. "I'm not sure if the driver who hurt me got a pardon for her conviction. At the time, the police charged Deborah with impaired driving causing bodily harm. She never gave any excuses for her behaviour other than alcohol. There were no raccoons sneaking out or bad brakes—only the inability to drive because of her being drunk. She had over double the limit of booze in her body."

I stare into Sofia's eyes, raising my voice as I say, "If you'd driven home last night, you could've hurt someone the same way I was or even killed somebody."

As I say this, I am reminded of Princess Diana again. To talk with Sofia about the princess's death would definitely help me make my point but I do not want to share this personal memory with her.

Sofia takes a deep breath. "You're right," she says, slowly shaking her head. "What you told me changes everything."

I believe she is saying this to end our conversation—and it does. On her way out, she promises to stop herself from driving drunk in the future. She closes the door behind her and I stay seated on the staircase. I shake my head in disbelief that she thinks she can change her behaviour so easily. It is ridiculous. She is fooling herself.

Over the years, I stopped talking about my head injury and facial scar, even to myself. It is hard to admit to anyone that I had brain damage. I struggled many times trying to explain my injury. It was almost as if I had to give proof of how I was hurt. I cannot even count the number of times I heard, "oh, everyone has that problem", when I would tell others about the challenges I faced in recovery. I never, however, had problems like the ones from the head injury before in my life.

I avoided talking about the accident, as well, partly to protect Deborah and her family. I copied the behaviour of those people in my life who did not want to hear about it. I thought they all deserved to get on with their lives. I sensed that the memory of the accident was a taboo subject for many. Sure, I wish I could have closed the door so easily but, to this day, the reminders for me are still constant. I tried to bury the story inside myself.

This weekend all the emotional guards I built to protect myself seem to be melting. I thought I had blocked those memories. I am surprised I just shared my story.

Standing up, I lock the door and start to tidy the living room. I grab some dirty wine glasses left over from the party and take them to the kitchen. After setting them down on the counter, I let Mya outside. She runs around the lawn in the backyard, sniffing the grass, while I hook the retractable leash on the patio door-handle.

I love looking outside, to see how a large rock, about five feet high, gradually cascades down to meet the grass. There is a green forest behind it. This thick wall of nature borders my entire backyard.[4]

Today, the early sun is shining on new leaves growing with the warmth of spring. I am mesmerised by the beauty of it all. The change of season, from winter to spring, is especially lovely to witness.

This tranquil scene washes away my concern of what could have happened last night if Sofia had driven home drunk.

3
Mya the Beagle

S ince 2005, I lived in this house just outside Ottawa, Ontario. I share it with Mya and the house is perfect for us. I rescued my dog when she was six months old. There is quite a story about how I found her.

As a puppy, through an ad online, Mya was given away with all her toys and food, to a couple. The owner, a young woman, was going through a divorce and she needed to find her beagle a new home. After giving Mia away (pronounced Me-uh), as that was her initial name, she missed her a lot. Because she could not stop crying and had regrets, she called the adoptive couple to see if she could get her back. The couple refused to return her—and changed her name to Mya (pronounced My-uh), as if to give Mia a new identity.

Then, through an ad online, they turned around and sold Mya to me a few weeks later. They had more dogs in their home when I got her so I am sure they had fooled some other owners into trusting them as well. They even showed me and my friend a playful thing Mya does, when she is scratched a certain way, by thumping her leg.

"Aww," we all said in unison.

They did this to show us how cute she was and try to prove the close relationship they had with their puppy. Later, I learned most dogs will do this if scratched this way.

I figured out Mya's story by getting her vaccination record. The couple who sold her to me did not want to give me the phone number for the veterinarian and that seemed strange. My persistence paid off however and I finally got a copy of the document from the vet. I was surprised that the record said the dog's name was Mia, not Mya. A different owner was listed on it than the couple I had bought her from. So I called that number.

The woman who answered cried when she heard what had happened to the puppy she gave away. We decided to meet for coffee at a pet-friendly café. Upon sight and smell (for Mya), happiness was obvious between the two of them. The woman explained to me that dogs were not allowed as pets where she had moved to and this was why she had to find Mia a new home. She was happy to learn that I would be her owner, instead of the untrustworthy couple who had taken advantage of her generosity.

Afterward, I assertively wrote an email to the couple who sold her to me, on behalf of Mia/Mya and the previous owner, explaining how we found out what they did and that I was not given any of Mia's personal belongings—not even her original collar or the bag of food which had been given with her, worth over one hundred dollars. I wrote that they should be embarrassed of their behaviour and left it at that.

A lady at the Humane Society told me that this often happens to dog owners. I hope the public gains awareness of this problem, to help stop this crime. I realize however, that without Mya experiencing what she did I might not have found her.

It is amazing that Mya does not act like she is a victim. On Facebook she speaks openly about her "puppynapping", as she calls it.[5] She does not look back to the "bad days" because she has an amazing life now. She even responds well to all her various names of Mia and Mya—as well as Happy. I gave her Happy as a middle name. I wanted to call her this but my mom talked me out of it. So her full name now is Mya Mia Happy Michael. I changed my name too, from Doris Stephanie Michael to Samantha Doris Michael, so Mya and I have this in common.

4
A Forgotten Life

Later in the morning, while still cleaning from the party, I realize that I am trying to distract myself from my thoughts. I am worried that seeing Sofia around at the dance school is going to be stressful. I do not want to stop taking my regular Latin and ballroom dance lessons. Creative movement through dance is important to me. As Doris, I started studying jazz at a young age.

I am surprised and confused that I told Sofia so much about myself. I usually keep secret what I went through in 1991. I still remember what a struggle this was for me and my family to deal with.

~

It was the Thanksgiving weekend of 1993 at my parents' house. Mom and Dad still lived in the same home where my brother and I grew up in the country, just outside Oshawa, Ontario.

We sat and shuffled through family photos. Mom and Dad were trying to help me remember the life I had before getting hurt. They told me how easy a kid I had been to bring up, good-natured and cooperative. I remembered I always got high grades in school but the other stuff did not register.

What got me most is when Mom said, "You came out in life a natural leader."

Despite the examples she offered, I found it hard to understand who I was in their eyes. I seemed popular among my friends but had no clue why. This all had changed.

At first, there was sympathy from a lot of my friends but gradually, many started to ignore me. Why they no longer wanted to hang out with me after the head injury was beyond my understanding. I have always been the type of person who easily makes new friends but many of these new friendships would quickly dissolve into nothing.

I could recall bits and pieces of my previous life but the memories were vague and fragmented. To look at my life as Doris was like looking at a movie about a completely different person. My previous personality, the way I spoke and behaved before, had become a blur in my mind.

"Why are you showing me these pictures?" I asked. "I was the family reject. It's obvious. There are no good ones of me as Doris."

I shoved some of the photos aside. I did not believe what they were telling me. I was glad I got in that car accident which wrecked the life I had. I could not find anything good about the person I was before. It was for the best to have amnesia.

"We love you. Can't you tell?" Mom said as she picked up an album and showed me a few of her most cherished photos.

"No," I said, "all I see are great ones of my brother. Mine suck. I was not important. I look like a little boy with that haircut. Way to go, Mom."[6]

This reminded me of the Italian barber she used to take me to. I remembered, as he spoke to Mom, he would cut off all my hair without care or concern for what I wanted. I was not going to tell her that what we were doing triggered this memory because it would have made the whole painful "family exercise" of looking at photographs more drawn out.

Mom glanced at Dad for support.

"We took lots more photos of you but they are on slides," Dad said.

"Let's show them to her," Mom said.

Dad got up to set-up the slide projector downstairs. Mom reached for a few more pictures while we waited for him.

"In this photo, what do you think of your outfit?" she asked, smiling.

The picture showed me sitting on a couch wearing a red dress and a red leotard of a different shade.

"What a stupid outfit. Nothing matches. Why did you dress me in that?" I asked. Mom laughed.

"You dressed yourself," she said. "You would never let me choose what you would wear. As soon as you began to work part-time, you happily bought your own clothes—my independent daughter."

Mom gazed at the photo, then quickly put it aside and picked up another. After a few moments, she rubbed her eyes. She could not be crying. What a ridiculous walk down memory lane this was. Suddenly I needed a smoke. I was a regular smoker at the time.

On my way outside I said, "After we see the slides I want to go back to university today, instead of tomorrow. Can you ask Dad to drive me?"

She was quiet and looked away. A part of her wanted me to ask him myself. She began to pack up the pictures as I walked out of the room.

To learn about my past did not interest me. This was why I changed my first name as soon as I set foot on the downtown campus of the University of Toronto (U of T) in 1992. Cutting the pathetic remains of my life as Doris off was the best way to cope and create a new life. Then—Samantha was born.

I had not particularly liked the name Samantha before but I knew without a doubt that it was the perfect new name for me. I chose to keep Doris as a middle name only to make life easier for the physicians and lawyers, who happened to be invading my life. I would not let anyone in my personal life call me Doris anymore. And I grew angry with those who did. The few things I still could remember of my life when I was Doris felt strange.

I do remember that before the accident, as Doris, in the summer of 1991, I worked full-time at Eaton's department store. I had been there for most of high school working part-time as a switchboard operator. From what I remember, it was a great job in high school because as Doris, I often studied while I worked. I could do this because the workload fluctuated with how busy it was and our office was away from the public eye. That whole summer, when I was eighteen and as Doris, I worked hard to earn even more than my board and tuition for university that fall so that I would have extra spending money. At the end of summer, to celebrate my success, I went with some girlfriends to party and relax at a new friend's cottage. This was when my life as

Doris took a turn for the worse. We got into trouble the first night there—big time.

If we had partied at the cottage, as we planned to, we might have stayed out of trouble. But Stacey, our host, wanted us—four young, attractive women—to go to a bar in the Muskoka area and drink with her. As guests, we passively went along with her arrangements. I do not even remember how we got to the bar; actually, I do not recall much of that whole day except for us singing away to songs nonstop. The lyrics of Lynyrd Skynrd, Led Zeppelin and David Wilcox, were well known by Stacey and me especially. Growing up in the country, I had been to many bush bashes and house parties where it was normal for classic rock songs to pound through the speakers. As a new friend, Stacey was one of the few people I have ever met who lived in the city of Oshawa and liked classic rock music. She was fun to hang around because she knew way more songs than I did. That summer she even made me a cool music mix.

On the day of the accident, all of us young women were bouncing off the walls with excitement. But again I do not really remember everything. I had no other group of friends like this group of girls. My choice of behaviour to get in a car with a drunk driver was out of character for me.

Twenty-one-year-old Deborah, who was Stacey's older sister, picked us up from the bar that night. She came to drive us back to their cottage in Muskoka. I was told that she arrived a bit before we were going to leave and she hung out with her friends sitting in another part of the bar. She had drunk too much before we left and should not have been driving us home—but she did. Because she was not sitting with us drinking, none of us were aware she was over the limit to drive and we did not think to question her.

On the way home, I was told that "Magic Carpet Ride" by Steppenwolf was cranked up, with Stacey and me singing along. Throughout the song, we were smiling from ear to ear and laughing. Life was good.

Then, Deborah suddenly lost control of the car when taking a right hand corner in the road and crashed into a tree. All I can recall is twisting in my seat to try to brace myself. I am told that the impact left me unconscious and severely hurt in the backseat, dripping with blood from my mouth and cheek. I was the only one injured in the accident. Nobody could tell if I was breathing. My friends panicked, thinking I might die and one even started to run through the dark forest looking for help.

Stacey had been sitting beside me and she slammed into me hard in the accident, crushing my head between her and the tree. This was before airbags were available in cars, so my body acted like one for her. I do not remember if anyone had a seatbelt on that night.

As I recall what I was told and the little that I remember, my muscles clench around my neck.

For that trip to Muskoka, as Doris, I drove up to the lake in Mom's car. But for the accident we were not in hers. Her car was left parked back at the cottage. My mom saw the car that we got in the accident with before that fateful crash. She usually does not remember my other friends' cars but as she was trying to calm everyone down when I was in the intensive care unit (ICU), she could see this car clearly in her mind. I think she felt as if she somehow knew the car was dangerous and that she should have stopped the accident. Sure this may have saved me from getting so severely hurt but moms are crazy with how much they worry. As a teenager, if Mom would have told me of her concern, I would have told her that she was paranoid. She needed to ease up and relax.

Later, Mom told me about the day when Stacey, my new friend, came to our house before our trip to the lake. That afternoon she was outside reading and enjoying the summer weather. Stacey parked the car right in front of her.

As my friend and I were inside, Mom looked up from her book and examined the tires and car closely. She would never normally do this. Usually she was confident I was okay. She had seen many company cars over the years, as Dad would bring them home. This car was different however, in some way. On that sunny day, something would not let Mom take her eyes off the old blue car. Maybe a part of her knew that if she got up and looked onto the backseat she would see a bottle of brake fluid. Stacey's father had given this to her for the maintenance of the car just the week before but she did not use it.

There could have been any reason why the car went off the road the night I was hurt. The only fact the police cared about though was that Deborah was driving—impaired.

5
An Apology

It is two weeks since my party and I am sitting at the kitchen table. I gaze into the forest as I wait for Mya to come inside. Sighing to myself, I can feel that I am still affected by what happened when Sofia wanted to drive home drunk. It is making me think of my accident in 1991 a lot.

To stop Deborah from driving drunk the night she hurt me would have been difficult. Later I learned how my good friend Lori and another friend Amanda who were in the car did not drink as much as Stacey and I had. In hindsight I wish they had spoken up. They were sober enough to stop her from driving, they knew better.

In fact, Lori and I normally behaved responsibly when it came to drinking and driving. We were not perfect but we tried to be careful. We always took turns as designated driver (DD). We went to different high schools and had been good friends since grade seven. She even volunteered to come to my high school prom party, dressed casually, to be my DD. In the early morning of August 20, of that same year, we threw responsibility out the window.

Peer pressure edged us to put our lives on the line. Stacey and her sister Deborah were risk-takers and we learned this the hard way. I think if we had better communication skills to express our feelings and concerns, one of us could have stopped Deborah from driving drunk that night. The accident should not have happened.

As a teen, I would sometimes repress my negative emotions. I tried to ignore my frustration and anxiety. A beer or smoke easily worked to camouflage stress and these habits were often my first choice for dealing with it. If I did not handle things in this way, my emotions might bubble over into anger; and my anger, as well as the anger of others, frightened me. Therefore, I learned to keep it inside.

An old friend gave me a mug for my birthday one year that said, *"Piss me off. Pay the consequences."* She learned one time, after we got into an argument about pretty much nothing, that as a friend I am tough to keep around if you make me mad. She thought the mug described me perfectly and gave it to me as a gift after the fight.

During that argument nothing happened between us but she could tell I was pissed off. She said she knew it from the look in my eyes which glared right through her. Without me asking, our friends took my side in this fight, so it was understandably hard for her. I kept that mug for years, as kind of a personal trophy, until a psychologist coached me after the accident in assertiveness training. My lack of communication skills was definitely an increased problem after the head injury and if they were not addressed through education, I would have had even more problems in my life as I tried to rebuild it into something that was worth living for.

What I recall happening the night of our crash was that we were away for a few days of fun; there was a warm, sunny blue sky; I was excited about going to start my first-year at McMaster University (Mac) in Hamilton, Ontario in a few weeks; I was moving away from home for the first-time; I was hanging out with good friends and new friends whom I did not know yet were irresponsible; there were no parents; and—we had booze. In hindsight, this was a recipe for disaster.

After the accident, Lori and I spoke about how hard it would have been to have had an alternative way to get back to the cottage. There were few cabs in the Muskoka area of cottage country and as students we could not have even afforded one. We therefore trusted Deborah. She was twenty-one after all, three years older and did not appear to be falling over drunk. Maybe she had been drinking before she came to drive us home from the bar—who knows? We would have needed to be fearless to confront her and we were not.

A few months after I was injured, Deborah wrote me a letter of apology. I read the hand-written letter often, at least a hundred times. I have memories of holding this piece of paper and crying while I was going through all the struggles from the head injury. It was depressing and so I finally destroyed the letter. I burned it in a personal ceremony almost a decade after I received it. I can still remember every single word. I memorized it from so many reads. The ink may have gone up in smoke but the words will stay forever etched in my mind:

Oshawa, Ontario
Fall, 1991

Dear Doris,
There hasn't been a day that has gone by that I haven't thought of you. I'm far from religious but I prayed for you every day and night. I cannot believe that I almost killed you and my sister, who happens to be my best friend.
I would've given anything to trade places with you. To be the one who was hurt, the one in the hospital, the one missing out on frosh week of first-year university. I felt upon receiving some discouraging news about your condition in hospital that if you were to not make it, that I would too take my own life. I realize now how this would have only been harder for all those involved, my family and yours.
I cannot believe that I scarred your beautiful face. I walked away without a scratch on me or so it may seem. My scars are internal ones. I hope your internal and external scars heal and that you can get on with your life. I also hope to see or hear from you soon, to learn how you are doing and progressing.
If you need any help, I'm always here for you.

Sincerely,
Deborah

It was about two years after the accident when I bumped into Deborah, when she was working as a bartender. I was studying part-time at U of T at the time. Everything in my life had drastically changed since the last time I had seen her.

That night, Deborah bought me and a friend a drink. She did not seem to have a clue as to what she had done to me. Here she destroyed the life I had and almost killed me by driving drunk. Then she was buying me a drink—how awkward. And despite her scatter-brained gesture, I had no clue what to say to her. I do not even know if she knew I had changed my name. This was the first and only time she had ever seen me with the scar on my face that was the result of her driving drunk in 1991. My scar really was unintentionally, personally hand-crafted by her.

6
A Permanent Scar

In front of a magnified mirror, this 2008 summer day, I stare at my facial scar. It is always the first thing I focus on when applying make-up. I learned over the years to use camouflage make-up to cover the red and white marks, as well as the shadows on my skin. I never leave the house without putting concealer on. I would feel naked without it.

I can make the indents of my scar visible to me in a mirror by tilting my head. By doing this, I can see if I have not covered a spot properly. In the elevator mirrors of the condo I lived in until 2005, I always checked to see how noticeable it was. The seven years I lived there, every time I looked, I think a deeper part of me was always hoping that one day this memory of my accident would be gone. It is now a habit for me to check for accuracy like this. I still do this tilt of my head daily in a mirror somewhere.

My reflection in a mirror is a relationship that life has taught me to build and foster. The need to focus on what is external, to who I am as a person, was never as important before I got scarred. The mirror is not always kind to me. Sometimes it has been my most critical friend, as well as worst enemy.

If I had been blind, as some physicians anticipated I would be, I would have had no clue as to what the facial trauma left behind as a mark on my face. Mirrors do not exist in a world without sight. I always said that without sight, I would have killed myself as I was recovering from the injuries I received. I tried a few times because of the problems from the head injury itself. If I had been blind as well, I know I would have succeeded—without a doubt.

Over the years, my ability to hide the scars on my cheek with make-up got better with practice. I developed ways to cover the scar tissue using techniques that are better than anyone has ever shown me.

The first step is to use sunlight to choose a colour for my cover-up. This concealer needs to match, as best as possible, the lightest part of my skin and sunlight is the best light to see this in. Then I use a neutral shade of powder to set the make-up and follow this by shading it with bronzer and blush. By examining the scars from my chin up to my eye I noticed that they are different shades of skin tone. To use many colours of cover-up always seems more noticeable to me and it is time consuming as well, so my technique makes it easier. After the marks are covered, to then conceal the lumps of scar tissue is impossible to do.[7]

My scar shows a private side of myself to others. I have no choice because it is visible. Time will slowly fade and minimize the scar more but it will never be gone. It is a secret from my past that I cannot hide completely and at times this is upsetting.

When I was a teenager I did some modelling. After the accident, I continued to model—this time for a cosmetician specializing in scars. She used me as an example to teach others who studied with her. The time I spent modelling for her, helped me to learn how to become an expert at concealing my own scar.

At the hospital, after I got hurt in the car accident, the plastic surgeons spent many hours picking the glass from the car window out of the cuts on my face. The specialists in Toronto were the best to do the job properly. My scar would be worse if it were not for their expertise.

One day, Stacey complained to me about two stitches on her chin from the accident and the tiny scar she had because of it. She went on saying how bad it looked. The Muskoka emergency room doctors were the ones who stitched them for her. I had no clue why she said this to me. The scars on my face were a thousand times bigger than hers. And these permanent marks were just the tip of the iceberg for me of all the injuries I had received. She did not realize that her petty complaint was thoughtless to share with me.

After the cuts healed, I learned that the scars would be permanent to some degree. It happened on a day when my only brother, who is two years older than me, told me he had listened to a radio program in the car featuring an interview with the author of a book on care for the face. "The author explained how facial scars are difficult for doctors to remove," he recounted.

The friends who were with me the night I was injured said plastic surgeons would completely remove the scar. They said this many times. This reassurance suddenly felt like a lie. So I immediately bought the book to learn if this was true. From reading I learned about how the skin on my face is different from elsewhere on my body, making a skin graft impossible. I sobbed while flipping through the pages of the book. This depressed me big time. I can only imagine how hard this must have been for my brother to hear my reaction to his attempt at helping me with this knowledge.

For the surgery to only be able to reduce the visibility of my scar and not make it disappear, upset me deeply. The mark on my cheek was obviously unattractive. I needed support and I began to speak to friends about my feelings. I tried sharing my struggles with the girls who had been in the car accident with me. They drifted out of contact, not wanting reminders of what had happened to us that night. They knew that I was at a low point in my life. I was the only one severely permanently injured from the accident. I had never experienced rejection like this before. My life began to slowly spiral into a dark, lonely place.

I am not insecure about how I look to others unless I catch someone's eyes examining my cheek; then I am self-conscious. This happens often. Sometimes people try to sneak a peek when they think I will not notice them looking but I always do.

A few times, unexpectedly, I have shown my feelings about my scar in public. One day, was when Mom drove me home from an appointment at the hospital. We were at a stoplight when I glanced over at the car next to us. A little boy sat in a car seat in the back. I had not yet learned how to put cover-up make-up on my scar. Once the boy noticed the red marks on my face, he frantically touched his own cheek, mirroring the scars on mine. Then I could lip read the words, "What happened?"

He realized I must have been in pain. His father heard his concern and looked over at me. Once he saw my scar, he immediately yelled at his son. To see the boy's shocked, open-mouthed confusion crushed me. He did not know what he had done wrong to be yelled at, so he looked back and forth at me and his father, trying to understand. Their car sped off as the light changed. My response was to start crying uncontrollably. The child had only been curious. He empathised with me for the pain I must have felt. The father's reaction and not the little boy's upset me.

A child's response to my scar is understandable but still hard to deal with. The last one who asked about my scar was a five-year-old girl. We were playing a game during the Christmas holidays in 2007 when the marks on my cheek caught her attention. Just like the boy, she touched her left cheek, which is the mirror image of my right and asked me what happened.

The game halted. More confident after fifteen years of experience, I told her briefly about the accident I had been in and said that these scars will be there forever. I let her examine my face up close. She understood how serious the injury must have been. It took her a while to take her eyes off my cheek.

Children's questions do not bother me as much as they would if they came from an adult. I find adults are more concerned at first for external reasons, which is different than a child's innocent curiosity about how I got hurt. Or maybe this is just what I believe.

To learn how to deal with my emotions again in situations like these was one of the biggest challenges I had after the head injury. My feelings were all over the map. To help myself, for eight years after the accident, I had to regularly meet with a psychologist. One neuropsychologist I went to for five years, specialized in women with facial scars. Sometimes I would call her in the middle of the night, crying uncontrollably and leave a message, while sobbing into the phone. Never would I cry this way before getting hurt. Anything could have set off my tearful episode. I was very emotionally sensitive as a result of the brain damage. After I left the message for her, I would feel okay. No matter how long until the physician called back, I would by then be fine.

She said, "I've never known another patient—let alone another person—as resilient as you."

This surprised me to hear. I had cried and I thought this was supposed to make me feel better. I am usually in a good mood, so to bottle up sad feelings makes no sense to me. Angry ones, however, I have been taught by people around me, as well as society's expectations, not to express. This made my head injury a challenge to recover from.

7
Dancing

S atisfied with the results in the mirror, I get ready to go to an
intermediate cha cha class. For me, dancing is a wonderful hobby. I
feel content as soon as I walk into the studio. I enjoy all the Latin and
ballroom dances. At the moment rumba is my favourite but next week
it might be a different dance.

On the way downtown, I want to visit my aunt Gisele, who is
seventy-three years old. My aunt and uncle just moved to Ottawa
from Calgary. Aunt Gisele just got back from hiking in the Austrian
mountains but Uncle Helmut is still there mountain climbing. She
says this activity is too challenging for her, so he will be gone a bit
longer. They often vacation like this and that, I think, helps them keep
their independence. They married after meeting through my dad's
engineering class at U of T in the late 50's, when Uncle Helmut was
studying to become an engineer.

Aunt Gisele and Uncle Helmut are supportive of my dancing.
Earlier this year, it was fun to perform for them a dance to a challenging
Brahms waltz piece with my instructor. Most waltzes have a regular,
rhythmic pace. Brahms's is a more romantic waltz with tempo changes.

Before performing I found out that my new dress had too long
a skirt and would make me trip. I had no time to fix it. I was really
scared I would trip on the hem and fall during the performance. I had
already stepped on the dress and stumbled during practice, which made
me especially anxious. Everyone was nervous this would happen while
performing. The last thing I wanted to do is fall and hit my head, so
this dress turned out to be extra stress. I was already anxious about
having to do a backbend in the dance and the dress added more worry.

It was special to me that Aunt Gisele was there to help me put on
my grandmother Omi's pearl necklace as I was getting ready for the

performance. Omi was my dad and aunt Gisele's mom and she left this necklace for me when she died at ninety-seven years old. She had loved classical music, so she would have enjoyed my waltz. This was why I wanted to wear her piece of jewellery for the performance.

I had purposely picked this piano piece because I knew Aunt Gisele was going to watch me perform. She plays piano and I loved listening to her while growing up. I have Christmas memories of standing around the piano with her playing and all of my family singing carols in German and English.

Before I performed that night, Uncle Helmut said to me, "Everyone here is happy. This is not normal. Does dancing do this to people?"

"Maybe," I said with surprise. I looked around the studio to see that everyone was laughing and smiling.

I hid the anxiety I felt to dance that waltz. I thankfully did not fall during the performance and we danced better than I ever expected.[8]

8
Money and Credit

As I am about to leave for downtown, I grab the ringing phone. It is the bank calling about an application I put in for a line of credit. I received some financial compensation through insurance as a structured settlement from the accident in 1991. It was not given to me as a lump sum but was invested instead. I would have, for sure, spent all of the money I received by now if it had not been invested well. My investments only give me a monthly income and it is not an earth-shattering amount. I still need to work like everyone else to pay the bills. Right now I work for myself part-time as an athletic trainer as well as in an office. I can responsibly looking after my finances and a line of credit would definitely make life easier.

I wait on the phone for what I am going to hear from the bank. My mood sinks as I anticipate the clerk's negative answer. This is not the first time I put in an application and banks always turn me down. I can get a credit card no problem but an account like this is not something they have ever given me. The other week I had the impulse to apply again for an account like this with the same bank as last time, even though they had rejected me before. I applied without thinking too much of it. Silently I wait on the phone and fumble with the phone cord.

"After assessing your application," says the bank clerk, "your line of credit has been approved."

"Really?" I ask.

My heart starts to beat rapidly. This is hard to believe.

"Yes and if you have any questions, please call us. I'll send the paperwork and cheques for the account to you by mail. Starting today, you can access this new account through your bank card," he says.

"This will sound stupid," I say, "but I'm surprised you approved me."

"I can't discover any problems. You are employed at the real estate office and have a good credit score," he says.

"Okay," I say with relief.

I notice that he is not even mentioning my self-employment as a personal trainer, which is where I make the most money. Self-employment has presented challenges for me when applying for credit. I wish I had realized before how easily I could get a line of credit if I had a different job. I would have taken one sooner elsewhere to be able to open an account like this.

I hang up the phone in disbelief. In a happy mood, I grab my purse and keys to drive downtown and dance some cha cha. During the drive my thoughts drift back to challenges I have had with money.

~

After the head injury I was not good with money. I had to adjust to my impulsivity and that my problem-solving skills that were once excellent, were suddenly terrible. It was not good when I learned that shopping helped me deal with the stress that filled my life. The new things I bought distracted me from having to face the problems I had from the head injury. The way I saw it was that any debt did not even compare to the shambles my life was in but others did not see it this way. My parents had to bail me out a few times with credit card companies. Therapists would constantly talk to me about "my problem" with money. I had no time to listen to them.

Eventually, I learned to better manage my money through reading books. I re-educated myself, over and over, until I outlearned the challenge. I had no difficulty handling my money before the accident. I hated to be criticized by others and this was what everyone seemed to want to do. I think they thought they were helping me by pointing out the faults in my life. So I got rid of the problem and their criticism stopped.

Presently, I have worked part-time for the past ten years as a personal trainer. After the injury, my stamina to work a full-time job is no longer there. The head injury has slowed me down in many ways. It is much harder to earn the income that I would earn with a full-time job.

I work from home, training people privately in Pilates exercise with the equipment I own. Despite my ten-year track record, the bank says that with self-employment, they cannot trust I will make money. This is hard to understand because I earn more money working for myself than I would for a company. The bank does not view it this way, however, which has been frustrating for me.

I had no dreams to become a personal trainer. The pay is decent but I did not need to complete a degree at university to do it. Before getting hurt, university had been my goal, so the rehab I needed always focused there. In the first few years after the accident, I did not enjoy my studies and was having a hard time. I had no problems like this in school before and I easily got marks above eighty percent. But due to the head injury, I needed help with note-taking during the lectures, required longer time for tests and had to learn how to study all over again. I also could only take one or two courses at a time because I no longer had the stamina to be able to study full-time and that really made me feel different. The Special Needs office of the university had to help me and I needed to rely on the assistance of tutors. It was embarrassing to me. I became more capable as the years passed after the accident. But the first few years were extremely challenging in school and this was a huge blow to my self-esteem.

At first I tried working on a Bachelor of Science Honours degree, majoring in Biology. I had liked science and medicine before and had wanted to become a physician but since I was a different person after the accident, my new dislike of studying science did not surprise me. So I switched to a Bachelor of Arts Honours, with a major in psychology. I took all the elective courses despite having no idea what I wanted as a career later in my new life.

The search for what would fulfil me threw me into confusion. I considered criminology, English, even Law School but nothing interested me. When I was Doris, I wanted to study psychology and science for my undergrad. Then I wanted to go on to medicine and become a paediatrician. I realized that with only being able to study part-time as a result of the head injury, it would be unrealistic for me to want to pursue this anymore as a career. And anyway, as Samantha I had no interest to become a doctor. But sadly, as Samantha I had no passion for anything else at university.

When not at university at the time, I spent the rest of my time seeing physicians, therapists and lawyers. Assessments, scans and treatment were a regular part of my schedule. I cried daily about how hard my life had become. After many years, I unfortunately grew to associate any schooling with my injury. I wanted and needed to forget about what had happened to me in that accident—so things had to change.

The summer of 1999, I hated every moment I had to spend going to a statistics class at Carleton University, in Ottawa. The course was compulsory for my degree. Studying all the numbers and formulas bored me. There was absolutely no room for me to think outside the box of what I was being taught.

As I looked outside of my condo at the nice weather I was missing that summer, I struggled to understand why I was doing this to myself. Finally the insurance company was out of my life as a result of settling through mediation. One night, I broke down and called Mom to tell her I would be dropping out of university. After she learned why, she understood. Her unconditional support felt incredible.

I had explained to her that since all the legal files were closed and there finally appeared to be privacy in my life again, I could do whatever I wanted. I had my freedom back. It had been stressful for that file to be active for so many years. So with the legal and insurance work over, the point of continuing to "learn" how to go to school for a Bachelor degree vanished. I was only really going to university for my medical team, lawyers and the insurance company.

The day after I left university for good, I went for a private Pilates lesson. As I waited for my trainer, I was reading a book about finding the purpose of your life. She laughed when I showed her the title.

"I dropped out of university," I said. "Now I'm trying to figure out what kind of work would make me happy. I want a job that would mean something to me. Where I can help people become and stay healthy. Kind of like what you are doing."

"I'm beginning a course in a few months that will last a year, to train new teachers. Why don't you join us?" she said.

This opportunity surprised me. Finally something clicked. I went on to take Pilates instructor courses in both Ottawa and Toronto from different schools.

Recently I also began working part-time as an office assistant for Sheila, a friend who is a real estate agent. I train her in Pilates. This office job gets me out of the house to work and that is enjoyable.

Today, I feel stronger with my new financial support, as I take the exit on the highway for my aunt and uncle's house. I never realized how much it bothered me to not have credit like this before.

9
Family Support

Before my cha cha class, I ring the doorbell at Aunt Gisele's house. She opens the door to greet me. In the kitchen we sit down at the table. She graciously offers me a cup of tea and a slice of delicious berry tart from a local bakery. As I eat, I begin to tell her about the party I hosted the other weekend and the incident with Sofia.

"A guest gave me problems. A woman from dance class wanted to drive home drunk," I say.

"What did you do?" she asks.

"A friend helped stop her but it was difficult. I stepped in but she threatened to hit us both in the head if we didn't give her the keys."

I wait for Aunt Gisele to respond. I laugh inside. I think I will leave the f-words Sofia used out of my recap of what happened. After a moment she says, "Well, that was inappropriate behaviour. How old is she?"

"Thirty-three," I say.

"What an immature woman," she says.

"I know. As I got older, I thought I would see fewer people wanting to drink and drive. Many still do it. Stopping someone is hard. I had nothing to drink that night and being sober didn't make it any easier or more difficult to step in to be a responsible host. Sofia couldn't have cared less who she hurt if she drove—or punched in the head," I say.

My neck muscles tighten with the memory of her threatening to hit me that night. My aunt senses my discomfort. We are quiet for a moment.

"I still remember you in a coma in ICU at the hospital," Aunt Gisele says. "Here you had this perfectly tanned body but then your head was massively swollen and you were bruised and cut up badly. The broken bones in your skull were numerous. The damage done to

34

you was severe."

There is deep emotion in her voice and I listen empathetically to what she shares. I have already heard this story from her many times before. I understand she will never forget this visual image of me right after the accident.

"Your cousin Rob came to visit you and fainted by your bed," she continues. "Your dad caught him just in time. As I was packing for our move from Calgary, I found the medical notes I started writing when you were in ICU. To do this helped me cope. I don't really know why I kept them. Would you like to read them?"

Normally I would say no to her and I have already said so once before in Calgary but something today makes me want to read them. I am surprised she wants to share her notes with me.

"After this incident with Sofia," I say. "I would."

I wait at the table while Aunt Gisele goes to get them. I do not know why I just said I want to see them because I do not want to relive my injuries, ever. Why would she have kept them? Sure I was seriously hurt but that is over with. If they were my notes, I would have destroyed them.

My aunt and I have always kept in regular contact. We enjoy talking about many things. To almost lose me in the accident brought us together even closer. I have always admired her. She is a retired medical doctor and as a child, I wanted to be like her. Mom believes the first words I spoke had been about how I would be a doctor. I had no desire to study for another profession. Aunt Gisele inspired me, although I did not realize this until years later, after the accident.

Before I got hurt, working in paediatrics had been my goal, partially due to the time I spent with children while volunteering for years at the Oshawa General Hospital. My plan was that after earning a Bachelor of Natural Science Honours degree, I would apply to medical school at McMaster University (Mac). Mac focuses on bedside manner more than many other schools do. Aunt Gisele had been on the Board of Admissions for the University of Calgary's med school and at the time she thought both Mac and University of Calgary offered excellent teaching approaches. A part of me wanted her to be proud of me for going to one of them.

Upon Aunt Gisele's return to the kitchen, she sets a spiral-ringed notebook down on the table in front of me. Tucked inside are some folded loose papers which make the notes bulky. I slowly pick them up. I do not understand why I want to touch, let alone read this. I cannot believe I am going to relive my past again in this way. It was a nightmare what I went through and I have better things to do, like to go dancing. I thought I always wanted to forget that accident ever happened but something feels different. What could have changed?

"I wonder if telling my story somehow might help stop irresponsible behaviour like Sofia's. I think prevention needs to be focused on more," I say. "We can't always rely on the law to control people."

I look down at Aunt Gisele's notebook I am holding. On the cover, she printed "Doris" and drew a heart around it.[9]

No one calls me Doris anymore. The name is foreign to me now. It feels strange to say the name Doris or even see it written like it is here because I am a completely different person than she was. As I open the booklet, on the inside cover, in plastic wrap for protection, is one of my grad photos or, should I say, one of Doris' grad photos. My heart sinks. For some reason I cannot stop looking at the photo. Aunt Gisele sees this.[10]

"That was my favourite picture of you," she says. "I still love it."

"Thank you," I say, "for sharing this with me."

My eyes are glued to the photo of who I was before the injury. To see a picture is different than reading or hearing my previous name. As I look at my eyes in the photo, I remember something Mom said about how the twinkle in them had faded after my head injury. She knew I suffered from dry eyes as a result of the injuries but she said it was a different kind of twinkle than that. I have no clue why I am opening this emotional door. The door is always locked in my life now and I do not have the key.

I slowly look at each word as I flip through the handwritten notes. I am being sucked emotionally back into the experience of what someone did to me and my family and a feeling of heaviness begins to grow inside me. I feel overwhelmed and cannot truly comprehend what I am reading.

It is almost like a part of me has now stepped back into the past, to the hospital and my injury. In my mind I am lying comatose on a bed. My heart is beating faster. These medical notes feel alive in my hands. My aunt is watching me closely. She can see my hands are trembling. I need to be more in control. I do not want her to see me getting emotional looking at this.

Aunt Gisele followed everything in the ICU and recorded the details of my injury and recovery. In her writing she particularly highlights how difficult the head injury was for me as well as my entire family. She wrote in the same medical detail as she would for a patient but her love for me shines through. I know that she cares about me a lot as Samantha. I am touched to learn how much she cared about me when I was Doris.

10
Medical Notes

At home after my dance lesson, I lay down on the couch to read every word of Aunt Gisele's notes. While I was at the studio, I kept thinking of them. Even dancing could not take my mind off them. Aunt Gisele suggested that I should not rush to read the notes but I cannot put them down. I have never stepped into another person's experience of what happened to me in this way. What she wrote is hard for me to read. Her emotions are etched on every page.

Aunt Gisele recorded things that happened while I was in the Toronto hospital. One day, she speaks about a nurse finding me trying to look in a mirror at the cuts and stitches on my face. I asked, "Am I going to die?"

This is heart-breaking to read. I must have been so confused at the time about what happened to me. I need to just put the medical notes down now. But I cannot. My grip on the booklet becomes even tighter. I have zero memory of this happening.

Sorrow for what I went through floods my body as I read about my family's experience. A part of me is embarrassed to learn things. It is hard to acknowledge that I was ever so weak in my life.

In Aunt Gisele's notes she talks about one day when my brother asked me in the hospital, "Can you open your eyes?"

"Why should I? They hurt too much."

I find it hard to believe that this really happened. After a one-month stay in the hospital, I only possess fragments of a few memories.

Aunt Gisele writes how, "It was very pleasant to spend almost all day with Doris. She was very sweet and appreciative. I did talk with her a bit about grief/anger/denial, etc. in the morning."

This too, is all a blur to me; the first few years after getting hurt are especially foggy. Her medical notes show how severe my closed-head injury was. Aunt Gisele kept a few letters I sent her during that time. Reading them is like looking at a letter from a complete stranger. It was almost as if, on an emotional level, I had become a child again and was no longer an eighteen-year-old about to start university. How I decorated the letters was childlike as well. As Doris, it would have been completely out of character to write my aunt in this way. The head injury had put a stranger inside of me. On the outside, aside from the damage done to my face, I still resembled Doris.

"She has certainly changed a lot—the denial stage is crumbling quickly and she is facing the various, often permanent deficits she may need to adjust to," Aunt Gisele wrote, "diplopia (double vision), visual problems, scar, hearing loss, dysphasia (choking on food) and brain damage. She is very brave and I am crying with her. I love her <u>lots</u>."

Aunt Gisele wrote about all the times my dad called her, stressed out with what was happening at home. As a family, we had many arguments. I did not require parenting in this way before, ever. I barely remember this as well. The words I am reading make the extent of my recovery disturbingly clear. I start to cry. To learn in more detail what my family went through triggers feelings I have not felt before. I cannot believe how I feel, like it was my fault to let someone do this to me. Thank goodness I was single and not married with children. To maintain a family, as I struggled through this horrible recovery, would have been impossible.

As I finish, I hold Aunt Gisele's booklet and close my eyes. My mind is racing. I begin to meditate, to help myself calm down. I am still crying. I focus on my breathing by taking a deep breath and then slowly exhaling. My thoughts gradually become quiet. I finally stop crying.

I know that crying is therapeutic but the injuries I received damaged my tear ducts. My eyes produce only slight tears now around my outer right eye when I express emotion in this way. I can easily wipe these away. I have no need to worry about wrecking my make-up. I know I am trying to look on the bright side of losing the natural ability to express myself in this way. A past boyfriend one time said I was not being real when I cried.

"You are faking it," he said. "No tears are running down your face."

He did not know much about my injuries. But I knew my emotions were real that day. It is hard to prove that to someone else. I still have to remind myself of this sometimes "yes, you are really crying; it's okay to express your feelings this way; don't hold back". This psycho-babble is a pain but it beats going to a therapist. After so many years of having my privacy invaded by professionals, my boundaries have changed in regards to what I am comfortable sharing with others.

Tonight, I am grateful that Aunt Gisele gave me her notes to read. They are obviously opening a closet full of memories though. I have always kept the head injury hidden from everyone, including myself, in order to protect myself. Maybe I was not admitting the reality of what had happened to me. Well, it obviously worked—until now.

11
The Lady in Pink

Moving some furniture in my den, I am trying to make the room more comfortable. In the bookcase, I notice Princess Diana's framed signature lying on top of some books. It has been there, since the night of my party.

Underneath the frame are some books I am reading. Some are from the period after my head injury. They had helped me build a new life. I remember reading Aunt Gisele's notes the other day. As if a light switch turned on in my thoughts, all of a sudden I am back in the hospital.

~

I needed to stay at the Hugh MacMillan Rehabilitation Centre, a children's rehab hospital and a special needs school in Toronto, for six weeks because of the injury.

In October 1991, I was standing in a gymnasium feeling bored. That day is one of the few I can remember from my recovery. I hated being there. Patients with "special needs" surrounded me. Despite my objections, they considered me to have brain damage and to be learning disabled, just like some of them were.

I did not believe them. I wanted my normal life back as Doris. I did not understand why I could not be an outpatient to do this. My family lived about forty-five minutes east. Mom could have driven me to the rehabilitation centre. Sure, the daily commute would have been stressful for her but I felt that staying there was worse for me. And what did it matter what Mom needed anyways?

From where I stood, I could see the gym's side door was the easiest escape out of my nightmare. This ridiculous thought made me laugh. I knew I would not run away but I needed the time I spent there to pass more quickly. My solution to help forget about the ordeal I had been thrown into was to go on a backpacking vacation to Australia. No one would let me go on this trip though. To be smothered by medical staff was becoming a pain in the ass and I was sick of it. Every specialist possible wanted to look at my eyes, ears, brain and more. I had never been analysed like this.

The accident happened two weeks before attending university. There was a university calculus textbook in my bedroom at home that I was apparently already studying before the accident. I could not remember picking up the books for classes, let alone studying calculus. I vaguely recalled calculus as being my least favourite subject in high school. I can just remember that the teacher I had made the class horrible for me. I had told others that the university textbooks were boring, from what I had read but I could not remember telling them this. This was going to be my first year towards a four-year degree.

I had already paid for the year's tuition and board by myself. Mom and Dad had offered to pay for this but, proud of my independence, I would not let them. Since I could no longer attend because of the accident, I would be getting that money back from the university; so my idea to escape on a trip was feasible. I saw myself on a beach, soaking up the sun but my family was stopping me from going and spending my own money. They were never such controlling parents before. I could not understand why they did not want me to go. I kept telling them all that I was fine. They seriously needed to lose their concern and get a reality check.

Everyone was acting as if the head injury was such a big deal. Of course I had a "head injury", look at all the broken bones in my skull that were still healing. The way they spoke about this type of injury seemed bizarre. I had not heard anything about it in my life. I did not understand all the problems they told me I was supposed to have. Brain damage from broken bones, I definitely did not understand how that could happen.

That day, everyone had been making a big deal about a visitor coming from Britain, named Diana. People and patients had dressed up for the occasion. I had difficulty understanding why they would do this. I had not put in any extra effort. I could not even see properly in the mirror anymore to do it. They acted as if Diana, whom they called a princess, was different from everyone. In my mind she was a person, like all of us.

I did not care to meet the Lady. But surprisingly, Princess Diana wanted to meet us individually, so I hung around with the other children. Mom was excited that I was meeting the princess. Sure the kids in this hospital deserved her attention but I did not need or want it. After the head injury, my life's focus was on me; my whole world became rehabilitation. I did not have a normal life anymore and I wanted one again. There was no time to read the newspaper and keep up with trivial stuff such as Princess Diana coming to Canada.

Really I had no choice but to be there for her visit. The staff chaperoned pretty much everything we did in the rehabilitation hospital. I did not feel like I fit in because I was older than most patients. They treated me as if I was a kid as well, as if I still required a babysitter as a young adult and I hated it. I felt like I was in jail.

We stood patiently along the gym wall waiting for Princess Diana's arrival. Part of my insecurity as I looked around, was that I did not want Diana, whoever she was—or anyone else— to see me right then. The nerve and brain damage from the injury left me with obvious problems. Along with the loss of use of some facial muscles, my eyes were dry, affecting my vision and I needed different kinds of eye drops to help. At night I applied a medical gel to them, leaving everything a blurry mess.

A disabled girl named Erica with whom I shared the hospital room got this prescriptive treatment as well. She could not apply the gel herself. She could not even speak normally. She too, suffered from a severe closed-head injury. When they applied Erica's eye drops, she moaned and cried deeply from the discomfort. Her suffering broke my heart. I knew how horrible this felt. It was an uncomfortable thing to need as a daily application. I could not remember anyone doing it to me but nurses had done so when I was comatose. I wondered if I cried as she did.

Erica and I did not talk about personal stuff in the rehab "jail". She was incapable. She made odd noises all day long. I wondered if she had been handicapped before she had the head injury but I was told she was not. It was difficult to believe a head injury did that to her.

My vision was no longer twenty-twenty. I needed to get prescription eyeglasses. I kept my left eye closed because of double vision. I could only open it slightly anyway. To stop me from doing this, they wanted me to wear a ridiculous eye patch. The medical team pretty much ordered me to wear this. So my compromise was to keep my weaker eye shut completely instead. For my eyes to focus together was impossible. The two eyes were literally looking at different things. Everyone called this "diplopia". I was so sick of hearing that word.

I would try to focus my eyes on something but it hurt to even move my left eye a little bit. The eye had become locked in one position. When trying to open my eyes, I looked in the mirror. I thought I looked crazy with my left eye looking off at nothing. Some facial muscles were weak from my injuries and I could hardly keep my eyelid up. Doctors told me I needed surgery to correct this and the double vision. I figured out however, that by lifting my head slightly, I could see a bit better straight ahead. This was how I looked for our British visitor to arrive.

All of a sudden, a hush came over the room as Princess Diana appeared. She was wearing a pink blazer with a black skirt as she greeted officials of the rehabilitation centre. The energy in the room changed as soon as she came through the door. You could hear the smallest sound as we all stood in silence. She slowly walked around the gym as she individually visited us young patients.

I could not take my eyes off her. Beauty shone from within her and I sensed her care and concern for us as she spoke with each child. I did not remember ever feeling this way around a stranger. Never had I been injured before, in a state where I needed or even deserved special attention from others. I was the one to always help them instead.

There was warmth emanating from Princess Diana. A girl beside me in a wheelchair spoke with her. A little boy dressed handsomely stood in part of a picture I took of them.[11]

As I watched the princess, I could see it was obvious she cared about us and I suddenly began to look forward to meeting her. Then she turned her full attention to me.

"Hello," she said, smiling as she walked over.

"Hello," I said.

She looked into my eyes and not at my scarred cheek and facial paralysis. She did not ask how I was hurt. All I felt from her was unconditional acceptance. This surprised me.

Mom had encouraged me to get Princess Diana to write in my Recovery Book. But I had no interest in this; it was just a piece of paper. I could not understand the big deal. Mom wanted me to take a photo for her as well. I knew deep down she was trying to motivate me to be interested to meet the princess. I was depressed and she wanted to cheer me up. I used to be a happy daughter.

I had watched Princess Diana get married ten years earlier, when I was eight years old. I had learned nothing else about her. I think Mom thought my meeting her would trigger memories of who I was before the accident when I saw her wedding.

That day, with enthusiasm in my voice that surprised even me, I asked the princess, "I was wondering if you would please write in my Recovery Book?"

Our visitor smiled and gently took the pen and open book from me. She wrote her first name with great care. I smiled and strained to open my eyes as best as possible while a woman beside us took a photo.[12]

After signing, Princess Diana smiled tenderly at me.

"Shhhh, don't tell anyone," she said. "I'm normally not supposed to do that."

"Thank you so much," I whispered back.

I took my Recovery Book from her and laughed to myself. Everyone was watching us, which made what she had done hard to keep secret. But in that moment, Princess Diana's focus was only on me and it was as if no one else existed in the room. I found her attention flattering. I was mesmerised and paid no attention to what more she said.

The princess then moved on to greet the next patient. Having met her, something changed in me. Her care and concern made me feel special. I did not think a visitor would ever be this important to a patient. I can remember a bit about my volunteer work at the hospital before the car accident. I began being a candy striper at age thirteen. I got to visit many child and adult patients. I do not remember but Mom says I was especially sad when one senior I regularly visited, died.

When I volunteered at the hospital before, I usually sat to talk or play with children. With Princess Diana it was not just a mere activity that made us feel so special, it was the weight and majesty of her presence which had an impact. It felt like we were part of a real-life modern fairy tale of some sort as this princess touched our hearts. No one took their eyes off her. We were hungry for attention and she reached out to us in a way that made us need her like that. Most of the young handicapped patients did not know who Princess Diana was. To them she was only a visitor. Their world, like mine, only consisted of endless physicians, therapy and family.

In that moment, as I watched Princess Diana walk around the rest of the room, any volunteer work of mine took on a different meaning. I realized that no matter why a patient is there, everyone needs support. I learned first-hand how important it was for me to know that I was cared about by someone who was not a part of the hospital.

Before my accident while volunteering at the hospital, I remember feeling comfortable being with patients. As a patient it was different to befriend other patients while staying there because I was classified as having problems that needed help. I had difficulty understanding and accepting the "learning disabled" label I was given because of the accident. A couple months before, I received A's in high school and graduated with honours. I thought I still was okay despite being injured.

The physicians and therapists were starting to accuse me of being in denial, they said it is a common way of coping after a brain injury. They thought this was one of the reasons I wanted to "escape" to Australia. I knew that they were just jealous since I would be away on vacation while they were stuck there.

Both my family and the medical professionals were chewing me out
for wanting to run away from problems I would not admit to. I did not
believe them because I was successful before and problems did not exist
in my former life. I understood how failure might be hard for anyone
to deal with but I just thought backpacking would be fun. And they
made me waste time listening to everyone talk doom and gloom about
me and my future. I was bored out of my mind.

A few days before meeting Princess Diana, a bunch of doctors and
specialists sitting in a line in front of me drilled me with questions—
almost like a prosecution. Boy was I nervous. What they wanted to
know seemed ridiculous.

"Where did you go to high school?" they asked.

"Just outside Oshawa, in the country," I responded.

"Did you graduate?" they asked.

"Yes, this year," I said.

"What can you remember from one of the last school courses you
took?"

I searched my memories. I had fast tracked through high school to
finish in four years instead of five, completing right away all the hard
courses needed to apply to university. So I had an easy last semester with
drama, English and co-op at a veterinary clinic. I remained quiet for a
moment. Suddenly, something from English came to mind.

"This year, grade thirteen English," I said, pausing for a moment.
"O that this too too solid flesh would melt, Thaw and resolve itself
into a dew, Or that the Everlasting had not fix'd, His canon 'gainst
self-slaughter. O God. O God. How weary, stale, flat and unprofitable,
Seem to me all the uses of this world…"

As I recited with confidence this passage from *Hamlet*, their faces
showed surprise as they scribbled madly in their notes. They were
testing me for any brain damage, yes, but they also were treating me as
if I was an idiot. So to prove them wrong, I continued.

"Fie on't, O fie. 'tis an unweeded garden, That grows to seed; things
rank and gross in nature, Possess it merely. That it should come to this.
But two months dead—nay, not so much, not two: So excellent a king;

that was, to this, Hyperion to a satyr; so loving to my mother, That he might not beteem the winds of heaven visit her face too roughly." I paused.

They thought I was finished. Dr. Rumney, the paediatrician, was about to ask me another question. But before he could say anything, I passionately continued.

"Heaven and earth! Must I remember? Why, she would hang on him, As if increase of appetite had grown, By what it fed on: and yet, within a month—Let me not think on't—Frailty, thy name is woman!"[13]

The specialists sat still, looking up and down from their papers. In school I got high marks for reciting this quote. Dr. Rumney, then quickly moved on to another question. I expected praise for remembering this but got none. Not one word and their silence shocked me.

I could not understand the point of the exercise. They called what we were doing a cognitive deficit test of some sort. Cognitive and deficit were words I was getting tired of hearing. I had not experienced anything in this way before. To be treated like I had become stupid overnight was hard. To need to prove my intelligence by answering those questions made me uncomfortable. I did not feel accepted by the "Rehabilitation Team". Rejection for me in this way was a first. I wanted to go home and hang out with friends. In short, return to a normal life, as Doris had before.

This was part of what made Princess Diana's visit seem special. She did not ask me to prove or explain myself or about any of the other "cognitive deficit" crap. Upon meeting me, she accepted me unconditionally.

I had many friends but nobody showed interest in visiting me at the hospital. I preferred things to be this way. It would have been embarrassing for them to see what a big deal the medical crew were making about my injury. Mom and Dad drove in every night to take me out to dinner. I was reluctant to eat in the cafeteria and they were concerned about that. They wanted to keep me from starving myself. My appetite had been non-existent since the accident and I could go days without eating.

Friends were no longer available as they once were. The social life I had months prior had dwindled into a distant memory. Only one old friend I had since grade seven came to visit me in Toronto. Shannon brought me back my Recovery Book. She had taken it to my old high school, where she still attended, to let people sign. I had been excited to read what people wrote. I opened the book with disappointment to read only her friends had written messages to me.

They said kind things, for which I thanked Shannon but the gesture was sorely lacking the support I desired and needed. I did not hang out with these people outside of class. Or maybe Shannon had approached my friends and they refused to sign.

Princess Diana's unconditional love helped fill a lonely spot slowly developing in my heart. She showed no judgment as she walked around visiting us patients. The strength of her character was obvious as soon as she walked in the room. I admired her ability to give herself to others. Before I met her, meeting a princess meant nothing to me but now I will always remember her as The Lady in Pink.

12
Head Injury

After looking at my aunt's medical notes I have been thinking a lot about the closed-head injury I received and its aftermath. Memories of what others told me after the accident have been swimming through my mind.

Being in a large city like Toronto for my injury, gave me the opportunity to have the best treatment possible. This was obvious from the first day in the hospital, during rehabilitation, as well as throughout the rest of my recovery. This helped me succeed.

At the hospital, when I was in the coma ophthalmologists said that with both my eye sockets being so severely smashed up, I would be blind. If not blind, then colour blind—for certain. They kept repeating this to my family. Through all the broken bits of bone on the scans, they could not tell whether my optic nerves were intact or not. They found no case in the medical records at the time of someone retaining their sight after this degree of damage. Miraculously, today, not only can I see but I can see in colour as well.

In the ICU, as I became partially conscious for the first time, I could not open my eyes because of facial paralysis. No one knew if I was blind or not. I am told that I said nothing about not being able to see. My family did not know how to react to my unexpected response. My body and mind tried to protect me from experiencing more stress than it could possibly handle at the time.

The first person to discover I could still see was Aunt Gisele, who lived and worked close to the hospital in Toronto. The nurses had me sitting in the hall to help stimulate my senses through the activity going on around me at the hospital. Walking towards my room, Aunt Gisele immediately noticed me looking at her. She saw my right eye was open a little for the first time. Despite my facial paralysis, I tried to smile.

Instantly, she asked, "What colour am I wearing?"

"Yellow," I said.

She urgently rushed up to me and gave me a passionate hug. My response confirmed I still had eyesight to a degree not believed possible by many physicians. The strength of my body was beyond anyone's belief.

My aunt had contacted one of her classmates, a neurosurgeon, asking about the blindness risk after my head injury. He gave her hope. He told her he had not seen a patient become blind in both eyes from a severe closed-head injury.

I understand how this lifted Aunt Gisele's spirits. I know, however, that it was more the eye specialists, rather than neural specialists who were talking about the possibility of my being blind for life. Head injury or no head injury, they were amazed at how strong my body was. They had difficulty understanding how my eyes were able to surmount such trauma to the orbits of my eyes.

But Aunt Gisele's classmate did warn her that I was likely to experience personality changes which may be difficult for our family to cope with. This had been a knowledgeable warning—because it did happen.

While in the Toronto hospital after my injury, eye specialists and medical students came to study me while I sat in my hospital bed. This happened because I was a patient in a teaching hospital. Many times my room filled with those wanting to learn. I remember one instance vaguely. Through my partially opened eye I could see they took extensive notes as they spoke about me. I was eating Jell-O to pass the time. This was one of the only hospital foods I liked consuming. At the time, I had no idea what they were talking about. What had happened to my mind and body was outside of my capabilities to understand.

When in a coma, my family kept saying to me, "You are a fighter, Doris. You are strong. You can pull through this." They were trying to help me regain consciousness and heal. Talking to me this way gave them hope. My family started asking me questions when I finally became somewhat conscious.

"What year is it?"

"Nineteen forty-two," I said.

I was not even alive in 1942. They tried not to show concern with my wrong answer or correct me. The physicians told my family not to be concerned because the purpose of questioning me was to stimulate my memory. It must have been hard for them to conceal their shock at my unexpected answer.

"What do you do?" they asked.

"I'm a student at McMaster," I enthusiastically replied and that lifted their hopes.

Aunt Gisele, after talking with a colleague who worked in rehabilitation, insisted that for my age I would benefit most by being placed in the children's rehabilitation facility.

Technically I should have gone to an adult rehabilitation hospital because I was eighteen years old at the time. Physicians were already sending me there but Aunt Gisele spoke to my medical team about it. Without her help, I believe there would have been even more challenges for me as I recovered. I also never would have met The Lady in Pink and that turned out to be pretty much the only memorable thing about being there.

As I recovered, personality change was probably the biggest thing I struggled with as Aunt Gisele's colleague had predicted. Before my head injury I did not have to think about being Doris. To this day it still feels like a new person is inside me.

In Aunt Gisele's medical notes a half year after I was injured, she claims that at some point I said to her, "I don't know who I am."

At the time Dad phoned Aunt Gisele and said, "She's got four personalities: a childlike one, a tart that is seductive, an angry one and her old self. We don't know which personality will surface at any given time." Of course, Dad would not have called me a tart, Aunt Gisele must have quoted him wrong. But a fragile part of me knows that he did say what he did. It is hard to accept in ways.

It was a morning in March 1992 when I walked into the kitchen and told Mom that I was changing my name from Doris to Samantha.

"Since everyone tells me I'm no longer Doris, I decided to give myself a new name. I learned in a dream that I will be Samantha," I said.

I had no interest in changing my name before but when the name Samantha just appeared to me, it felt perfect to use and my announcement surprised me as well. That morning, Mom stopped making breakfast. She turned to me with a sad expression and I could tell it was hard for her to accept but I did not care. I was tired of people rejecting me as Doris and suffering because of this. My old friends were not in touch with me anymore, so I figured no one would care if I changed my name. At university I would be known as Samantha. The life I had as Doris ended in that accident and I was tired of trying to scrape something from the remains and become her again. I would never be able to succeed at this. Samantha was a new name for a new life.

The recovery from my head injury was the hardest challenge I ever had in my life. It affected all areas of my body, mind and soul. Most of my "deficits" were invisible to others and many were invisible even to me. I did not get a printout list of the damage done to my body and brain explaining what had changed. I had to undergo hundreds of hours of tests and assessments but this in no way informed me of everything. The specialists doing the tests did not know who I had been before. I needed to experience life again and suffer through problems I did not have before—to learn. I wish there had been an easier way to recover. Getting support from people not familiar with head injuries was always a challenge and it still is to this day. It was and is an isolating injury from which to recover.

13
Perfect Prizes

On a warm yet overcast summer day in late June 2008, I am driving with the sunroof open, hoping it will not rain again today as it has been a lot lately. I just picked up my new car with tinted windows from the dealership. I have the music turned up, trying out the speakers. This six-speed manual shifts smoothly, different from the five-speed I traded in. My thoughts drift back to the first time I drove a stick shift car with this many gears. I was eighteen years old and it was before I graduated from high school.

~

My dad spent his whole career at General Motors as a mechanical engineer. Test-driving company cars was part of his job.

The day when Dad pulled up to our home in a brand new, white, six-speed Corvette, I was drooling. Mom would not go near the sports car, saying how it was too low to the ground for her. I, however, had no problem with it. My brother got to drive these cars when Dad brought them home—talk about envy. But GM changed the age rules for those allowed to drive company cars from sixteen to eighteen just as I got my license. Because of this I had to wait two whole years before I could drive any of the cars.

So, Dad decided that day to let me drive the "Vette" with him as a passenger. And was I ever nervous. I started the car, revved up the engine and drove out onto our country road.[14]

I shifted gears as carefully as possible. No one had ever shown me how to drive a manual transmission. I taught myself, by driving and shifting gears in my mind to practice. I could not believe Dad was giving me a chance to show him I knew how to drive stick shift.

The sports car seemed like a gorgeous animal in my hands. For our road trip, I was quiet and let Dad tell me where to go. He said he wanted to see me shift and drive at a higher speed. The tour along Highway 2 was totally exhilarating. My heart was pounding in my chest and when I stopped at a red light, I was shaking in the seat. Dad said nothing the whole trip and I could not even look at him. I believed and understood from his silence that I was doing okay. I knew he would not have let me off our country road, if I were not able to drive manual transmission properly. That was only the second time I had driven stick shift since getting a driver's license at age sixteen. I knew I could do it and failure was not a thought.

After we had the car out, I drove back to the three-acre wooded lot we called home. I parked the car. As I started to thank Dad for our trip, I could see behind him the large vegetable garden and the chicken coop. I was about to pull up the emergency brake and turn the engine off when he looked at me with surprise.

"What are you doing?" he said. "Go out for a drive by yourself."

I almost did not believe what he had said. He could not have been serious. My heart was about to explode.

As I drove the car out alone onto the road I had more anxiety than when Dad was in the car with me. If I stalled, I would have looked like such a loser. I knew he was standing in front of the garage listening to me. I made a slow shift of gears to prevent this from happening. I relaxed once I was out of his earshot. What a fun time I had out on my own!

Memories such as this, that somehow were not lost from the amnesia caused by my head injury are endearing. Dad letting me drive the car that day meant the world to me.

Today, driving my new manual transmission car, with the music streaming from the speakers, brings back these memories. It also reminds me of something I read recently in Aunt Gisele's medical notes. I had not remembered until now the experience which happened around the time I met Princess Diana in rehabilitation, when Dad and I drove down Aunt Gisele's road, downtown Toronto. I think my dad would have done anything for me at that time in my life to put a smile back on my face.

She wrote "Her dad came to the house to pick her up—and take her for a spin in the black Corvette he is presently driving. They roared off!"

The safety features of my new car give me a feeling of security as I drive and that only adds to the pleasure. A song by Nickelback on the radio fades into a commercial for the Ottawa Hospital and Children's Hospital of Eastern Ontario lottery.

"The grand prize for the Ottawa Hospital & CHEO lottery, *We All Win* is $1 million dollars, a furnished cottage by Guildcrest homes which is on display at Scotiabank Place, a car, boat, plus more," they say.

This definitely sounds like a perfect prize for me but I do not buy tickets and I will not start to. My former fiancé used to buy lottery tickets all the time and it was annoying. I could not understand him. The only time he would check the number of his ticket, to see if he won was upon reading in the news that the big winner had not come forth yet to claim their prize. He had hundreds of tickets, everywhere.

One day, this habit of his got on my nerves and I wanted to stop myself from becoming anxious. So I grabbed his tickets and took them to see if any were winners. I knew he would not change, therefore, to complain to him would have solved nothing. He saw no reason for me to do what I was doing. I came back and gave him a couple hundred dollars he had won with the tickets. Now I want to avoid reminders of him, so I definitely will not be getting one of those lottery tickets for the hospital's draw.

The prize for this *We All Win* lottery reminds me of the legal work I had to deal with after the accident. My theme song during that stressful time was Barenaked Ladies' "If I Had $1,000,000". I did not own a copy of the album or purposely play the song or even choose to hear it. It was heard everywhere in those days. The playful lyrics helped me find the inner strength to be able to finish my legal work with less anxiety. I have learned that reframing my thoughts about something stressful can often help me a lot.

The cottage prize would be great because I also eventually want to own a year-round cottage on a lake within an hour's drive from home. When I was young, there were cottages in the family. Mom and Dad even met at a lake where my mom's family had one. I will get one when I am married someday because I want to share it with a husband.

I enjoy being close to water. A creek, covered by trees runs through the front of my parents' property just before the road. In the summer I hear it running at night. When snow melts in spring, the creek might flood and water can go over the bridge that is a part of our driveway. Sometimes my brother and I could not go to school because of a flood. Dad usually drove through the water to go to work. The bridge was old and the water rushing over it could have damaged it. There was always the danger of him not making it across and getting stuck. I remember standing inside with my mom and brother, watching from the living room. His passage to the other side brought us relief.[15]

My university friends were shocked by one story about Dad. In the morning while we ate breakfast he would go outside for a smoke. He would be dressed for work wearing a suit. From where I sat I could see the end of a small pellet gun out the breezeway back door. One by one he would shoot the blackbirds off the bird feeder. He held his smoke in his teeth and shot them as they landed. When he successfully hit one, the other birds scrambled as dark feathers flew everywhere. Mom would look over from cooking our porridge and cringe at the sight.

Growing up, this became an unforgettable image, of my masculine ideal: a handsome man with a gun, smoking and wearing a suit. The pretty cardinals, grosbeaks and blue jays needed the food. Not blackbirds; they are scavengers. Dad complained, "They poop in our pool. I am tired of picking it out."

I tried my best to help my friends from school picture a world outside the big city. As Doris, I always loved birds. To read Doris' Kindergarten Thought Book, after my head injury, helped me to understand who I was before.[16] I could not believe how many pictures of birds Doris drew and wrote about. There was a robin, an owl and even a yellow canary that my dad found one day, that were a few of the birds that were a part of My Thought Book. At one point the teacher in her comments said,

"Oh you are a real bird watcher". This understandably led her to want to discover for herself, the source of my hobby.

So one day, when I was in kindergarten, me and the other seventeen students walked the fifteen minutes to my house in winter and crammed into the kitchen for a bird lesson. Mom taught everyone, including my teacher, about the two feeders loaded with birds. Kids climbed on top of one another to see all the action. Many had not seen anything like my backyard. I lived surrounded by forest, unlike my classmates whose homes were in subdivisions.

That day we spoke of the blackbirds stealing food from the other birds in spring. We witnessed only good birds getting the seeds now. We were proud of them because my mom told us they would stock up this food somewhere. She explained how some birds are going to have little birdies soon. It was their job as "parent bird" to gather seeds for them to eat.

Enthusiastically, I added my two cents to the group discussion. I was confident helping my mom out because two years before I had attended my brother's kindergarten class. I would have been four years old. Mom was a volunteer in his class every day and she would take me along. I learned a lot from quietly watching the older kids, the teacher and my mom.

This gave me leadership skills for my own kindergarten class. I was knowledgeable to help the teacher and students if they needed my help. I could explain to others how they were doing something wrong and try to show them a better way to do it.

Years later, when I was sixteen, I met a guy who went to school in downtown Oshawa. We went to kindergarten together.

"I always remembered," he said, "the trip to your house to learn about the birds from your mom."

To talk to him about this turned on a real life movie in my mind, one for which each second was a delight to relive.

Today, while driving, the thought of a cottage and the million dollars reminded me of all these things. As I drive past a small convenience store, the commercial drifts from my thoughts. The fresh air coming in through the sunroof is refreshing.

14
Alignment

"Ms. Michael?" a woman asks when I answer the phone on Saturday morning.

"Yes, this is she," I say.

"I'm calling to tell you that the owner of the dealership has a gift for everyone who bought a car this Thursday and Friday. It's a ticket for the Ottawa Hospital and CHEO lottery, *We All Win*. The grand prize draw will be on the news at noon on July 3."

She tells me the ticket is at the reception desk to be picked up. She cannot be serious that I am getting one of these tickets. I had no expectations to get this. It is interesting how the commercial stood out to me yesterday in the car. I wonder why I am getting this. Well, I now have a shot to win. I would not want the prize because to get a large amount of money handed to me would make me uncomfortable. To earn money is different however and more of a personal accomplishment rather than just getting lucky winning a prize.

Next week I am busy with Canada Day and work, so I better go and pick the ticket up today.

In the distant sky above the car dealership an air show has begun. I watch how graceful the planes are as they perform choreographed movements. I have never seen anything like this from the small airport in the village of Carp that is north of the highway. I enter the showroom and the receptionist greets me. I give her my name.

"Please thank the owner again for me," I say, as I accept the ticket from her.

"I will. You can view the grand prize cottage over there," she says, as she points across the road.

Walking outside, I notice that the prize cottage is underneath the air show as well. The air show, cottage, dealership, ticket, car and I—are all in alignment. What perfect timing! It seems dramatic. On the drive home this visual image of the planes doing a performance as if they were dancing in the sky over the cottage and the dealership stays on my mind.

I am self-conscious about money. I try not to flaunt what I have. I am modest, so to get a big prize would not make this easier. If I win this prize, what will I do with the million dollars?

15
Thoughts with Nature

At home, I decide to meditate. I learned how to do this to help myself cope with the stress and to rebuild my concentration after the head injury. This enabled me to overcome the challenges I sustained to my memory, attention and emotions. In my recovery I was determined to become capable again and restore my once sharp cognitive acuity.

After taking many meditation courses and reading books as well, I found most of the techniques to be relatively simple. Learning about different approaches helped me deepen my practice into something which works well for my needs. There are spiritual or religious reasons why someone may meditate but for me, it is for the health benefits.

As a result, I discovered a calm reflex within myself that has become stronger now from regular practice. Using my thoughts through meditation to trigger this, I can make everything automatically settle down inside of me. This feels different from going to sleep. I can slow down my breath and heart rate with ease. Because of all the benefits it brings me, I meditate daily. The experience makes me feel almost like I am purring. A cat does this because it feels good and this is no different for me and my meditation.

Today, my eyes effortlessly close. Thoughts about the lottery ticket and air show drift from my mind. For twenty minutes, I lie on the couch in the TV room with my knees bent and feet flat. This position seems comfortable for me today. Next time it might be another. No technique I studied told me to practice this way. I enjoy improvising on what I need and the variety in this way helps keep me committed. Otherwise I get bored. I can sit, lie or stand. I do not care. Every day my needs change. Following my breath or reciting a mantra or affirmation are some other choices. I let my body decide what it needs as I close my eyes. Having a laid-back attitude about it helps me do it regularly.

For my meditation today the word that comes to my mind to say to myself is the word happiness. I never judge what word I choose. I leave it up to whatever my needs are at the time. Sometimes it is the same word or else a mantra I have learned before but often I will let my subconscious mind decide for me what to focus on.

Today on my breath "in", I say to myself, happiness. On my breath "out", I concentrate on slowing my breath down and trying to empty my thoughts of distraction. When I catch my thoughts drifting off, I repeat the word happiness, to remind myself of my practice.

After I am done meditating, I sit up and remember how everything lined up when I picked up the lottery ticket earlier. That was an interesting observation. Everything appeared to be in sync.

But I am not going to win this lottery. What am I going to do if I do win though? I cannot control everything that happens in my life. Really, I think I should just give the ticket to someone else. That is an idea or maybe I could help others with the money? The cottage is something I could keep but the money could go elsewhere. There has to be a cause I could help with some money. My thoughts suddenly are reminded of Sofia the night of my party, when she wanted to drive drunk.

Mya rings the bell that hangs on the inside of the patio door, bringing my attention back to what is around me in the room. I get up to let her out. The magnificent forest, lawn and rock garden are full of life with radiance, even underneath the cloudy sky. My dog does not run off the porch but lies down instead and gazes into the dense trees to enjoy the warm weather. I decide to take a seat on a chaise lounge and join her. The fresh air and outdoor smell adds to my relaxation following the meditation. I feel at peace.

Thinking about Sofia again, I wonder what could have stopped her from wanting to drive drunk. Every host at some point may experience a challenge when trying to control a guest's behaviour. To help others assertively confront another who wants to behave irresponsibly, would be meaningful to me. Different ideas start to come to mind and drift through my thoughts effortlessly.

I can speak from a place of strength about my accident and the injuries I received, as I did with Sofia the morning after my party. What happened to me in 1991 was preventable. If I win this lottery I could give the prize money to charity to help prevent irresponsible behaviour like hers. That is an idea—so maybe it would not be so bad to win a prize like this after all. How interesting that by just changing the way I think about something that was stressing me out, my entire perception of it changes.

Sofia's behaviour is an example of why I need to share my story. For personal reasons, I do not talk about the depth of my head injury and the struggles I had. I worked through the horrible experience and it is over. Learning what happened to me affected her but for how long, is something that I question. There is no guarantee that I could do the same for everyone. Sofia needed something more to permanently change her.

To just speak about my injury and give away money would not help others in meaningful enough ways to me. How could I have been more confident that Sofia would change her future behaviour? At my party, the police could not have stepped in to stop Sofia unless she drove drunk. I wish she could have prevented herself from wanting to behave in a way that could hurt others. Jason and I needed confidence and courage to confront her. Not everyone would be brave enough to do what we did.

She did not need a babysitter but an adultsitter. I was safe in my home from her driving drunk. I wanted to prevent her from hurting others. She scared me when she threatened to hit me in the head—I still remember it. My heart begins to beat fast. I brush off my thoughts.

After the party, Sofia's friends told me of the stress in her life. They were trying to get me to sympathize with her so that I would excuse her behaviour. Anyway, it is obvious the woman does not handle stress well. Deep down inside she was angry and this is something I learned first-hand when she threatened me. Stress management might help her. Many people do not know how to relax.

Mya, suddenly jumps up onto the chaise lounge and walks in a circle to curl up near my feet. The leaves in the forest beside us rustle with the wind. The chimes I placed on a maple tree a few years ago gently cling with a soft melody. I bought these chimes as a Christmas gift for Mom and Dad but Dad did not like them. Now they are hanging in the forest here, giving off their lovely sound.

Something interesting happened after I hung them. In winter, most leaves fall off the trees. This maple is now different however and the leaves will stay on around the chime, even on the coldest of days. I thought leaves naturally fell from trees but these seem glued to the branch now, every year. With new leaves in spring, these old ones fall off. Never before had this particular tree shown so much resilience.[17]

One reason this might happen is because no squirrels go on the branch with the chimes now. But I did not think these bushy-tailed creatures were responsible for the falling leaves. So I watched and observed that they do run around that branch and the leaves with the harmonic sound. The squirrels might be using it as camouflage to hide from Mya, their "predator", who is always watching them from inside the house. Often wind also rushes through the forest stirring the chimes. This weighs more than a squirrel and the leaves still stay on the tree. I wonder if the sound from the chime and the vibration of the musical notes it carries somehow strengthens the connection the leaves have to the branch.

Hearing them just now gives me an idea about how to help someone like Sofia. Relaxation exercises would take practice to master but music for relaxation might work more effortlessly. It would need to be slow in tempo and something a person can listen to whenever they want help to calm down. With practice, their body and mind can chill out effortlessly once they hear the music, just as mine is right now, as it hears the sound of the chimes dinging in the tree and the nature which surrounds me. I have become conditioned to relax to this. This is the lifestyle that I choose for myself.

This is my experience with music as well when I volunteer downtown as a hostess in the Patrons Circle Lounge at the National Arts Centre (NAC), a performing arts centre in Ottawa which is home to classical music, opera, English theatre, French theatre, dance, variety and community programming.

Volunteer work is important to me. Since I was a teenager, I have continuously volunteered in many different areas, including an animal hospital, a university law school's human rights centre, a physiotherapy clinic and more. I am passionate about whatever work they need me to do and I am as reliable as a volunteer as any paid worker. After I met Princess Diana, who was renowned for her own volunteer work, volunteering became even more important to me. She was an inspiration to me.

I started volunteering at the NAC in 1999 to host and help donors get drinks and be comfortable in a private lounge they have access to. These patrons donate a certain amount of money a year or are emeritus donors, which means they bequeathed money in their will. I am a patron myself. The lounge is staffed only with volunteers. We open one hour before the performance and at the intermission. To pass time between, we can see the production in Southam Hall when it is a NAC production. We are not allowed to attend when the show is put on by an outside promoter renting the hall but we are still able to look through the door.

Live music has always been therapeutic for me. Even if I arrive feeling okay that night, no matter who is performing, everything slows down for me inside, making me feel relaxed and at peace. It is like I have an internal relaxation switch, similar to meditation. The music from the instruments becomes part of me, changing the energy of my body in ways that make me feel good. Just like the chimes on the tree somehow changed the connection the leaves have to the branch by strengthening them. I look over at the chimes in the forest again. Sound is vibration, so maybe this plays a role.

Over the last ten years, I have enjoyed many fantastic performances. My favourite operas are *Carmen, Madama Butterfly, Salomé* and *La Bohème.* The NAC Symphony Orchestra plays concertos I always love but piano and cello are my absolute favourites. I also like listening to Harry Connick Jr., Chris Botti and Diana Krall.

The Kirov Ballet from Russia is mesmerizing. The National Ballet of Canada also impresses me with their performance. Especially since

Karen Kain, the former prima ballerina, became the Artistic Director of this ballet in 2005. Seeing her dancing in Swan Lake in Toronto in 1980, when I was Doris, is something I obviously could never forget. I recall how excited I was at the time to be watching the performance and I was hardly able to sit in my seat. I only remembered this after my head injury, when seeing her dance once at the NAC for her Canadian farewell tour in 1997. It happened when Mom came to Ottawa for a visit. This was before I started to volunteer at the art centre. Being there with my mom beside me and seeing Karen dance in the *The Actress,* triggered this memory of her dancing when I was Doris.

The tap dancer Savion Glover gives a stunning performance. I studied this style of dance for many years when I was Doris. I can no longer remember all the dance moves, only a few. I have a special appreciation for watching Savion dancing tap. And any Argentine tango is lovely. I can dance the Argentine tango a bit with a skilled partner but ballroom tango is easier for me.

Some music to help people cope with stress could be used as an alternative to negative habits. The music would need to be different from typical songs for relaxation, though; more popular music but with no vocals. Also, I believe it should be a solo musician performing to help a listener build their concentration and focus. Piano would be nice, especially for its full range of notes on the bass and treble clef. This is probably my favourite instrument. I took lessons before and own one.

Relaxation is now an important part of life for me. When I was growing up, no one ever taught me how to relax.

One time at a dinner party I hosted the other year, three friends and I gathered in my den and spoke about a massage chair I own. A few of them tried it. I was telling them how massage helps me deal with stress. These were attractive, smart women, a little younger than I. One woman was a lawyer, a piano teacher and another finishing her PhD in children's education.

Suddenly the conversation shifted to the different pills all three women were on to help them cope with anxiety and depression. This shocked me. Names of medication were mentioned because the mom of one of the women was a pharmacist. I knew nothing about the topic they were talking about. I immediately stepped back from the discussion. I never took the kind of medication like they were. To help myself deal with challenges in life naturally, was always my priority. What I have also been told is that someone with a current or past brain injury should be cautious about taking sedatives. I will not complain about this rule because it gave me no other alternative than to learn to cope without pills.

Because I felt uncomfortable that night, I avoided getting involved in the synthetic drug talk. Even though I believed something else—a natural alternative—might work better, they did not need me to tell them how to look after themselves. They should try meditation, exercising would help as well and so would eating and sleeping properly.

While practicing medicine, my aunt Gisele would not prescribe medication to a patient, unless it was absolutely necessary. Despite the prescription pad sitting blankly on her desk, she tried to help them through conversation and stress management skills, before resorting to a pharmaceutical option.

My friend Kim, one of the friends on antidepressants, met Aunt Gisele last summer in 2007 when we drove out west for the Calgary Stampede. This was just before my aunt and uncle moved to Ottawa. We stayed at Aunt Gisele's country home not far from the Rocky Mountains. Kim and her husband camped out on her property while I slept inside.

For me to be sleeping in the house was a relief. The moderate hearing loss in my right ear from the car accident challenges me at times, however, I usually can manage without wearing a hearing aid, as physicians have prescribed for me. Surprisingly, to not have this aid with me on this trip made me anxious about being in a tent. In Northern Ontario it was pitch black out at night—the kind of heavy darkness that makes one afraid. When I was Doris I lived where it was dark at night—but not this dark. As Samantha I felt like a wimp and could not do it, so for the drive to Calgary I slept in the car while they were in the tent. My logic was that at least this way I had a security alarm to wake me up if needed.

During our visit, Kim confided in Aunt Gisele about the challenges she was facing. My aunt did not tell her that upon returning from Alberta, "I think you should take more medication." Instead, she helped her find her own support and guidance within. After this conversation, Kim felt able to cope with things stronger than ever. She wished my aunt had not retired because she would have gone to her for professional support after she moved to Ottawa.

If I had stress management tools to help me when I was young, I may have avoided getting in the car with a drunk driver that fateful day. My mom always said that as Doris, the summer of 1991, I was bouncing off the walls with excitement about attending university. To be able to relax without booze and smokes would have helped.

One idea comes to me that if I win this lottery I can use some of the prize money to make a CD with music for relaxation and then give away the rest to charity. By selling a CD like this I can raise even more money to go towards helping prevent irresponsible behaviour. A non-profit company could be created to do this and I could share my story on talk shows as well. I do not know much about these types of shows but I do feel they would be a good platform for my message. On a show, if someone would want to give to my cause, they could buy the music CD I created. This is something I would not normally want to do. I do not even watch much TV.

I am having fun playing with my creative ideas. While taking a deep, slow breath I gaze into the trees. With nature surrounding me, my ideas feel as effortless as the beating of my heart.

I could even ask my new friend Andrew to help me. We have been friends since Christmas. He works in communications as well in the non-profit area. He helped the NAC start the TELUS Gala, which has been hosted by other companies as well, since then. The gala now raises money specifically for the NAC's National Youth and Education Trust, of close to $6 million dollars so far.

Mya suddenly jumps off the chaise lounge, running full tilt until the end of the retractable leash halts her in her tracks. She is barking and I tell her to be quiet. She hears someone walking along the path in the forest. The thought of strangling herself is never a concern when she runs likes this. She lives without fear.

As I take a deep breath of fresh air, I think again of my idea about the relaxation music CD. I am surprisingly confident I should make this. Never did I think that I would want to speak out to the public about my injury but after reading Aunt Gisele's medical notes recently, I see no reason to stop myself. To sell something and raise money as I tell my story is a good idea. All I am imagining to do seems to be meaningful to me and that is the important thing. I am trying to figure out how to cope if I win this prize. If I do not do this, I will be stressed out about it possibly happening. My head injury made me more sensitive to stress so I need to look out for myself ahead of time for challenges likes this. This does not mean worry but simply mentally preparing myself by thinking through things that could happen.

Sitting outside with Mya, surrounded by nature, I feel less anxious now about the possibility of winning any prize money. Spending time acknowledging my feelings was important. I trust I can deal with things like this on my own. Therapy is no longer necessary for me to cope. Over the years my inner strength has increased from my success in looking after myself. To think about a challenge and then find a solution is a form of mind exercise for me. I will not let myself be a victim in life. I am a survivor and I know I can successfully deal with any challenge like this that comes my way in life.

As it starts to get cool, I open the patio door for Mya and I to go inside. I call Andrew and tell him about my idea to do public speaking and create a music CD for relaxation to raise money. He says that he believes my idea has the potential to make a difference which could benefit others.

"I will definitely help you with your charitable work," he says.

I do not tell Andrew about the money I will give as well to charity from winning the lottery. If I do not win, I can say I changed my mind and do not want to do public speaking and selling a music CD. He would understand. I would not need to explain to him how I did not have the money to do something like this without winning the prize.

16
Confirmation

The evening sky is getting dark from heavy rain clouds. I am walking to the kitchen to make something to eat. The green trees and lawn catch my eye. Nature needs this weather to grow. Tonight, dinner will be a salad with stir-fried chicken. It is simple for me to prepare and this is the way I like to cook. I do not enjoy cooking.

I remember back in the summer of 1999, Mom and Dad came to visit me at my condo. I had not told them that I had done decorating with a bit of money from my investment from a legal settlement I received. This happened when all my files finally closed and I was relieved. To help myself recover from the years of stress I endured, I chose to decorate my place.

Mom walked in and set her bag down. As she was taking off her shoes she started laughing.

"Is something funny?" I asked, concerned.

"I'm not surprised you've put a pool table where the dining room table should be," she said. "That's my daughter for you."

"You can see me cooking for ten people to eat, right?" I asked.

The question made me laugh because we both already knew what the answer was.

"No. I remember even when young, you never wanted to learn," she said.

Mom and Dad let me be independent growing up. Through the good and the bad, they unconditionally tried to accept the choices I made. To force or try and persuade me to be someone I am not, goes against who they are.

This evening, the rain is still coming down. As I stir the chicken, my mind drifts back to the lottery and how July 3, later this week, I feel, is somehow important. To not be anxious about this, I have already researched how to create a non-profit organization and a charity. I can build something which can be both of these but different rules apply to each one. A charity has more restrictions, for example, the ratio of family members to non-family on the Board of Directors is closely monitored. Also there are many rules about what we can and cannot do as a charity and to simply tell my personal story would not qualify. To be a non-profit is not as restricted. On a non-profit there needs to be only three members while a charity needs five. Andrew has agreed to be on the board, which is amazing but I need more people.

I can get the non-profit established soon, whereas to create a charity will take time because if it qualifies, there is a waiting list to get the application approved. My focus now needs to be on creating a non-profit and a music CD for relaxation. I feel a non-profit organization gives my creativity the freedom to do more right away. This seems to be important to me.

I wonder who else can help me with this work. I stir the chicken in the frying pan.

The thought that my aunt Gisele could be the person pops into my mind with absolute clarity. At the exact same moment, a sharp, loud crack of thunder booms, shaking everything. I jump back from the stove, gasping. I do not move as the weather continues to rumble throughout the house for four whole seconds. There has been no thunder today, so the noise really startles me.

I take a deep breath to help calm myself. I note how in sync my thoughts were with this dramatic expression of nature. Mya is looking around the room, trying to understand what just happened.

Of course, Aunt Gisele is the best person to help me! She lives in Ottawa now. It would have been impossible for her to offer her support in this way if she were still in Calgary. She knows what happened to me and our family from that accident. Her expertise in medicine and psychotherapy would also serve her well as a board member. She definitely can add strength to my story.

As I finish cooking dinner I turn off the stove. An impulse has me go get Aunt Gisele's medical notes to look at while I eat. I really wonder how I can share our family's experience. I worked continuously hard on my recovery and this helped me succeed. But I had almost given up on life a couple of times by attempting suicide. Something within me pulled me through. Doing this work without Aunt Gisele would somehow not be right. I need her support. I believe there is a purpose for us to help others in this way.

I flip through the pages of Aunt Gisele's writing as I eat. Even though I looked at this already, it still feels new. More than ever, I see clearly what happened to me. I lost the life I had before as a teenager named Doris. I learned first-hand how a head injury's impact affects every facet of one's life. To read again a conversation Aunt Gisele had with Dad makes me cry.

"Suicide note—told doctor about it—she gives no advice to parents on how to handle things—they may discuss further."

Mom and Dad never told me they found one of my suicide notes. This is heart-breaking.

"Parents did not talk about her suicidal ideas or feelings with her."

Maybe I should stop reading this. I set the notes down on my lap. I close my eyes as I take a deep breath and talk to myself. I am okay, all of this is in the past. I survived that accident. I repeat this over and over until I feel myself become less anxious. Calmly, I once again pick up the booklet to read.

Aunt Gisele writes about the many phone calls she received from Dad and how distraught he was. He apparently even spoke with my neuropsychologist when I was in rehabilitation at one point, to tell him how much I was in denial about what had happened to me. The physician he spoke to did not believe him at first but then realized that my dad was right. I was very good at masking my problems to others. I could talk my way out of a lot.

I am shocked to read again how long it took me to come out of denial and admit to myself that something horrible had happened to me. At the time I hit a level of unhappiness I had not experienced before in my life—ever. I had no clue of who I was anymore. It was a struggle to naturally be Doris again. I did not have to think about how to be her before; I just woke up as her every day.

In her notes, Aunt Gisele writes of my friends and their lack of support. This brings back memories. I set the medical notes down again and listen to the negative thoughts that are running through my head: it is over; don't get emotional about this stuff; the chapter is closed; this is a waste of time to look at; I read it already; I don't need to look at this information again. To help myself, I start to repeat confidently to myself on every "in" breath, that I accept this challenge in my life and that I am strong. As I do this I notice I sit up a little taller and my thoughts slow down.

After eating, I take Aunt Gisele's medical notes back to the den. I place them down where Princess Diana's signature is. The frame is still in the same spot I put it the night of my party after the argument at the door. Carefully I turn it over so that I can see again the last piece of my Recovery Book. As I observe these two meaningful items from my past I am totally in the moment. I cannot take my eyes off them. It is almost as if they are surrounded by an aura of mystery.

There is no more thunder for the rest of the evening. It oddly feels like it was a confirmation, expressed by nature that I am on the right path.

Aunt Gisele and I are planning to celebrate Canada Day, July 1, 2008, at a private dinner on the rooftop terrace at the National Arts Centre. The event is for qualified patrons of the NAC. I am one as well. Afterwards, we will watch the fireworks over Parliament Hill.

"First I want to see the performance in Southam Hall," I tell her as we make arrangements over the phone. "Pinchas will be conducting the orchestra, while some children's choirs from across Canada sing. Dinner is after."

Pinchas Zukerman is the conductor of the NAC Orchestra and is well-known to my aunt and uncle. He is also a violinist who performs worldwide.

"It will be lovely," she says.

"On a different subject, ideas are still coming to me of how I'm supposed to do something about the accident I was in," I tell her. "The other day, I spoke with my friend Andrew. He works in the non-profit area. He helped the NAC start one of their gala events. I think you went once when Yo-Yo Ma performed," I say. "Anyway, I asked him to help me begin a non-profit and he said he would, no problem."

"Good for you," says Aunt Gisele.

"I want to try to get on a talk show to share my experience. This surprises me but I really feel inspired to help others in some way. I want to prevent irresponsible behaviour like that of the guest at my party. I came up with an idea to create a CD of relaxing piano music to sell to raise money. I feel that everyone should have stress management tools under their belt. And listening to music is definitely one," I explain.

"Very creative idea," she says.

"It would mean so much to me if you were on the Board of Directors as well. I want you to help me speak about the effect this had on our family. You know exactly what we went through. I do not think I am strong enough to speak out on my own about things," I say.

"Definitely, I'll help you!" she says. "We should get together as a group. I'm interested to meet Andrew."

"Thanks for your support," I tell her.

"No problem, I'm very excited about this, Samantha," she says.

"Great, I look forward to seeing you Tuesday," I say, hanging up the phone.

Aunt Gisele and Andrew would do anything to help me help others by sharing my story of how people can find and use their inner strength to cope with adversity. However, there is a small detail they are not aware of. I need to win money to create this non-profit and music CD. Well, July 3 is when I will learn if this is going to happen or not.

17
Canada Day

As Aunt Gisele and I arrive at the National Arts Centre downtown, we show our tickets to the police officers at the road block set up for the July 1, 2008, Canada Day celebrations. They let us through. Thousands of people usually join in the celebrations on the streets near Parliament Hill in Ottawa, the nation's capital.

The art centre is busy. We wait for a seat in Southam Hall. Most people are wearing red and white, carrying Canadian flags and other patriotic icons but Aunt Gisele and I did not dress festively. We take our seats for the concert to watch the Unisong Choir perform with the NAC Orchestra. The lights dim and the audience grows silent.

The performance is wonderful with the instrumental accompaniment to the singers. Over three hundred children are on stage, with at least one choir from each province in Canada. The symphony orchestra sounds its usual best as Pinchas conducts it. Without asking, I can tell Aunt Gisele is enjoying herself.

After the performance, we go to the rooftop terrace for a barbeque and to watch the fireworks. On the stairs, I bump into a few patrons I know from the lounge and we say hello. Seeing them here is different than when I volunteer as a hostess for them.

After mingling for a bit, we sit down. The President and CEO of the NAC, Peter Herrndorf stands in front of us and addresses the group. He expresses his gratitude for the generosity of the patrons. With sadness, he announces that Mr. Hamilton Southam, the first Director General of the NAC and the person for whom the main concert hall is named, has died. He was one of the founders of the art centre. His family is well known in Canadian publishing. How sad that he passed away but touching that his memory will live on through music.

Dinner is delicious. We share a table with four others and when I look around, I am surprised to see my friend Andrew sitting at a table behind us. We catch each other's eyes and I notice his surprise as well. He quickly gets up and comes over smiling.

"Hi, Sammy," he says.

He is the only person to call me Sammy. He gives me a kiss on each cheek. Andrew is originally from Toronto. The double kiss is the French way to greet one another around the capital.

"Hi, Andrew," I say returning his smile.

"I didn't know you'd be here!" he says.

I had not mentioned to Andrew that I am a patron as well as a volunteer, the reason why I am at the event.

"Andrew, this is my aunt Gisele," I say. "I want her to help us with the charitable work I spoke to you about."

The two of them greet one another.

"We must meet to discuss Samantha's work idea further," Aunt Gisele says to Andrew.

"Definitely," he says. "I'll let you enjoy dinner. I look forward to meeting soon."

Andrew walks back to his table to sit down with his girlfriend.

"What a handsome gentleman," Aunt Gisele says.

"Yes. I didn't expect him to be at this event. And seated right behind us," I say.

"It's almost as if we are sitting in a triangle here," she says.

"Maybe it's another sign," I say, "I'm meant to do something."

"You told me about him when we spoke the other day and I meet him almost immediately without any planning," she says.

"I know," I say.

The fireworks later in the evening are spectacular. As we stand outside and watch, I look over at Andrew and his girlfriend and then at Aunt Gisele, standing beside me. Life is showing me that no one could help me more than these two people. It seems I am on the right track with this idea and that makes following any of the signs being shown to me effortless. Now I need the money to pull this off. The lottery draw is this Thursday. I cannot wait to find out the result. This date of July

3 is still popping up everywhere. I hear people mention it whenever I am out. This makes me feel as if things are reminding me about the lottery prize I could win that day.

In this moment I sense a connection between the three of us beyond words. I have never felt this way before. I make note of how the first time we meet as a group is on a day of celebration. I have not been passionate for work like this since before my accident, when I was about to go to university. To have something in common with my previous self, Doris, is unusual but I welcome the feeling, savour it, as the fireworks burst brightly in the black night sky.

18
Scarface

While getting ready for work, I inspect a magnified mirror to see the scar tissue I am trying to conceal on my cheek. This takes me about ten minutes every day and then five minutes more to wash off at night. Unbelievable, how the nearly two hours a week I spend on this activity add up to almost a hundred a year. I have been doing this now for seventeen years, which adds up to almost fifteen hundred hours or nine solid weeks of my life so far. Despite the time and energy, the task is obviously important and necessary for my emotional health.

I still remember my former fiancé's response when he saw me without make-up for the first time. He looked at me with disbelief.

"You are so good at hiding the scar," he said in a surprised tone. "I never realized how bad the marks are."

I looked at him in shock. I did not know what to say. I felt shy and vulnerable as he stared at my bare cheek. I had to look away until he stopped inspecting it. I wondered, at the time, if he realized that he was making me feel self-conscious by saying what he did and staring at me the way he was. I learned later that he had no idea how his words hurt me until I told him. He apologized when I shared my feelings but the damage was done. To protect myself I stepped away from him emotionally a bit.

Then I learned something else that forced me to step back even further. It was during an argument that my former fiancé had with his older brother one time that something was said. Apparently his brother aggressively called me a name. He was trying to upset my ex and it worked. How I found out about this was by questioning my ex's mannerism when we spoke about his brother. He seemed really insecure to talk about him. I sensed that he was trying to protect someone in some way. It was important for me to understand what was going on for him.

He finally broke down and told me what his brother had called me in a fight they were having about money his brother owed him. He had called me Scarface. I was hurt to learn this but for different reasons than one might expect. I was disturbed at this guy's lack of empathy and how childish he was behaving.

After I found out, my mind assertively went to work on how I could help myself. I reviewed what my needs were, which was to express my feelings and what could be done to make him not get away with the immature behaviour he was showing people. I knew that deep down he was jealous of my boyfriend, his brother. I had to understand him as best I could, to be able to successfully confront him.

My solution was to call his brother when he was at work and leave him a short message. I did not tell my ex I was doing this. I thought there was no reason for us to speak to each other. I was not going to attack him, just give him a heads up on what happened and what could happen. In the approximately one minute long message I left him, I politely told him how I knew that he had called me names and that their whole fight had to do with money and not me. I then suggested that he better pay back the thousands of dollars he owed his brother, otherwise I would encourage my boyfriend to legally go after him. A few days later my ex got all his money back from his brother, over ten thousand dollars.

After this happened, my former fiancé and I went back and forth for years as lovers and friends, until I finally figured out that our relationship would not meet my needs long-term. I have too good a memory. I always remembered his insensitive, awkward compliment about my scar and the ability I have to cover the marks up with make-up, as well as his brother's hostile welcome to their family.

As I finish putting on make-up today, I step back to check my reflection. My left eyebrow is starting to droop. I begin exercising to strengthen the muscles, so that I can naturally keep this area of my face lifting on its own.

My grandmother Omi inspired me to learn how to do this. She gave me a book by Senta Maria Rungé, called *Face Lifting by Exercise* written in 1961. With the book I learned how to do exercises to help with the facial paralysis. I have exercised this way since the accident, in front of a mirror as well as with an electrical muscle stimulation device that I got through physiotherapy. By using this I was able to regain a lot of the muscle control. I will have to do this type of treatment long term. It increases my confidence every time I do the exercise.

Helping myself in this way makes me think again of my life's experience. The work I am being shown to do to share my story is coming to mind a lot. I am having doubts whether I can help others. Plus, Sheila needs me to work at the real estate office. If I start public speaking, I will not be able to continue working for her. I cannot quit. I would feel bad leaving her to find someone else to do the work I am doing. I will stop then wasting my time with this idea to help others.

19
A Disappearing Job

For eight years I have trained Sheila once a week in Pilates exercise. Last summer, I started to work for her as an assistant in her office as well. Three days a week I help her with odd jobs, from answering the phone to working on her web site or whatever else immediately needs attention.

Sheila and I still talk sometimes about how we got to know each other in 1997. I had been using a real estate agent I met at a coffee shop on Elgin Street and wanted him to look for a condo I could buy. My mom and dad were generously helping me with the down payment to buy one. The building must have extra security. He said: "You'll never find anything like it here, maybe bigger cities but not Ottawa."

I told him I was positive there was a condo building in the city that would meet my needs. He finally did help me find the building I had been looking for but I did not buy a condo there with him as my agent. I had to let him go. I did not want to work with him—at all.

There were really several reasons for this. The biggest was about what happened on a day while we visited a unit for sale. When he showed me the steam room in the spa of the building, he looked at me and said, "You look like you just had an orgasm."

I stared at him, speechless. After this remark, I canned him. Despite his pleas of apology, there was no second chance at all I would give him. Later we bumped into each other and he thanked me for not excusing his behaviour.

"I learned a lesson from you I still remember to this day," he said. "In the end, I still respect your decision to work with another agent."

I believe there are two ways to deal with problems like this. One, you either work through it, or two, you walk around it. To give the agent another try to do business with me would have been stupid. I would not let myself trust him again as a businessman—ever. So there was no point in even trying. I would be wasting my time.

After letting him go, I became positive one of those condos in that building would be mine, however, I had no agent. To make the days go by faster until I found one, I took the floor plan for the building, the same for each floor and taped the piece of paper to my wall. I highlighted in yellow the unit I knew I would find and buy.

Then I decided what floor I wanted to live on. I realized I did not want to be up too high. I got the idea to go to the local fire station and speak with the fire-fighters to learn how high they can reach with their ladder. They told me. I would not buy above this level but I did not want to be too low either. This left me with five floors out of thirty and this meant I was only interested in buying one of five condos in total. So I waited for one to appear on the market.

At the time I was having problems with my landlord. This was the main reason I wanted to move. I moved to Ottawa to go to university at the end of 1995. Some of my legal matters had settled in Toronto and I wanted to get as far away possible from that city. It was full of bad memories for me. In Ottawa I rented an apartment in a heritage house near the University of Ottawa, across from an old church. These homes are protected by government in Ontario for their historic value. It was a nice place to rent but I had to move. I was not happy living there.

Then one day, when I drove around the city to try and cheer myself up, I gazed at the condo building I knew would be my next home and I decided to stop at Starbucks. This is where I met a British couple, Sheila and her husband James. They sat next to me. Sheila was reading an article on Reiki, a Japanese method of hands-on healing. My mom has her masters level in Reiki, so I started talking with her about it.

I explained to her why I was in that area of the city, concerning the condo I wanted to buy. I then told her I had to stop working with a male real estate agent, who was helping me.

Sheila immediately asked, "Who upset you and what did he do?"

I spoke about my agent's inappropriate behaviour.

"Now I need a new agent," I say.

Then she said, "I'm an agent myself."

Right away, I knew she would help me find and buy my condo. She said she would keep an eye on the listings. I asked her to do something different instead. I wanted her to write a personal letter to the owners of the five condos I had chosen, telling them briefly about me and how I wanted to buy their condo. She had never done anything this way before. She was not even sure how to get the owners contact information. I knew of course she could find this info with a bit of research and I encouraged her to search in a few different areas.

"It's a gut feeling I have. But one of those owners wants to sell," I told her. "And that condo will be mine—watch."

Sheila stared at me with surprise. My approach was creative and I was determined to succeed. Eventually Sheila was able to find the contact information and she wrote the owners. She told them I was studying at university and was interested in buying their place. After she did this, believe it or not, I succeeded in getting the exact unit I wanted in a ladder-high floor in the building!

The owner who sold it to me did not introduce herself right away. She had flown back from her winter stay in Florida and at home, while reading her mail, came across Sheila's letter. Surprised, she phoned because she had decided before coming home that it was time to sell the condo. She no longer lived there but had been renting it out. The last time she called that place her home would have been with her late husband and since he passed away, the memories were hard for her.

After this woman contacted us, I was positive she owned the unit which was going to be mine. My idea to approach the owner this way worked. I had not heard of anyone doing this before. It just appeared to me to be the most logical way to find and buy the exact condo I wanted.

I then lived there for seven years and then sold the place by myself when I moved out. To sell my condo, I created a website, advertised and even had an open house that the condo corporation approved of. This took imagination to dream up. They were really strict with the condo rules. My method was to first learn why our building did not allow an open house on the property at the time and then I thought up a way that respected this but still allowed me to have one.

I had no idea why they wrote the rules like that, however I politely followed them. I did not want to start conflict with anyone in the condo corporation. With the legal battles I had been through before, this would not have made me happy. It was fun thinking up an assertive solution to the obstacles the condo corporation had placed in my path.

My solution was that each visitor to my open house would be personally escorted to my condo. My fiancé at the time and his sister helped me do this. I wanted always to be available to help the guests and answer questions inside. By doing it this way, every person was technically considered my guest, so the condo corporation could not stop me. I had no open house sign out on the road for the public to see, something they did not want. It was only through advertising online and in the newspaper that I informed buyers of the opportunity.

There were a few offers on my place. At the time, my lawyer thought I should jump at taking an offer less than my asking price. I explained to him how I had already met with a couple and that we had verbally agreed upon a sale price and this was what I was expecting to receive. My lawyer looked at the document and told me that it was a very good deal without an agent. I did not think so. It was three percent less than what we had agreed on and I would not accept it.

After going assertively back to the negotiation table with the couple a second time, I made the sale that I wanted, on paper this time. I then met with my lawyer and confidently handed him the signed documents. He was speechless. I got my exact asking price with no real estate fees to pay on either side. With the way I found and sold my property Sheila thought I should become an agent myself but I am not interested, even though I did enjoy the whole experience.

At the office, this morning, Sheila arrives after I get the routine jobs done. We talk for a bit about her daughter; family is important to her.

We start to work. Her team, which includes her son and husband, is busy. With summer beginning, this is common in real estate. She complains about some work I did and I know something is wrong because it is unlike her to be nit-picky. I am capable of doing a wide range of tasks for her and if I do not know how to do something, I will learn and I will learn fast. Today however, she is being argumentative.

"Sheila," I say. "I can change what's done, no problem."

"We won't need your help anymore," she blurts out, looking down to avoid my eyes.

"Oh," I say, surprised. "Okay."

"Samantha, it's not you. I know you don't want to become a real estate agent but we need to enlarge our team. So we've decided to add Tara. She does the staging for us and is writing her real estate exams later this summer. Until then, she's going to do the work you're doing. You were helpful in terms of getting us launched as a team and I'm so thankful to you for this," she explains. "I still want to come to you for Pilates."

"No problem, Sheila. I understand," I say, oddly relieved.

"I shouldn't have told you yet," she says. "We decided to wait a bit until we did. I never planned to blurt this out today. I don't understand what came over me!"

As I leave the office, I remember that earlier this morning I thought I could not stop working for Sheila in order to do the charitable work I have been dreaming up. Almost instantly my job dissolved into—nothing. I wonder if this means something.

20
Private Investigators

Home from work, I grab some lunch. On the counter I notice the hospital's lottery ticket for the cottage and the million dollar prize.

Well, I now might as well go check the prize cottage out. Maybe I will really win it. The draw is tomorrow. Doing this would help distract me from the news I just got from Sheila about my job ending. The office job was enjoyable from the social side of things. I now might need to win this prize if I am no longer earning this income because I do not want to work more hours as a personal trainer.

After lunch, I get ready to leave and grab the car keys while saying goodbye to Mya. Having come close to dying in an accident before makes me always want to pay attention to her before I leave. To drive a car is important to me but this also means facing risk daily. I sometimes worry that my dog will be left alone if I do not come home. I attribute this to simple realism, not paranoia. I try not to take my life and the good things I have in it for granted.

Mya always can tell when I am about to leave the house and today she positions herself on a slipper-back chair at the front window. She will stay there the whole time until I return.

As I put my shoes on, I glance out the patio door into the backyard. The trees and grass are a deep green. The atrium window above on the second floor I call *My Live Painting*. As the leaves change with the seasons, so does this framed view.[18]

I have no favourite season; they all are eye-catching. Even winter is because the backyards on the other side of the forest are visible then through the branches of the trees. An ice rink is lit in one backyard at night and sometimes this offers a picturesque view of people skating.[19]

Mya has fun watching anyone or anything in the forest. Being a watchdog, she tells me when something is visible. Her barking does not annoy me because the main reason I got her was to help me with my hearing loss from the accident.

In order to not need to wear the small, modern hearing aid, I taught myself how to manage by lip-reading. No one suggested I take lessons to learn how to do this but it just seemed to me the most logical way to cope with this problem. I learned and practiced enough to understand what is being said by looking at the mouth as well as the eyes of the person I am speaking with. I do this when someone is talking more to my right ear. Usually, I do not mistake what they are saying. Turn out the lights and talk to me in that ear and it is a different story.

Whenever I misunderstand someone, I am easy on myself and laugh about it. I cannot worry about it because this is just the way life is now and I accept it. I will never hear perfectly again. To expect different would be stressful; and stress like that is something I do not want or need.

To have Mya as a roommate helps me with this challenge because, when my former fiancé moved out, I was nervous to live alone in a house. The reason for my anxiety was that since I am a sound sleeper and sometimes I sleep on my left side with my right ear up, my bad ear, I might not hear the house or fire alarm. I know realistically this would not be the case but I needed something more to feel secure. When a party is happening next door, the hearing loss is useful but not when safety is a concern.

My uneasiness about not being able to hear well anymore started to surface when I began to live alone, without roommates, at age twenty-two. Mainly this was because after the accident in 1991 private investigators (PIs) had been regularly following me. They worked for the insurance company which was helping me with my injuries from the accident. So, unbeknownst to me, the insurance company would sometimes check up on claimants receiving benefits by using a PI. I learned they do not even need to tell you they can do this, when you sign the policy.

My head injury left me with many problems that required endless professional support and claims for related expenses, so a file had been open for almost eight years. To be investigated for this long was not fun. Deep down, I sensed the PIs around me, kind of like when someone stares at you from across the room and you can feel it. So this made my hearing loss an even more uncomfortable challenge for me.

Buying a condo staffed by two separate 24-hour security guards was one way I coped, although in hindsight, they did not help much. One time around five in the morning, an investigator got past security at the front gate. That night, he spoke with the guards in my building. How my guards knew the PI was who he said he was, baffled me. He just told them he was a private investigator and did not even show identification or indicate for whom he was working. I seriously could have been in danger from a strange man following me!

The PI asked my building's security questions about me. One was, if I shielded my face with my hand or a scarf when leaving the building to cover the scar on my face. The investigator showed how this might look to see me cover my right cheek. Also he asked, if I cried in public from insecurity.

They had to be kidding. How embarrassing. I had more confidence than he was insinuating. He was portraying me as a victim. I know the PI was asking these questions to help build the defence for the insurance company to close my file through mediation. My lawyer and the insurance company had already met a few months prior and were unable to find resolution.

They were then trying to use the PIs to scare me into settling for less than was being offered on the table. My file was an old file from a company the insurance company had bought out. This file for them was unwanted baggage. The agent on my file at the time we settled was a shark. As soon as he got his hands on my case, he started to aggressively pursue closing it through my lawyers. So the PI's inconsiderate behaviour did not surprise me but it did piss me off—big time.

In recovery, I did not claim to cover or cry about my scar in public because I would have been lying. The PI's questions to my security made me uncomfortable and I objected to the invasion of my private life. The insurance company had access to this kind of information through the physicians and therapists who were working with me. To allow a PI to speak of my personal life to others in this way shocked me.

My security guard did not tell me about this PI visiting until much later. The guards in my building were not strangers; they were a part of my daily life. They worked for me—or so I thought. When I investigated further I learned that PIs would also park across from the gatehouse of the condo complex waiting for me to leave home and then they would follow me. My guards at the gate sat and watched them the whole time and did not say a word to my building's indoor security guards or to me. A few NHL hockey players and some established professionals lived in my building. I am sure they would want to know if they were ever being followed as I was.

Most of the PIs were male, between twenty-five and forty years old. I would date guys this age. I did not talk about the injuries I had sustained anymore at the time but to think a PI may have wanted to see my facial scar up close under the guise of dating me, made me nauseous and insecure. I learned there are, alarmingly, no rules for insurance companies to follow when they hire these investigators to work for them. I am friendly and easy to talk to; any one of them could have approached me. I had to seriously wonder if the insurance company would have kept my best interest in mind in the process of hiring these guys.

At twenty-five years old, I hoped to settle down and marry and the whole experience was building a distrust of men. It stressed me out—big time. This surveillance had to stop; I wanted my privacy back.

I found out about all this during the Christmas holidays of 1998. I still remember, during that time, looking out the window as I was about to go somewhere to see if there was any car parked. If there was, I would not leave the condo. After the holidays, I had my lawyers in Toronto get rid of the insurance company. I did not speak directly to anyone at the insurance company ever again. I saw no need to because this was what I had hired a lawyer for. I especially did not want to talk with the last agent—the shark. The PI experience had violated my boundaries and I was angry. There was no reason for me to confront this problem assertively myself. It was over between us and we had nothing to work through. My lawyers would then speak on my behalf.

A legal assistant called to tell me they had advised the insurance company to back off. Knowing this made me more comfortable to leave home again without looking outside first. It was too late however to repair our broken relationship, since I no longer trusted them. As a result, I finally agreed to settle and close the file with them. I knew that the internal scars I was building to protect myself needed to heal. My lawyers were able to negotiate an amount for a settlement that both sides found acceptable. But I knew it was for less than I needed and deserved. To get rid of them, I had no choice but to accept their offer and move on.

To close this case allowed me to open up emotionally and express the anxiety and discomfort I had felt for so many years of being under surveillance. The hundreds of reports written by others over the years were a huge weight on my shoulders. Cognitive evaluations, physician's assessments and lawyers letters where overflowing in many offices. After we settled, the invasion of my privacy appeared to be over. As I would look out the window of my condo, I still would check sometimes to see that no car was waiting for me to leave. It took me awhile to trust that things were really over between us.

I am relieved to this day that I chose to close this policy. I know I had sincerely wanted and deserved help to achieve a successful recovery. As a result, private information of mine was everywhere. Physicians' offices, insurance companies and law firms, all had personal details about me. After the entire legal case was resolved, my legal assistant said my file had more than sixteen thousand pages on microfiche films.

Even though it was stressful for me to have had the insurance company and lawyers around for so many years, I desperately needed their help. They assisted my recovery by giving me valuable support and resources. I will always be grateful for this. When I was ready, however, life pointed me in a direction to learn things about the PIs to help me grow and change and move on, stronger than ever.

21
The Cottage

As I look around at the country side while I drive, it reminds me of where I grew up. I wanted to take the backcountry roads route, to go and see the grand prize cottage for the hospital's lottery. Scotiabank Place is the venue, in the west end of Ottawa, where concerts and NHL hockey games are played. There is a lot of farmland on this route but this area will not be fields and forest for much longer as construction starts up. Builders are going to be putting new subdivisions here for thousands of homes.

After parking, I walk up to the portable cottage to go inside. The man showing the model is talking to a couple. I overhear him say that the cottage is structurally solid and movable to any location. The two bedrooms unit is decorated in a mixture of styles. It is as big as my condo was. I look around, noting how comfortable the place seems. I sit down on a couch and wait to ask the gentleman a few questions. The people soon leave. The man comes over to talk with me.

"The cottage is cosy," I say.

"I agree," he says, sitting down to join me.

"I got a ticket as a gift from the dealership's owner," I say, pointing to their building right across the road.

"Oh, I know exactly what tickets you are talking about. I just sent in the other day the names and addresses to officials looking after the lottery at the hospital. What's your name?" he asks.

"Samantha Michael," I say.

"Think I remember yours," he says. "So you thought you would come and check out the prize?"

"It's not like me to want to win a lottery. I never buy tickets. Something has been showing me I may win the grand prize, if you can believe it," I say. I closely observe his face, trying to sense whether

I should continue. "Unusual stuff has been happening to show me I'm going to win. The date of July 3 appears to me everywhere as well. I know that if I win, I'm supposed to use the money to help others. When I was eighteen, I almost got killed in a car accident in Muskoka."

It is amazing how in a few sentences I told him my story. Today, I am not as guarded about the topic.

"You are going to find this interesting," he says. "Here's information you'll want to see."

He hands me promotional paperwork for the cottage. As I flip through the pages, I stop at the floor plan for the model and gasp. I look up to see the man smiling.

"See the name of the cottage?" he asks.

"Yes!" I say.

The cottage is called *The Muskoka*. Muskoka is at least a five hour long drive from here. The builder is from the Ottawa area. What an unlikely name.

"This is what I mean! Stuff like this is happening, every day," I say, feeling confusion mixed with excitement. "I wish I knew who's writing the script and directing this experience. My ego would never dream about winning this. I'm fortunate to not need this money at the moment. Already I have enough to make me content; not many people can say this."

"If you're drawn to help others, I'm like you," he says. "I'm a mentor in Alcoholics Anonymous. Over twenty-five years ago, I quit drinking. After I helped myself, I decided to help others."

"Good for you. Interesting that in the accident I was hurt, the driver was drunk. I met Princess Diana in a children's rehabilitation hospital in Toronto after my injury. The circumstances around her fatal accident were different," I say. "I cannot judge the facts but I think it was a mixture of irresponsible behaviour and driving under the influence. Her driver was under the influence of alcohol, as well as prescription medication. I'm being reminded of meeting the princess with what I'm supposed to do if I win this lottery."

"On my TV set there's a box of candies named after Princess Diana and her boyfriend who was in the accident with her," he says. "It sits there and I don't know why but something won't let me toss or eat them."

"Maybe now you are learning why you kept them," I say with a smile.

When I get up to leave, he wishes me luck with the draw. If I win, we both say we would look at life in a new way.

As I leave, I decide to stop by a café for a cup of tea. A friend owns part of the business. Or an "instant friend" of mine as Andrew calls them. He finds it amusing how I meet people and get close to them effortlessly. I have met many people this way and Andrew himself is actually one of them.

I go to this café because I like the food and the seating. Today as I walk through the door Carl, the owner, greets me.

"Hi, how are you?" I ask while ordering tea.

"Okay but a bit frustrated. Grab a seat and I'll come over and fill you in on what has been happening," he says.

I choose a table away from people. As I sit down, I flip over a newspaper. I am surprised because usually Carl does not have any around to read. The headline reads about a million dollars available for teen rehabilitation. I notice that it stands out to me to see a million and rehab. I read the title again.

The lottery grand prize is one million and I want to use the money to help children. The amount also reminds me of when I was in recovery settling my legal matters and I was hearing "If I Had $1,000,000" all the time.

I read the story and learn about drug rehabilitation centres the Ontario government is putting money into but it was the headline that really grabbed my attention. At the bottom of the page is an advertisement for my car dealership. I have never seen one in this paper before. For me the ad ties in with the headline above. I am confused why I am being shown this.

Then I flip the page and read another headline about a drunk-driving accident in the Ottawa area. My jaw drops. The news story explains how new policing rules are going to be put into place as a consequence. But I know that more needs to happen than just punishment. I wonder what does this mean for me to see all this in the newspaper. I quickly close the paper as Carl sits down.

"Hey, there's never usually any newspapers here. Do you mind if I take this home?" I ask. "I want to read the rest of it."

"For sure you can take it. I bought it earlier to read at lunch but I'm done now," he says.

I tuck the paper under my purse. We talk for a bit and he tells me about some problems with his business partner. Carl is having a hard time dealing with this.

"You need to get more emotionally detached from work. A way of relaxing would be good for you," I advise.

We talk a while longer. My mind is multitasking nonstop. I am trying to make sense of everything: the lottery ticket, the job with Sheila disappearing and the airplanes doing a show over the car dealership and the cottage on the day I picked up the ticket for the lottery. I am confused and overwhelmed as thoughts swirl around in my mind. I wonder why I am sensing I will win this lottery. I have had no dreams of winning a prize like this before, ever.

Talking with Carl about his challenges makes me realize I am experiencing my own stress as well. It might be difficult for me to sleep tonight. Since the accident, sleep is still a problem on occasion. I did not have insomnia before the head injury and without proper sleep I am not at my best. Once I get home I will take a warm bath to relax.

22
Stress Management

Checking the temperature with my hand, I adjust the water for the bathtub. As I wait for it to fill, my thoughts drift back to how much I have learned since my accident, to help myself when I am under stress. As Doris, the smoking and drinking beer on weekends never would have been able to help me the way I needed it most after the head injury.

After seeing a neuropsychologist on a weekly basis for a few years after 1991, I found it was lacking something. Sure, it was helpful to acknowledge some topics of anxiety in my life and to have someone with whom I could share my feelings but I did not want to cry about my life forever. It was getting boring to talk about what and why stuff happened to me. I was introduced then to biofeedback therapy, cognitive therapy and Mindfulness Meditation. These therapeutic approaches aided my recovery tremendously by giving me valuable skills I could use to once again build a happy life.

In 1993 I started biofeedback therapy, working weekly with a therapist named Heather. She taught me, in many different ways, how I could monitor some of my involuntary nervous system behaviour and control my body's way of dealing with things. At the time, I was unaware how stress affected my body. What she taught helped me learn better ways to cope.

One way, was by using a special thermometer on my fingertip throughout the day. Heather showed me how I could monitor the temperature of the skin on my hands with this unit that was small enough to keep in my pocket. She scheduled me to take breaks throughout the day and take my temperature and then record it for us to look at when we met next. If my temperature was low, I was to survey my breath and body, as she showed me how to do. I was taught exercises

I could do, to raise the temperature.

I learned by doing this that my hands become cooler from stress due to a lack of circulation possibly caused by shallow, rapid breathing and/or muscle tension, particularly in the shoulder and neck area. At the time of my therapy, when I would take a breath, I would tend to lift my shoulders, resulting in shallow breathing. At first it was way easier for me to breathe shallowly and go outside for a smoke than to deal with my anxiety and try changing for the better. What I was doing was a habit for me I had for many years. But when I became conscious of the fact that part of the reason why I enjoyed smoking was because it forced me to take deeper, slower breaths, even though I was breathing in something toxic, my perception of my relationship with cigarettes changed. I seriously then wanted to quit—without question. And two years later after many failed attempts, I finally succeeded and kicked the habit.

By learning to maintain more correct posture it helped me reduce the problem of muscle tension. By working with a physiotherapist specializing in posture and Pilates exercise I became stronger. Breathing deeply and expanding the mid-chest area, where the diaphragm is, while keeping strong abs, is part of the focus of this method. There is no lifting of the shoulders while inhaling, which was the way I used to breathe. I learned a lot of valuable information from this physiotherapist.

Heather also taught me that by changing my perception of challenges in my life, I could help myself become independent and capable again in ways I was before the accident. As Doris, I would not have been able to cope easily with stress, head injury or no head injury. My injury enabled me to rebuild a new source of support and strength within myself.

As I continued with my biofeedback therapy, one day, Heather asked about my dating life.

"Who are you seeing and how's it going?"

This had been around the start of our working together, so I was loaded with problems. I had come out of a long-term relationship with a guy named Brian and was just starting to date again. She thought I sounded like I lacked self-esteem. She said, "Next week we will try increasing your self-confidence. There are a few books I want us to read parts of together."

I wanted to do this right away and not wait until our next meeting. After our appointment, on my way home, I went to a bookstore and bought a couple of self-help books about self-esteem. I enthusiastically jumped at the chance to help myself. And then, burning with this new passion, I took out more books from the public library. In residence, where I lived at university, I read for hours and hours, devouring every word. Reading these books, I realized that I held the key to overcoming many of my problems.

Before the accident, I would not have opened a book like this. But the information I discovered inside, was like a life-jacket being thrown to me in the sea of my fiasco. I desperately needed this kind of knowledge. I soon realized that re-learning skills which were destroyed by the brain damage was the best way for me to cope. I had the power and ability to rebuild the many damaged parts of my life. For my next session with Heather I confidently walked in and told her I had increased my self-esteem. I was positive from what I read that I had addressed the core of my problems and not only the symptoms. I could already see the effect this was having while relating to other people in my life. That day, Heather stared at me, speechless.

This was not something I would tell her if it were not true. I did not understand why she looked so surprised to learn this. She must have had other patients who did this. With skepticism, she started to quiz me about my problems to assess what I had learned and how I was coping. She was impressed as she realized I really had become stronger. She asked me if I was having fun when I saw the new guy I was dating and what were we talking about, as well as how I felt then about my scar. I answered her questions with more confidence and strength than I ever could have before.

At this point Heather started to videotape some of our talks. At the end of our session, we then watched part of it.

"Tell me what you see and what you like about seeing yourself?" she asked.

"I look and sound confident," I said. "It's different than a picture.

I can hardly see my scar. I'm outgoing—cool. I like my jawline when I speak. That sounds weird to say but I never noticed it before. I like to laugh. This is fun to do!"

Heather was quiet while I shared my observations. My self-perception had changed remarkably. From then on, after every session, I would find self-help books to study. I had no idea before how interesting and helpful they were to read.

Heather also helped me learn to become stronger, using resources outside of biofeedback. One time during a session, I told her, "My concentration's not good anymore since the head injury."

"You should take the Mindfulness Meditation course at Toronto General Hospital taught by Dr. Paul Kelly," she said. "It's an excellent course. It would help you."

Heather told me that he started one of the first hospital-based meditation programs in Canada. I jumped at the chance to study with Dr. Kelly. I worked with him once a week for eight weeks studying and practicing meditation. It was fun because my mom and a friend of hers took the course as well.

This training in meditation made me aware of how my concentration is like a muscle and needs exercise—regularly. Now I practice daily. As a result, focusing and studying no longer give me problems, unless I am not sleeping well. If I did not learn how to meditate, my recovery would have been even more difficult—without question. I know that meditation has been probably the most important thing I learned how to do to help myself. It has enabled me to rebuild the best life possible.

Heather also taught me to take personal responsibility for my problems. Not just for correcting them but for having them in the first place. Sometimes mere small changes in my perception and interpretation could make huge differences in how I was dealing with things. Learning to cope in an assortment of ways increased my confidence.

Every time I saw Heather, she asked about my life and guided me to become better at dealing with and resolving any problems. She was a therapist as well as a mentor. For example, one day I had been arguing with an insurance adjuster, something that became a frequent occurrence. Problems like this for me, before the head injury, were non-existent. I told Heather about the fight we had and she immediately zeroed in on why we were arguing.

"You are using passive-aggressive ways to express your feelings and needs to him," she said.

She wanted to help me become stronger and referred me to Dr. Shelagh Emmott, a cognitive behavioural therapist, who specialized in assertiveness training at Toronto General Hospital. This therapy is much more skills-oriented then psychotherapy. From working with Dr. Emmott, I walked away with tools under my belt—for life.

Cognitive behavioural therapy helped me develop more effective communication skills. I learned enthusiastically and I did not need to be a patient there for long, the goal of this type of therapy. By examining my thoughts to learn what I was saying to myself, I could see the effect my inner commentary and perception had on my well-being. This therapy focused almost entirely on my mind when dealing with stress, whereas biofeedback focused more on my body.

I learned through this therapy that I was sometimes unkind with what I said to myself. Examples were: I sound stupid; nobody likes me; this person is an idiot and I am going to get mad to make my point.

Dr. Emmott taught me that I was the biggest part of the problem I was having with others but at first I found this difficult to believe. She had me work with a cognitive behavioural therapy book by David D. Burns, MD called *The Feeling Good Handbook*. In this book, along with my therapy, I learned about the different types of thinking I have and how they can affect my feelings and moods. I learned to recognize them within myself and to accept or change them. I also learned to talk back to myself when I was not speaking nicely to myself, as well as how to reframe my thinking.

Whenever I saw Dr. Emmott, she would ask about how some challenges I was having in my life were coming along and whether there were any new ones. One time I told her about a problem I was having with a roommate. The girl annoyed the heck out of me. Dr. Emmott had me write down what happened, what was being said, my feelings, her feelings and the outcome I hoped for. After evaluating my feelings it was really helpful for me to put myself in the shoes of the other person for a bit. I hated stepping into my roommate's shoes but to get the outcome I hoped for I needed to understand her better. After I acknowledged and accepted everything, it did not seem so bad after all. My perception of what was and had been happening changed for the better as a result.

Slowly, over the following weeks, my skill level in assertive communication got better and better and I was becoming capable to deal with things on my own. When I would present a challenge to Dr. Emmott, I could outline for her all the details of where my thoughts were. I was already two steps ahead of her. This therapy helped increase my emotional strength to deal with stress in my life in a different way than psychotherapy ever could have. I was learning skills and they were becoming tools I could use in my life, by myself. It was giving me back my independence that I had lost as a result of the accident.

I worked hard with Dr. Emmott. I learned that by taking responsibility for things happening in my life, I could positively influence just about anything. This therapy was tremendously helpful and gave me a powerful skill that I still carry with me to this day. After this therapy, I then studied cognitive therapy a little more in university, to further my knowledge.

Another thing I was passionate about learning more of after biofeedback therapy was learning to breathe better. I wanted to study it further. I worked with the physiotherapist who specialized in Pilates and then I continued to train in this area. Now I train others in Pilates, teaching them the same lessons I learned about how deep breathing and carrying good posture can help anyone deal better with stress. One of my clients, a physician, said, "In medical school, we never learned anything about this."

I was eager to recover in these ways from my head injury and that motivated me to learn. My recovery became top priority. All of my therapists taught me, each in different ways, how I could cope, no matter what challenge I faced. I was like a sponge, soaking up every helpful suggestion they gave me. I researched everything and will continue to do so, for as long as it is necessary in my life.

To combine cognitive behavioural therapy with biofeedback therapy, Mindfulness Meditation and Pilates was an incredible opportunity for me. It was a leap forward in my recovery. It privileged me with life skills I would not have received without my injury. I wish I had been taught skills like this in school before the accident however, so I did not have to get severely hurt in order to learn them.

I am grateful to Heather, Dr. Emmott and Dr. Kelly for helping me discover many proactive ways to help myself. I try now to take full responsibility for the challenges I am facing, instead of blaming others. To sleep right, eat well, practice relaxation, exercise and drink enough water throughout the day are all important. To pay attention to my needs helps me manage any stress I experience. To look after myself independently in ways like this, always boosts my confidence, which enables me to handle whatever life puts in my path.

Now if I ever get challenged by something in life, I ask myself questions like: what is my perception of what is going on; how do I feel; how might others feel; and how is my body dealing with this? I survey my body and check my breathing, the temperature of my hands and whether or not I am holding any unnecessary tension. If I have a problem, I will often immediately know what to do or where to go, to learn how to better cope. I may need to change or study something new in order to deal with whatever is challenging me in my life. It might sound like this takes a lot of time but it does not. Because I am more conscious of what is going on in my life it keeps me on top of things.

My mind and body are like a lighthouse. As the storms of life swirl around me, I remain steadfast, shining brightly. The determination I have to take care of myself is strong. I want my lighthouse to be dependable for me, no matter what the "weather" is like. My goal is to live the best life possible. I do not need everything to be perfect but I have learned that it is worth the effort to take responsibility and improve what I can for myself.

The warm bath for me tonight was deeply relaxing and helps me get a good night sleep.

23
July 3

It is Thursday, July 3, the day of the hospital's lottery draw and I am keeping busy doing work around the house. At lunch I am going to watch the news on TV, to see them choose the winning ticket.

I am glad this will soon be over, one way or another. I am open to receiving the prize but only to support the charitable work I would like to do. Few people would give away money they won. As I turn on the TV, I am reminded of my former fiancé. This is unlike me to be sitting here with a ticket.

"We are here now with officials from the Ottawa Hospital and CHEO lottery, *We All Win* for the draw today. About forty-five thousand tickets were sold," the newscaster says.

"Okay, let's get started and spin the drum," the official says.

First they will draw for the smaller prizes, then the grand prize, *The Muskoka* cottage. Many names for the smaller prizes are announced. No surprise there. But for the grand prize draw, I am nervous. I cannot wait for this experience to be over.

They spin the drum and pull a ticket. I hear them announce a name—other than mine. My heart sinks. I stare at the television screen while frowning. I grab the remote to turn the television off and I throw the ticket aside. Looking over at Mya, watching the forest, I sigh.

"I don't understand at all what has been happening the last week because something had been showing me I'd win this cash prize and *The Muskoka* cottage," I say. "I never felt this way about winning money before. July 3 appeared to me everywhere as a date of significance. My feeling was that this day, today, would be a huge step forward with the work I was supposed to do."

From practicing meditation for so many years I have developed solid concentration as well as intuition. Usually I trust my hunches but after this I may start to question them more. The motivation I had to speak about what happened to me when I was young felt good.

Confused, I look at Princess Diana's signature from my Recovery Book that is sitting on the side table. I brought it out from the den the other day, along with Aunt Gisele's medical notes. One day, I held them together while I meditated and my relaxation was very deep. I was especially looking forward to working with Aunt Gisele.

Frustrated, I pick up the small frame and notes and take them back to where I hid them before in the den. A sudden impulse makes me want to throw them against the wall in frustration, however I stop myself. I have not wanted before to do anything like this. With care, I place the two items behind a row of books, this time to hide them better than I did the other month. There, this will now help me forget what happened and be able to wipe my hands of the whole outrageous lottery experience.

On my way to the kitchen to make some tea, a painting catches my eye. I received it as a gift from an Asian man I dated a few times. He had painted me a flower with Chinese writing beside it, which translates to *Always Happy*.[20]

He said this is how he would describe me. Today *Always Confused* would have been more appropriate.

Later in the day, before bed, I am online looking at Google News. The top story is about an accident in Muskoka, north of Toronto. During the afternoon four young adults had been at a country club, drinking heavily. On the drive back to their cottage, they did not make a corner in the road. Their car hit the guardrail, smashed into a tree and plunged off, tumbling into Lake Rosseau. Three men in that car died, including the driver; only a woman survived the accident.

Deep, heavy feelings flood my body. I cannot take my eyes off the article. I am speechless. What a tragic story. I wanted to speak out to try to prevent these kinds of tragedies. I do not understand why I am seeing this now when I can do nothing.

I am amazed by the similarities with my accident. The driver of our car, Deborah, was not sitting with us drinking but like the boys in the story, we were all young, up in Muskoka and there was no other car involved. Like the driver of the boys' car, Deborah also missed a corner in the road and slammed into a tree.

Confusion and sadness overwhelm me as I read more. I thought I was to help others, to teach people so they would learn ahead of time the effects their irresponsible choices might have. The importance of sharing my story is obvious. People need to realize the decisions they make can have severe outcomes for themselves and everyone around them.

Deborah was not the only person at fault. I am partly to blame as well because I drunkenly got in the car with her. It was my choice. Even though I normally would not behave like that, I could not use it as an excuse.

I can do nothing to influence change without winning that money. I feel helpless. Going to bed I have trouble falling asleep. I cannot stop thinking of what happened to those guys in cottage country and what happened to me in 1991. I can recall few details of the actual accident I was in but my imagination is hard at work. From my rapid heart rate and breath, I know I am anxious. I wish I knew where the off switch is for my thoughts.

A memory of when my intuition was one hundred percent accurate and saved my life, comes to mind.

~

After the accident my gut feeling always told me I needed important surgery to fix my ear. When I say always, I mean—always. As time passed my feelings became more intense and I was scared. To about twenty different Ear, Nose and Throat (ENT) doctors that I was a patient of, I would tell I needed surgery.

All the ENT's said that with one of the little bones in my ear, called the incus, being out of place from the accident, it was not worth the risk of putting it back into place. This was the surgery they thought I was talking about. They claimed that usually someone with this bone being dislodged would have more severe hearing loss. My hearing loss was moderate but not as bad as they thought it should be. So they were concerned that moving things around might damage my hearing even more and not help me.

I agreed with them but this was not the surgery I knew, deep inside, I needed. I always told them this. Their apparent lack of concern about my intuition was distressing. I knew, without a doubt, that if I did not have a certain surgery on my ear, my life was in jeopardy. Every doctor shrugged off my fear—until Dr. John Rutka came into the picture.

I first met Dr. Rutka one day in 1995, after I saw my family doctor who knew Aunt Gisele. I felt more comfortable sharing my fears with this doctor because he knew my aunt. I told him how I needed some important surgery on my ear and that my life was at risk. I asked this family doctor to refer me to another Ear, Nose and Throat specialist. No, actually I begged him. He said, "Samantha, you have seen all the best doctors in Toronto. I will send you to one more but that's all. After this, I will only recommend you speak to your neuropsychologist about this developing anxiety of yours."

I would not give up on myself until I got the medical support I needed and my anxiety was resolved, so off I went to the next ENT doctor, who worked out of the Toronto General Hospital. During the course of the exam the doctor surprisingly discovered a lump in my ear drum.

"Oh look, what is that? There is a bulge in her eardrum," Dr. Rutka said to a medical student while examining my ear closely.

This doctor then booked me for an MRI scan to make sure that it was not brain tissue that was bulging into my ear. When the results of the MRI showed nothing unusual, I was immediately booked with Dr. Rutka for an exploratory surgery.

The day of my operation this surgery turned out to be much longer than anyone had anticipated. While operating, Dr. Rutka discovered a hole about the size of a dime in the lining of my brain, behind my ear. This area was leaking cerebral spinal fluid (CSF) intermittently.

This damage was a result of the accident and it might eventually have been fatal for me. The reason this leak was never detected before was because my body had creatively produced scar tissue into a mass, in an attempt to plug this hole from leaking. This was what the doctor and the medical student had seen bulging into my eardrum. This plug worked so well that when I lay down for CAT scans, the dye they injected to show my spinal fluid never showed a drop of leakage for my neurosurgeon. Had I been asked to stand up for the scan, it would have been different but who stands up for CAT scans?

I kept a copy, printed as a photograph, of the MRI that Dr. Rutka had taken of my brain, in my guest bathroom at the condo where I used to I live. Even though it had shown nothing unusual, I had a sentimental connection to this picture and Dr. Rutka.

I always found people's reaction to the photo to be amusing. One time after a guest came out of the bathroom she asked, "Do you mind if I ask you a question?"

"No, of course not," I said.

"What is that picture of in there?"

"My brain," I said.

I left her standing in the hall in shock. I did not want to explain to her why I had a picture of my brain.

I will always be grateful to Dr. Rutka for helping me. It was his curiosity about what he did not know which led to his success.

In bed, turning onto my side, as I fall asleep I think about the mixed messages I have been receiving about winning a lottery to help others. I guess my intuition let me down this time.

24
Abandonment

The following morning, I look through the Saturday news online about the Muskoka drunk driving accident. The eerie similarity between their accident and mine is sending shivers up my spine. The flashbacks I am getting about my own accident, memories I have never had before, are intense and make me cry. This is not good. I have read enough of this sad stuff. I put my computer on sleep and decide to go grocery shopping to get my mind off this tragedy.

Tonight, I want to stay in and cook dinner. Friends asked me to get together but I am not interested. Socially, as Samantha, I am more distant than when I was Doris. I have heard this often happens in life as people get older and busy with families. However, when many friends abandoned me after the accident, when I was suffering and most in need, I withdrew my emotions somewhat from many different friendships for protection.

Sure, it was easy for me to meet new people when I went away to university. Something, however, changed for me. I grew cold through lack of trust. Others could not tell because I was still more open-hearted than most people but I knew I had changed.

I focused instead on developing a more meaningful relationship with myself. I learned that whenever I need to, I can give myself approval and support in life. To not expect anything from others spares me the fear of getting hurt. This may sound harsh but it is not. I love people and with nothing to lose, using this approach works best. By not being scared of the outcome, I find I can give more of myself to those I meet. I keep no tally of the many positives I put forth to others and what I receive in return. I know when to stop giving though because I am not a pushover, I am self-confident.

To remember what I experienced in the past with friends, as Doris, is important. This helps me put healthy boundaries around new friendships. *Once bitten, twice shy* is not my attitude but *once bitten, twice smart* is.

The disappearance of friends in sudden and unexpected times of need is not unusual. It makes me wonder if they really were my friends to begin with. One friend told me how people drifted out of his life after his dad died. In the beginning, everyone had sympathy for him but when he took time to move on through his grief, a different side of his friendships emerged. They showed less support and availability.

After the accident, many friends stayed at arm's length from me. Sure, they were relieved I was alive. However, they wanted to get back to partying in their seemingly carefree lives. As well, perhaps those who were in the accident with me felt guilty around me because we were all partly responsible for what had happened to me. Or maybe they preferred to ignore me.

The easiest solution was to avoid me entirely. This way they did not have to see my scar. At the time I did not wear any make-up to cover it. I wore little make-up when I was Doris before the accident, so I needed help to learn the difference this could make for my self-confidence, as well as the comfort of others. The noticeable marks on my face would have reminded everyone of the mistake we made. By avoiding me, they did not need to witness how much I had changed as a person. By not acknowledging my struggles, it became easier for them to accept. I wonder if they realized how hard it was for me to lose my social network.

Many people I knew before the accident, appeared to care only about their own needs afterwards, seemingly not interested in helping me rebuild a life. Even a call to see how I was doing would have made me feel I was not all alone with my struggles. Instead, my parents sadly had to watch as their, once popular, daughter gradually became isolated due to lack of support.

What hurt me most was the abandonment, especially by the girls who were in the car with me. We had been celebrating how good life was when everything—including these friendships—came to an abrupt halt. Amanda, one of the friends in the accident, was studying occupational therapy at university. After the accident she did not ask once how I was coping with my head injury. I am sure she was studying at school a lot about the type of injury I had received.

Lori, my good friend before the accident, said she cried every day after. She claims she still cried years later, whenever at university she looked at our picture—the last taken without my scar. I still remember how excited we looked in that photo. Looking at it, there was no way anyone could imagine our fate later that night. I angrily destroyed this photograph one day. I hated the reminder of the life I had lost. Doris was gone. There was no point crying about her.

Often I thought Lori lied to me about her crying episodes. Sure, maybe missing the person I had been before my injury might have made her cry. But this is an understandable, yet pathetic excuse for her lack of support. If she was upset, she should have contacted me. We were still friends. I was still alive.

"I did not get anything after the accident as a cash settlement," she once told me. "It's hard for me to see you being able to buy things now."

Lori clearly thought she deserved compensation for her emotional hardship because of the accident. The money I received had nothing to do with emotional hardship; it was to help me because I will not be able to work full-time. They gave it to me so I can maintain the same quality of life I would have had before being injured.

If I ever shared my struggles with Stacey, after the accident, she would immediately remind me how we were all responsible for the accident. She yelled at me once how my injuries were my fault only and no one else's and that I could not ever get off blaming her sister for any of my problems. After she aggressively spoke to me this way we drifted apart, losing touch. I wonder if we have ever been true friends.

The appearance of Deborah on television has not only affected me but some of my family members as well. Dad leaves the room grumbling and Mom quickly changes the channel whenever she comes on. It upsets me that her appearance does this to them. My parents remember that over the years I complained and cried to them often about all the struggles in my life that were a result of the accident she got us into. They are less upset by what happened the night she hurt me, as they are with her and her family; they showed a complete lack of support. Deborah and her family's self-centred attitude upset them both.

Deborah's irresponsibility destroyed my life as Doris. I was the one smashed up and unconscious in the back seat. What did they all do to help me? Nothing, other than Stacey's father passing along through her, that my parents had his "permission" to legally go after Deborah's insurance if need be. I might be able to only ever work part-time now and he was telling us that we had his permission to seek reimbursement for this. I do not think we needed his stamp of approval to do that.

Stacey also told me her father understood how serious my injury was and the effect this would have on my quality of life. It was interesting that he knew so much about head injury before he even laid eyes on one single medical report about my diagnostic status. To get this message passed on for him through his daughter was awkward. I had no idea why Stacey was his messenger. What a burden to put on a teen. My parents were not impressed with this and neither was I. If this had happened at a cottage my parents owned, they definitely would have tried to be available for support in whatever way they could.

One time, about ten years after the accident, I looked up Deborah's number and called her. After seeing her laugh and joke around on television for a few years I needed to talk to her. Something deep inside compelled me to pick up the phone. Why exactly I did this, I do not know. I was brave.

During that call we spoke about her sister Stacey. We both understood she chose to defend Deborah and that explains why we lost contact. It was an unusual conversation; I did not know what to say. I simply felt I needed to call her, even though a decade had passed since I was hurt in the accident.

Deborah told me that her family had sheltered her from learning about my injuries. In other words, she did not know how seriously she messed my life up. They kept her from knowing the results of her behaviour. She seemed pleased that they did this for her. This bothered me to hear. She did not realize how thoughtless it was to tell me she was ignorant of the damage she had done to my life.

I knew that Deborah's family also received information about my progress for legal reasons. Because her father kept everything a secret from her, she knew nothing of my failures and successes. To learn that what I went through was a solo journey for me, hurt deeply. To know that all the hundreds of hours I spent crying and struggling, that I was even more alone than I thought I was, was hard to accept. For her father to try and protect his daughter from the consequences of an accident she caused, touched a nerve deep inside me. Although I did try, by using denial as a coping mechanism, I never could have turned a blind eye to what she did to me.

Deborah also told me she was not close to many people and that she had difficulty forgetting about the accident she caused. She lived in a small apartment and spent most of her time at work and at home.

For Deborah to have been sheltered from learning about my injuries made me angry in a way that I could not understand. I always believed that she was compassionately following how difficult my recovery and struggles were. Sure, I knew that for her to hear how much pain and suffering she caused someone else would have been hard but she was being protected from reality—a luxury I was not allowed. All I can say is that Deborah is lucky our lawyers were able to settle outside of court. In court she would have had a huge wakeup call.

Without giving it much thought during our call, I started to share with Deborah my experience about meeting the late Princess Diana. I wanted to tell her how the princess visited me at the time when everyone started to reject me in different ways, when I most needed support. For some reason I wanted her to know this. As I was about to tell her how no one visited me in that rehab hospital, including her sister, Deborah interrupted me. She immediately started to speak about the death of Princess Diana.

"I can't believe how much the media milked Diana's story," she said. "I thought they never would shut up about it. Every time I turned on the TV or opened a newspaper, there it was!"

She went on and on, seemingly more angry than sad. Deep down, I understood why she disliked hearing about Princess Diana's tragic death so much but I do not think she did. The Lady being killed by a drunk driver reminded Deborah of how close she came, to killing me or even someone else in the car with us that night. Deborah had something in common with the drunk driver of Princess Diana's car; she destroyed the life of someone else.

I found her words self-centred and uncaring. To listen without telling her off was hard but I did not say anything. Not one word of compassion came from her. She showed little empathy for anyone in the Princess's life. While I listened to her go on and on about her discomfort of seeing this death being reported in the news, I remained quiet. My heart was beating fast. My cheeks were hot. I bit my lip. I did not call her to fight with her.

Deborah's reaction to Princess Diana's death as a result of a drunk driver appeared to reflect in many ways my own reaction to seeing Deborah herself on television: every time I turned on the TV or looked in the mirror, I was reminded of her and what happened—just as she was when she heard about Princess Diana's story. I did not think it would be kind to share this with her, so I kept these thoughts to myself. I sensed she had not worked through stuff. I felt compassion for her.

"We should meet to both get closure on this," I said.

We spoke about getting together, without making plans. A few weeks later, I received a letter from her in the mail. She said she could not meet with me—ever. She said she had decided this by going to a counsellor after we spoke and talking for an hour. Together, she explained, they could not see the point for her to start a friendship of any kind with me. She told me that we were not friends before she hurt me, so there was no reason for us to be friendlier to one another now. She then had the nerve to tell me she would love for me to call and tell her how I am doing occasionally.

Her words enraged me; I was stunned by her self-centred attitude. I would not treat another person the way that she was treating me. She had said in her letter in 1991, that if I ever needed help, she would—always be there for me. To meet me this one time was the only thing I ever asked of her. After I reached out graciously to her, I was verbally smacked in the face with her uncaring response. Then she wanted me to call her long distance to check in. There was no way I would ever do that. It was obvious she was scared to acknowledge the damage she had done to my life, especially the scar she gave me.

After receiving Deborah's letter, when I knew she would be at work, I called her. I felt that to write her back would be a waste of time. I had no interest in speaking with her directly. I only wanted to leave her a message. I needed to respect her feelings with what I said but I also needed, in as non-aggressive a way possible to tell her what I thought of her attitude.

"It was nice talking with you the other week. Thank you for the letter you sent. I just want to respond and say that you are—a fucking bitch. Not for the accident because I believe we all were responsible in ways but for afterwards. Your complete lack of support makes you—a fucking bitch. I feel sorry for you and will not be contacting you again. Have a nice life Deborah. Goodbye."

After hanging up the phone, relief flooded my body. I ripped up her letter, walked into the bathroom and threw the small pieces of paper in the toilet. The sound of the flush was soothing as I watched everything disappear.

Back in the living room I sat down to meditate. I could tell from how quickly I relaxed to a deep level that a part of me was pleased I had stood up for myself. A huge weight was lifted off my shoulders. I obviously needed to move on with my life and maybe this was why I had phoned her in the first place. I could not believe I called her those names. I usually do not swear. I have never before in my life called a woman a bitch in her face, let alone put the f-word in front of it, so I was really surprised. But I had no script for what I was going to say. I simply, spontaneously expressed my feelings in the best way that I could, trying to be as assertive as possible.

I did not tell my family what happened. I felt that it was meant to be a confidential conversation between Deborah and me. There was no need to dig up the past again for them.

25
An Aid

I t is dinnertime and I am sitting at the table. My thoughts are caught up with how the Muskoka accident that happened last week triggered memories and anxiety about my own experience and how I am finally feeling a bit better now. The thought of helping others with that lottery money was so persistent and then the whole idea just dissolved into nothing and that is strange.

The signs pointing me in the direction of helping others were obvious. I thought that the walls I had built around my past were crumbling, to enable me to finally share my story. I was remembering more and more the circumstances surrounding my accident. I thought the painful memories of friends lost and the lack of support I experienced, were all meant to prompt me to do work to help make things better in the world. I was being shown I would win that money and *The Muskoka* cottage, so there was no choice for me but to open up about my injury. And then I did not win.

It was as if someone was watching and playing a game with me. Like an invisible director somewhere was creating a real-life movie and doing things to see my reaction. It definitely was a learning experience but not in the way I imagined. I am not a person who worries, so I can easily let this go.

Tonight, I am enjoying dinner of grilled salmon with salad, while the patio door is open. As I eat, I am looking into the trees to exercise my eyes. This is something I do regularly. I taught myself how to exercise my eyes at my parents' house. I did this at night when my bedroom lights were off. I would see the small orange light switch for the top light with my right eye. Then I would try my hardest to bring my left eye which was looking off to the side, to focus on it as well. Then I would hold my eyes there for as long as I could.

At first, it was nearly impossible to do that. The pain was intense but with practice this got easier—as do all things. Without these exercises I would have needed the surgery to correct my double vision. Physicians were not interested at all that I was doing this. They just wanted to keep on telling me about the operation I had to have. They told me I could do the exercise but it would never work and that I should not get my hopes up. But it did work. After seeing my success, they shrugged it off and said my body must have healed itself. No—I healed myself.

I also do not need to wear prescription eyewear now because of regular exercises I do to strengthen the muscles controlling my eyes and improve how they change focal points. I use eyeglasses my mom's friend brought me back from Britain in the 90's, that are called pinhole glasses.[21] They are exactly as the name suggests and have hundreds of little holes over the entire dark opaque plastic lens. They are not corrective lenses but are glasses only meant to be used for eye exercises. This kind of therapy could be classified as a form of behavioural optometry.

I wore them occasionally to watch TV. While watching, I would look back and forth from the TV to outside of my condo. This variation in distance back and forth, between near and far was important for this exercise to work for me. It was like lifting weights for my eye muscles. The glasses look ridiculous to wear, however, they worked well to strengthen my eyesight. After using them my eyes were always tired for a day or so. It kept on getting easier and my vision definitely improved.

The ophthalmologist needed to gradually lessen my prescription. I actually had to beg him to do it. He always wanted to keep the same constant strength but I asked for a weaker one so that my eyes could get even stronger. He also thought that what I am doing would never work. My eyesight is twenty-twenty now. I do not need reading glasses anymore, although I still have a pair for driving. They are the lowest prescription possible for anyone and only need to be worn in case my eyes tire, something that can happen from dry eyes, especially at night.

This physician, after witnessing my success, did not speak to me again about how my eyes were getting better. He acted as if he did not care. It was like he chose to ignore what I did because it was not something that he had ever prescribed for a patient. It was beyond what he had learned in med school.

Now, if I ever strain my eyes on the computer or while reading, I will put the pinhole glasses on and have a coffee as I look into the forest with Mya. Maybe a few times a year I might need to do this. I think it might help Mya strengthen her eyes too, if she wore them while watching the forest. Sometimes I put them on her to wear and she likes them.[22]

I have been able to keep the same weak prescription now for over ten years and whenever I get new glasses, the people at the store do not understand why I am using the same prescription. I love watching the look on their face when they learn how strong my prescription used to be. I let them know that I still see my eye specialist once a year for a check-up and the prescription remains the same.

Tonight, at the dinner table, my thoughts are quiet. I am at peace. A sudden realization comes to me with new clarity and I understand more about what has been happening to me.

I did not need to win the lottery to do the work I wanted to do after all! I already have access to money to do almost everything I have imagined to help others. The bank gave me that line of credit the other month. This financing is available right now. I can still make a music CD for a non-profit to sell while I do public speaking and try to get on some talk shows to share my story. I can start a non-profit. I can definitely do this work for my cause. Nothing heroic needs to happen like I would have done with the prize money. To create a CD and raise money while speaking about my experiences is enough. This is a normal charitable vision.

To think I might win the hospital's lottery forced me to imagine what to do with the prize money and maybe that was its only purpose. I had many guards up around the story of my accident—big time. Dreaming up how to cope, if I won, helped melt my defences.

I get up from the table to get Princess Diana's framed signature I hid in the den. I place it down beside me while I eat.

I now know that most of what I imagined the last few weeks is still going to happen. Using my own money is perfect. This is my idea. I choose to do this work. Nothing can hold me back now from helping others.

Those deaths in Muskoka were preventable. Their tragedy motivates me to tell my story and make a difference in our world. I am sad to think about what the family members of the three young men killed must be going through. The night I was hurt, my parents and brother had no idea if I would be dead or alive when they got to the Toronto hospital. That night Mom awoke to the phone ringing quite a few times after one in the morning, with no one at the other end. She was anxious. But finally she received that life-changing phone call when there was a nurse who was speaking on behalf of a doctor who had laryngitis. She was told that I was seriously hurt in a car accident.

"Doris is now being helicoptered to a larger hospital in Toronto. Please meet her there."

"How hurt is she, aside from the closed-head injury?" Mom asked.

Finally, the doctor who had difficulty speaking got on the phone and tried to explain my injuries as best he could. My family had no idea what a closed-head injury was. They had no idea what condition I would be in when they saw me in the Toronto hospital. I could have died or been permanently stuck in a comatose state.

Late that night, when Dad walked into the ICU and saw me, he burst into tears. No one had ever seen him express so much emotion. My head was swollen massively and bruises were developing. My face was full of cuts and stitches. The devastating sight probably opened up old wounds for Dad. His dad died when he was ten years old. My aunt Gisele, his sister, is older and she never saw him cry about it—ever.

At the hospital, my mom found the strength to support others. Everyone needed her; she had no choice but to be strong. My hair was a bloody mess, adding to the visual display of my trauma. The nurses wanted to cut it all off. Mom remembered how much I loved my long hair and refused to allow them to do this. They spent many hours untangling my hair and cleaning my scalp, knowing if they were not careful, I would be in more pain.

While I was there one of the ambulance attendants from Muskoka came to see me and learn how I was doing. My parents were touched by his concern. He was from cottage country three hours away.

My thoughts return to what is triggering these memories: what were those young people thinking; why was Tyler, the driver of the car in Muskoka, not more careful; why did his friends and girlfriend not speak up to stop him from driving drunk?

When she wrote me the first letter in 1991, Deborah had expressed regret about her not being careful with our lives the night she smashed up the car. Many people young and old still drink and drive. Sofia was thirty-three years old and would have driven drunk if we had let her.

Picking up Princess Diana's signature I take a deep, slow breath. Thoughts drift from my mind as I focus on what is around me right now in the room. I hear the ticking of the clock above the patio door, the roar of the highway in the distance, birds chirping and the hum of the fridge. I look out into the forest.

Suddenly, I see an image in the branches and leaves of the trees. I have seen images like this looking up at clouds but nowhere else. Mom sees things like this in the forest when we go for a walk with Mya but I would not be able see it without her pointing it out. What I see in front of me, unbelievably, is what appears to be Princess Diana in a pattern of nature. I am amazed. It resembles her head, looking off to the left side, like the picture I took when I met her.

I cannot be seeing this. I look down at her signature. This is not real. My mind is playing tricks on me. I look again into the forest and still see her. I now understand why I am seeing this, as my purpose for speaking out about my experience becomes obvious. There is a deep inner knowing surrounding everything I am supposed to do, that I cannot put into words. If I am the only one who can see this image in the forest it makes no difference because the message is loud and clear to me.

I am grateful for Princess Diana visiting us kids in the rehabilitation hospital. I wish to do my philanthropic work as a tribute to her. I could not do non-profit work like this unless it was in pursuit of a higher purpose. It is just the way I am. Kind people like Princess Diana, are losing their lives because of the irresponsible behaviour of others. Children in hospitals need people and gracious visitors like her.

Sure, I have many permanent challenges from the trauma I experienced but I am still alive. My experience can help others. I could just consider myself a victim in an accident caused by a drunk driver but I will never do that or act like one. People usually cannot tell how badly injured I was other than the scar on my cheek. I want to inspire prevention, different from supporting only increased police enforcement. My scar makes my story even more real, to both myself and others. I cannot ignore this permanent mark.

I look closely at Princess Diana's signature. I wonder what I can call the organization I am going to create. I gaze at the letters of her name: d, i, a, n, a; then this time, backwards, a, n, a, i, d.

I think anaid might work. No, it makes no sense. A naid—is a definite no. I wonder then about—an aid—I like it. Maybe it could be An Aid Foundation. No, because it might be mistaken for other work. An aid—for what then? I like how Diana's name could be a part of the work I want to do. It could be—An Aid to Help! Yes, An Aid to Help Foundation—sounds perfect. When I get a chance, I will call Andrew, to see what he thinks.

26
Déjà Vu

It is now later in the evening and the way Princess Diana's name feels so right to be part of the name of my non-profit—an aid—has been bringing back memories.

~

It was a dark winter morning in January 1997. I woke from a vivid dream about Bill Cosby, Princess Diana and myself. I had not had dreams like this before. I would not call it a nightmare, more a vision of what we could do to promote responsible behaviour in the world. All I felt throughout my dream was deep unconditional love surrounding everything.

I would occasionally see my thoughts more clearly this way and feel emotions more deeply and that was new for me. I think my daily meditation was causing this. I had just taken a course in Transcendental Meditation which deepened my practice. This experience was different for me than the Mindfulness Meditation I studied before.

Right after the accident, my thoughts were fuzzy and pale in colour as a result of the post-traumatic stress. I hated this and tried not to pay attention to it. There was nothing I could do to change it, so I could see no reason to worry about it. But through meditating deeply on a regular basis I was able to then visualize things much better in my mind's eye—better than ever. And this was making my dreams more clear and memorable than I had ever experienced before in my life.

A few days before this dream, Cosby's son was killed, so what I dreamt about did not surprise me. The newspaper said he pulled over on the side of the road to fix a flat tire and a man shot him. How tragic.

In my dream, Bill Cosby, Princess Diana and I were teaching people how to behave responsibly in the world. It was not a dream with conversation but with emotion. We were influencing others. I cannot describe it but it was clearer than daylight. I shrugged it off as unimportant because I met Princess Diana before and I had also just learned about Cosby's son being killed.

A few weeks later I read in the paper that Bill Cosby was coming to Ottawa to perform a comedy show in the spring. I was surprised he would want to do this so soon after losing his son. I wondered how much he could smile and tell jokes after his tragic loss. I was curious to see him perform.

Immediately I called for a ticket and asked to be as close to the stage as possible. This was something I would not normally do. I usually sit farther back because it is easier on my eyes. However, for this show, I wanted to be close to Cosby because I thought he must be going through a lot and part of me was curious to see how well he could cover it up. I was pretty sure he would not be able to hide everything from me. His eyes would give him away.

Because I called so quickly after seeing it in the paper, I got a front row seat.

At the show, Bill was a true gentleman. I enjoyed his sense of humour. He started to joke about high school teachers.

"Everyone here can remember a bad one," he began. "How students dreaded getting this teacher."

Cosby asked the man sitting to my left, "What was the name of that teacher for you?"

"I never had one," he said.

Cosby started to make fun of him for not remembering one. The man was getting red in the face. My heart went out to him for being singled out. Without thinking, I softly said, "I had a teacher."

"You did," he said while looking at me, deciding whether to take his attention off the man.

"And what was his name?" he asked.

"Mr. Adair," I said. He was the calculus teacher I hated.

"Mr. Adair," he said pausing for a moment. With an obvious smile in his eyes, he continued, "And what's your name?"

"Samantha."

"Samantha," he said. "Well, come here, Samantha and let me introduce you to everyone."

He reached down and invited me to stand. While holding my right hand, he turned me around to the audience.

"I would like you all to meet Samantha. Did anyone else have Mr. Adair?" he asked.

One person yelled. I paid no attention. I was more concerned about what had happened to Cosby and how he must have been dealing with the loss in his life. In that moment, as he held my hand, my heart went out to him. From having seen and heard of my own dad's struggle after I was hurt, I have a soft spot for dads.

"Thank you, Samantha," he said looking at me as I sat down.

I watched him closely as he performed the rest of the show; somehow making people laugh must have helped him cope. I understood better why I wanted to see him and sit close to the stage. Cosby had acted as a dad on TV but he was also one in real life. He has feelings and vulnerabilities just like everyone else. He did not mention his tragic loss during the performance. I did not expect to see the man break down. I just thought he would say something. It is understandable that he chose not to.

Occasionally that summer, my thoughts would drift back to the dream I had earlier that year about Cosby and Princess Diana. Then in August, Princess Diana was killed in that fateful car accident. Her tragedy was a result of irresponsible behaviour, which was what I dreamt we were trying to stop in my dream.

After I learned about her accident in 1997, I immediately knew her driver had been drinking. My dad said, "Nothing in the news says this."

But I was not surprised to later learn that her driver's blood tested over the legal limit for alcohol. The accident which killed Princess Diana had a few similarities to mine. Their car was taking a corner in the road and she sat in the backseat, just like I had. Her driver was someone who picked her up that night, just like mine had as well.

"Watching Princess Diana's funeral was like déjà vu for me," Aunt Gisele said one day. "She died from the same type of accident that she was visiting you as a patient in the hospital for."

Her words sent shivers up my spine. I thought I alone noticed similarities.

My uncle Dieter, who is Aunt Gisele's brother and Omi thought the same. In a letter I surprisingly kept, he wrote:

Calgary, AB
September 8, 1997

My dear, dear Samantha,
… As I told you, the only reason why these happenings in Europe meant so much to us here, was the strange parallel of what happened to Diana— and what happened to you!
… Diana was definitely different! Her only and main mistake was marrying Prince Charles. On the other hand, had she not married him, would you ever have met her?
I am thinking about you more and more these days and I often curse the distance that separates us. How nice would it be if whenever something were bothering you it would be possible to drop over here, sit in the garden with Omi, Gisele and me and talk your heart out!
… So let us remember Diana—not for what she was supposed to stand for but for who she was. Mainly, however, let us not forget that she died after her accident—but you are still alive and have loving people around you, even if they are very far away! Isn't that wonderful?

Love
Dieter

After Princess Diana's funeral, Mom gave me back the piece of my Recovery Book that she had kept; she thought I needed it for support after what had happened. This seemed odd to me but after I realized on a deeper level, how upset I was, I agreed with her—which was a surprise. I met Princess Diana at a time I was trying to forget. It had slipped my mind that Mom still had this part of the book. To have this piece from my past was not of importance to me—until she died. The rest of that book I had already destroyed by tossing it in a fire at my parent's house during one of my many dramatic attempts to get rid of the past.

Now, seeing Princess Diana's signature, framed in a small beige frame, evokes different emotions. Sometimes I remember her kindness while visiting me and writing in my Recovery Book and I am grateful. Other times I remember her death and I am sad. Deborah was right, in that we do still see a lot of attention placed on Princess Diana in the media. For many, she will never be forgotten. I am motivated to raise money for a cause as a tribute to her, so I guess that makes me one of those who will never forget.

Within the frame, behind her signature, I had put a business card from someone I met in 1999 who works in injury prevention in the Ottawa area. She said to call her if there ever came a time I was ready to speak out to share my story. I did not have any reason to follow up with her because I was not open to sharing anything, especially in public. But I did not know what else to do with her card, so I put it behind Princess Diana's signature. I always remembered it is there when I look at the frame. It is as if every time I see this piece of my Recovery Book, there appears a question mark in my mind. Just like the night of my party, when I sat on the stairs holding it.

After I finish eating, I take my dishes to the kitchen and then let Mya out. My beagle would stay outside on the porch for hours, if possible. To gaze at the forest, from either inside the house or outside, is her form of meditation. Winter and fall are her favourite times because when the leaves have fallen to the ground and nothing impedes her view, the action unfolds before her in all its wonder.[23]

I have taught Mya that if she barks more than once outside, she will be brought back into the house. This works unless something interesting happens in the woods. As a compromise, after the first bark she woofs quietly under her breath. There is no problem with her changing the rules to suit her needs. She has learned to control her behaviour. Learning to behave in life is something dogs and children respond well to; it might even help some adults. After my recovery from the head injury, I definitely know that this is possible.

As I finish cleaning up the kitchen I see Mya standing at the patio door, waiting patiently to come back inside. It is one of her cute habits; she does not protest if I am not there immediately. She will just scratch again. As I slide the door open, I take her leash off and she runs quickly to jump on a chair to watch the forest, this time from inside.

"What a simple life you have, Mya," I say. "You never get bored."

27
A Living Ghost

Late in the afternoon, this summer day in July 2008, I turn on the
television to watch while I make dinner. A talk show guest discusses
problems in his family and I half-listen as I cook. A different program
comes on as I sit down to eat. I look into the forest at the leaves blowing
softly with the wind. Suddenly from the television—Deborah begins to
speak. I slowly turn my head to her image now on the screen.

Heavy emotion floods my body as I sink down into the chair. I
sigh in despair. Plugging my ears with my fingers, I look back into the
forest. My cheeks are now hot and my heart is pounding in my chest.
I feel somewhat light-headed and not well.

So glad you came to dinner Deborah, I think to myself. My door is
always open to her—no, it is not but there is no other choice for me than
to change the channel or turn the TV off. That will not stop me from
feeling stressed out as a result of seeing her in my home. Great, I am
trapped. This memory is wasting my time. I cannot label my feelings
but they are more intense than normal. What can I do to help myself?
I have to be able to do something.

A memory comes to mind of one of the last times I watched
Deborah on television many years after we spoke on the phone. I
used the unexpected sight of her to help find closure on some of the
unexpressed feelings I still had about what she did to my life. It happened
this past New Year's Eve for 2008 after dinner at Aunt Gisele and Uncle
Helmut's. Everyone stayed until midnight but I preferred to go home
earlier.

To drive on this celebratory night makes me nervous, considering
the abundance of risky drivers out there. I know that for a fact from a
couple of sources. A young man I know told me one time, "Many of my
friends drive stoned. They go downtown for the night and drive back

baked." Thanks for telling me. As a result I am even more concerned when driving.

After I got home that evening I poured myself a glass of wine. Sitting down on the couch I turned on the TV set. All of a sudden, before her image even appeared on the screen, Deborah's voice echoed throughout the room. What a surprise for her to be working at that time of day. This traumatic memory of mine was really beginning to bother me.

Anxiety welled up inside me. I closed my eyes and looked within to see if there was something I could do to help myself feel better. This was a night of new beginnings for me and here she was. I felt like she was intruding. I was feeling good about my life—until then. Even though she was not doing it on purpose, her continuously interrupting my privacy at home was becoming hard to deal with. I would not let her ruin my New Year's. It had been years since we last spoke. Putting a life back together for myself was not easy and she was not welcome in it. But there she was smiling and talking on the television set, as if she did not have a care in the world.

Speaking quietly to myself as I watched her image, I was able to lift a huge weight off my shoulders. I became aware of the many words not spoken between us, the conversations we did not have but should have. I could tell it was important I speak with her in this way by myself. To ignore my needs would have given me more emotional baggage than I wanted or needed. Before I left the telephone message for her almost ten years after the accident, when I called her those names, I wanted to meet her in person to do this in a friendly way. She rejected me. I can live with that. But I still had to do something with my feelings, which were a reaction to her actions. I thought that the short message I left her on the phone would have freed me from this stuff but I could see that some stuff still remained.

That night at midnight, I focused on the television and put my fingers up in a peace sign to her, a gesture I had not made before to anyone, ever. What had inspired me to do this was someone I recently met and who knows Deborah. It was my neighbour, Derek. Mya and

I see Derek a lot around the neighbourhood. Every time Derek, Mya and I see each other from afar, whether I am walking Mya or in the car, he sends me the peace sign with two fingers on his right hand. So the connection between Derek and Deborah helped me choose to do this on New Year's Eve to her.

One time, after seeing him send me this sign, I somehow felt more comfortable talking with him about my past. I told him briefly about my accident. My unexpected openness about the subject caught me off guard. I did not speak about the severity of my closed-head injury with him.

"That's the effect I have on all women," he said sarcastically.

I mentioned how the woman who hurt me is on television. He asked what her name was. Turns out he met her some years back through a friend at a concert for the band The Guys. He thought she was funny. From the few times I spoke with her, I thought so too. I had not met anyone who actually knew her, other than people from Oshawa.

But I thought I forgave Deborah that New Year's Eve—and yet here she is, still haunting me on TV—in my own house. This is not fair. As I look outside into nature I force myself to acknowledge that seeing her still upsets me. Obviously there are a few cords between Deborah and I that were not cut and possibly never will be. My feelings are different in a way I cannot figure out.

I learned in assertiveness training how anger should be toned down and then expressed appropriately. When I called Deborah that word on her voice mail, I was calm, cool and collected. Previously as Doris, I had more of a snappy edge to me. There was little trace of her in the message I left Deborah. I miss this aspect of Doris, the capacity to get passionately pissed off.

This might have not been the best thing to do to control myself like this; anger is a natural part of life. It was okay if I were to be more emotional with her—she was not nice to me. Most of the time, being assertive translates into effective communication. However I may have taken self-discipline too far by stopping my body from automatically expressing itself.

I wonder why this is so difficult for me. I have tried in almost every way possible to resolve this but unwelcome reminders are always showing up, making me feel like shit. This is hard. It is as if I am in a vicious circle that I cannot ignore. I think these reminders are telling me something. There is absolutely no way I will go back to a therapist to help me work through this. I refuse to let files about my personal life build up again. I need my privacy. Somehow, I will figure out how to work through this by using the skills that I learned in the past.

My buried feelings seem to spin my thoughts, around and around in an endless circle of anxiety: 1) I do not like Deborah as a person because of how she treated me after she hurt me and because she changed the course of my life forever; 2) I then see her image and hear her voice in my home on the television and/or hear about my family's reactions when they see her there as well; 3) while I attend to my make-up in the morning and evening every day, I will, on some level be thinking of her for giving me the scar; and 4) driving away from home, I see my neighbour and that reminds me of her too. Start at number one all over again. I am getting dizzy.

It would be helpful if we were able to forget bad experiences with a memory dimmer dial, a delete button being even better. Our accident is no secret; the police charged Deborah and the case became a matter of public information. Her conviction gave her a criminal record. Her sentence was to spend a single night in jail followed by several months in a halfway house. While she stayed there she was still allowed to attend university.

Sometimes while reading her letter I would cry feeling confused about my feelings. I am not a jealous person but I realize now that I envied her. She would still have gotten her university degree in the same amount of time as she always planned. I sunk deeper into depression over the years as I realized that university was going to be a struggle for me, unlike it would have been before I was hurt.

I do not seek revenge against Deborah for getting us into that accident but the sound of her voice in my home is like a ghost speaking. The alternative, to not do work like I feel guided to do, is to continue to suppress my feelings like I have already done in different ways over the years. This would not be hard to do. I question whether this is healthy however.

When I look back I am actually startled to realize that I have never—once spoken to a therapist about Deborah, other than to say that she was Stacey's sister. I kept the letter Deborah wrote to me to myself. There was so much therapeutic crap on my plate at the time that if I were to have thrown my feelings about her into it, I would have been in therapy forever.

For my happiness and well-being, I understand what needs to happen. I have not been ready to speak out until now. I need to respond to what happened to me, in 1991, instead of only reacting to the consequence of that accident. Being faced with flashbacks and unpleasant reminders, such as seeing Deborah on my television set, has to stop. But unless I allow myself to grow beyond the original physical and emotional pain I experienced, I will not be able to move on. I have to be strong enough to do this. I have no choice. I hold my happiness in the palm of my hand right now.

Suddenly my mind is free from thought. I sit up in my chair. Deep inside somehow I feel an emotional door is closing. I pick up my dishes to take to the kitchen. Getting up I look over at the television screen and notice that Deborah's ghostly image is gone.

28
Crossroads

L eaning back against the headboard this summer evening, I am in
bed reading some notes I have taken for my dancing. To sit like
this always reminds me of the life I had as Doris. In those days I used to
study and read this way in bed all the time. When Mom saw this unique
bed I have now in a news flyer one day, she knew right away that I would
want it. After I told her I bought a new bed she guessed which one I got
and she was right. Mom thought it was cute how I bought something
like Doris would have. I cut her off from analyzing it too much. I am
not Doris anymore, period. I hate it when she gets all nostalgic.

Wanting to write something in my notes, I grab a pen from the
nightstand. This action brings a suppressed memory into my thoughts
and I clearly picture at one time sitting in this position in bed writing
before.

Since the Muskoka accident that killed those young men, I have
been having a lot of flashbacks about who I was as Doris and what I
went through after being hurt. I feel like I am on a bit of an emotional
roller coaster.

~

It was a Friday night in 1992, the spring before I was to attend U of T.
My social life had withered; no friends wanted to spend time with me.
I sat in my bed at home writing a note. Living in the country, without
street lights the sky was black.

Becoming aware of all the damage done to my body and mind from
the accident depressed me. The list of permanent problems or "deficits",
as the medical crew and lawyers in my life called them, continued to

grow. I was finally starting to admit that there had been changes to my body, such as a constant runny nose, ringing in my ears and a lack of smell and taste that were just a handful of the many physical problems I chronically had. For the insomnia, depression and memory challenges that I had, I could really only talk with physicians and therapists about them. I felt alienated from others and this was something I had not experienced before in my life. The brain damage had left me in a nightmare. I did not know who I was anymore. When people called me Doris, I had no idea who they were talking about.

My denial was weakening by the second and I could not stop crying. I had tried to make excuses for almost every problem I was suffering through as a result of the accident, by using denial as a coping mechanism. It was easy to do because much of the damage done to me was invisible, even to me but it did not get rid of the problems. It was only a matter of time before I would be challenged again by my damaged mind and body. I was waking up to the fact that a normal life of mine as Doris was completely gone.

I looked at the bottom of my door. A towel blocked air from the hallway. I lit a smoke and took a drag as I read what I wrote.

Dear Mom and Dad,

I cannot live anymore. Life is horrible since I was injured. It destroyed everything. No friends call and I sit alone on weekends. I have no reason to go on. Things would be easier for us all had I died. Sorry to do this.

Love,
Doris

None of my friends returned calls that week. My boyfriend Brian, whom I met after my accident, was out with his friends. I loved him deeply but we unfortunately did not have much of a social life together beyond the two of us. No one invited me to any parties on the weekend anymore, which was so different from before I got hurt. At that time in my life, during the week I focused on work and school and then to have the weekend full of social activity was normal. That previous life socializing, working at the department store and studying had disappeared for me.

Friends no longer wanted to spend time with me. In the hospital I was told that some friends tried to be available for me but I do not remember anything. To get to Toronto to visit was a bit of a commute from the Oshawa area. A handful of girlfriends I had for a long time sent me a poster with pictures and souvenirs from times we spent together. They taped one of my favourite brands of cigarettes to it. My family ripped the smoke off right away because everyone wanted me to quit. I started the habit when I was finishing Grade 6. They were treating me like a baby.

In the hospital, I begged for a smoke. Dad and my brother lied when they went out for one. The withdrawal I experienced was intense. Apparently, while comatose, I moved as if lighting a cigarette and smoking it—to the shock of everyone. Maybe I was having a smoke in my dream. My family all tried their hardest to hold me back from smoking but it was not long before I picked up the habit again. I figured it should be my decision if I was going to quit or not and I did not know why I should. My life sucked as a result of the accident and it did not matter if I smoked.

Finishing my smoke, I butted it out in a jar. With care, I picked up a sharp piece of broken glass on the night stand and started to press the tip of it into the soft part of my left wrist. My ability to feel physical pain had greatly decreased due to the head injury. So even if the cut hurt, I did not care. The depression and struggle I was experiencing would never end, so I had no choice. My emotions were up and down like a yo-yo. I never cried so much before at any point in my life, other than at times fighting with a long term boyfriend I had for almost four years in junior high and high school. I did not want to live anymore.

Blood started to trickle from my skin. I pressed harder. I looked at the suicide note again, feeling suddenly overwhelmed by a great sadness. Life was good before the accident, when I knew who I was. What a waste.

The phone on the night stand rang as I was about to slice across my wrist. It startled me and I immediately stopped pressing the glass into my wrist. The call was coming through on a private phone line I had in my room. If I did not answer it, my parents would think it was odd, so I needed to pick it up. I set everything down and picked up the phone while grabbing a tissue.

"Hello?"

"Hi, Cutes," Brian said, using one of his nicknames for me. His other one was Dodo. He usually called me that when I was crying, which had been the majority of the time since he met me.

"Do you want to go for a drive tomorrow evening?" he asked.

I thought for a moment while looking at the sharp glass, blood and note I had written. I had no idea why this guy cared about me. No one else did anymore. I should have said no but I liked him—a lot.

"I'd like to," I said softly.

"Great, I'll pick you up tomorrow night around seven."

When I got off the phone I stared at the bloody tissue from my self-inflicted wound. I seriously almost just killed myself. A huge weight of emotion pressed down on me and felt overwhelming.

I reread the suicide note and started to quietly cry. I thought about the time Brian and I had spent together. His concern for me was genuine and he enjoyed spending time with me, even when no one else did anymore.

I touched the scar on my cheek. My life before the accident was nothing like I was experiencing at this time. I could not deal with all the problems I had as a result of the accident; I was upset about way too much stuff. In the fall I would be at university—a new start for a new life. I needed to hang on for a bit longer. I felt a glimmer of hope inside me.

I quickly hid the note and broken glass. I did not tell Brian or anyone else what almost happened that night.

I met Brian in the fall of 1991 at a friend's house party. His name was all I remembered at the time. I have no recollection of having spoken to him because our first encounter took place right after my head injury. He had gone to a different high school and he was a year older.

A friend's friend had a big crush on him and spoke about him a lot. That is why I knew his name. My good friend Lori, who was in the accident with me, went to his school as well. She says she also had a crush on him for years and she was not exactly thrilled when I started dating him. I always wondered if she was jealous that he was my boyfriend.

Brian was a handsome guy. He showed signs that he wanted me to be his girlfriend. How he figured out where I lived, I have no clue. But he arrived at the door one morning after working a night shift at a grocery store and gave Mom a bag of gummy bears for me. I was still asleep. After the accident, I was tired all the time and I needed to sleep a lot. He told my mom he would call me. Mom mentioned his visit. But I had no clue who the guy was. I ate the gummy bears though. What a nice guy he was to bring me a gift.

My memory lapses plagued me on a daily basis. I did not remember simple things such as how I used to do my hair and put make-up on. I still had make-up from before my accident but no clue what to do with them. So I wore a new hairstyle with the sides pinned up. Before the car accident, I would have thought this looked geeky. It felt okay to me after. This was another mark of the drastic changes because of the head injury.

The damage inflicted on me continued to depress me. My denial was disappearing. In its place was a person whom I no longer knew. A new person occupied my body. It was a struggle even trying to be Doris again.

Brian was one of the few people to pay attention to me as the months passed after my accident. This might have been because he did not know me before I was hurt, when I did not have brain damage.

I cared so much about him that I would not smoke around him. He hated it and I did not want to push him away. Brian loved me when I did not yet put make-up on my facial scar and he encouraged me as I was learning to hide the marks.

We went for drives in his dark grey Mustang GT a lot. He usually drove us around on road trips while I sobbed about problems. He also owned a Ninja sport motorcycle and he took me out on it once.

When Brian came to take me for a ride on his motorcycle in the spring of 1992, we sneakily had decided that he should park out on the country road. I knew I should not be going for a ride on the motorcycle but I did not care and I was determined to go.

I did not tell Brian much about my injury. He saw the scar along with the facial paralysis and knew I had problems but he did not know all the details. Maybe I should have told him my rehabilitation team advised me not to do stuff where I could hit my head again so soon after the head injury.

That day, I casually said to Mom, "Bye, see you later."

She had an odd look on her face. Walking out over the bridge to the road, my heart was pounding. I still remember how excited I was to watch Brian pick up the two motorcycle helmets he had hidden in the trees. I smiled as he handed me one.

Getting on the motorcycle and putting my arms and legs around Brian was incredible. I knew I was safe with him. Brian started up the bike and we rode off. He shifted gears easily so that the engine would not make much noise. Neither of us wanted my mom to hear the motorcycle and spoil our fun.

Brian drove carefully, especially in Oshawa on the corners of Highway 2. I hung on to his waist as tight as possible, enjoying the feeling and even though it was probably too tight for Brian, he did not complain. When I was young, Omi used to hold me like this on car trips if we did not have enough seats for everyone. She was only 4'11" and her hold around my waist was solid. I trusted she would not let me go. And she promised she would not. Back at that time seatbelts were just becoming mandatory in cars in Ontario.

That day, my hour long tour with Brian was incredible. As he would accelerate at a stoplight and shift gears, my heart pounded when the force of acceleration pulled me backwards. When he got up to speed, we would just coast along without anything holding us back. The freedom during those blissful moments stood in stark contrast to the state of my screwed up life. At that moment, I was living the life I wanted to live, with no one setting up my schedule and demanding I rehabilitate from an injury I did not even understand. I was independently doing my own thing, like I had always done before.

Getting back to the house that day, we were in for a huge surprise. Mom was in the kitchen, teary-eyed and red in the face. In my whole life I have never seen her like this. As soon as we walked through the door she exploded. She rambled on and on about how she had noticed something was different when Brian did not drive over the bridge to the house but parked out on the road instead.

"Usually I hear your car," she said, pausing to hold back tears, "as you come down the road. Not today."

Brian and I stood there silent. I forgot that Mom had been trained to hear my brother as soon as he turned his car onto our country road. The bass in his audio system as well as the engine would wake her up. Of course Brian's Mustang would make even more noise. Stupid move on our part.

"I watched from the front window as you two strutted out to the road, with not a care in the world," she said sternly as she dramatically pointed out towards the front of the house.

Brian started to respond, to defend himself but she would not listen.

"Why did you take her out on your motorcycle?" she asked. "Do you not realize how seriously injured she was in that accident last year!"

Brian was being blamed for the ride he had taken me out on. But—I was the one who got on the motorcycle, he did not force me. I tried telling her how I was an adult and I could do whatever I wanted. She would not listen to anything I said. She kept her focus on Brian. I was tired of everyone treating me like a kid. I had no freedom anymore. Life was no longer fun.

"I stood there guessing with horror what was about to happen as I saw you pick up the motorcycle helmets through some of the trees. I could hear you start your motorbike up and ride off," Mom said.

She loudly told us how she wanted to stop us, how she quickly decided not to drive after us, realizing she might cause us to be in an accident by distracting Brian from the road. Mom usually would not yell at me so this was shocking. It was as if a tap opened inside her and emotions unrelated to the motorcycle ride poured out. She went on and on about what could have happened until we grew scared listening to her. Her voice and words were tinged with paranoia about me ending up in ICU again. She was turning even redder in the face than when we had first walked in. I had to promise Mom I would never go on his motorcycle again. It was hard to promise her this because I did not understand why I could not go.

Tonight as I sit in bed. I realize my thoughts have taken my mind off of looking at my dance notes. I close the booklet and set it on the night stand. I turn out the light to go to sleep.

Brian and I dated for a couple of years after the accident and I will always love him as a person. I think he would say the same about me. The last time I saw him, we hugged each other dearly and thanked one another for helping each other grow in our lives to a place that would not have been possible without this support. With the depth of my gratitude to Brian for all he had done for me, I always wanted to help him. I could not take him for granted.

He had been planning to go to college before wanting to apply to the police force. With my help he ended up getting a Bachelor's degree, with some courses in law enforcement from U of T. He would not have been able to achieve this without me. He had not completed the proper high school courses for application to university. I helped him and encouraged him to attend as a mature student.

Had I not had Brian's support, suicide appeared to be my only other choice in life at the time. I have small scars on my wrists from trying a couple of times. I used to make excuses for how I cut myself. I was really clumsy from the head injury and the damage done to my eyes and ear so it was easy to lie about: I fell down a few steps from lack of depth perception; I lost my balance and toppled over; my eyes were dry and blurry and I did not see I was about to get hurt.

After a few years, Brian ended the relationship with me and that hurt deeply. He finally admitted, in one of the hardest breakups I ever had, that all the stress my life was surrounded by was way too hard for him as a young man. He did love me but my crying, the recovery, the lawyers—it all finally became too much for him. He wanted a girlfriend who was not going through what I was, someone who was not depressed all the time, one who had a normal life. Someone like myself when I was Doris—the girl he never knew. I understood his needs and wished him well, however, it was hard to let him go without protesting. I tried to be supportive.

"I love you and want you to be happy," I said, choking up. "If your happiness is not with me then I can't hold you back. So I guess this is—goodbye."

Brian had accepted me, unconditionally. I later learned that this is rare. I will be grateful to him forever for helping and loving me. Without him I know I would have thrown in the towel and killed myself, or, should I say, the remains of the life I had as Doris.

If there is such a thing as angels, I believe Brian definitely was one for me.

29
An Assertive Choice

Turning on the TV, I start making dinner. I am sautéing onion with green peppers and grilling some steak. Onion is an interesting vegetable for me. When I was Doris, I hated them; as Samantha, I love them.

Mya is tempted by the smell of the meat that sits on the counter. What I am cooking is her favourite. I once heard how dogs are not supposed to eat fried onions but Mya seems to like them, so I give her a few.

When I cook, she lies in front of the stove on the tile floor and I put a small mat there to keep her warm. If she does not get anything she will not complain, so I do not consider it begging. Spending time with me is her top priority or at least this is what I like to believe. I wonder who is fooling who, here.

As I turn around to put a utensil in the dishwasher I look at the television screen. I freeze on the spot—oh no. I am looking directly at Deborah. The stove's fan is going, so I cannot hear what she is saying. And I do not care. After a moment the image on the screen changes as it goes to a TV commercial.

After having seen her, I cannot ignore my feelings. My heart is pounding. Anxiety floods my body. Her appearing repetitively in my home is really getting to me and I am beginning to understand this better. I do not know what to do. I thought that I had dealt with things when I saw her on TV the last time. This is like a never ending problem. These old memories are intruding and are unwelcome, in my current life. I cannot pretend I did not just spend the weekend crying over what happened in that accident in 1991 and the lengthy recovery I had to endure afterwards. My needs have changed—I have changed.

"Mya, I'm tired of seeing her," I say and hearing her name she tilts her head as I speak. "It's time for her to take a hike." Mya seems disinterested in what I am saying and looks back at the stove top to wait for food.

Sure Deborah has been creepily haunting me for years. Maybe she needed to resurface all the time to show me that I need to work through something. Well, this is going to stop. This is a difficult challenge I face and I must be able to eliminate the problem somehow. It is time Deborah and I have a final departure.

"Hmm, I have an idea," I say, while stirring the vegetables.

I am not a big TV watcher. And the few times I do turn it on to enjoy are counterproductive if I have to see her. As she said to me, we were never friends, so she is not welcome in my life.

"We are getting rid of cable TV Mya," I say. "I can't get the channel she is on here with only an antenna. No more *Dog Whisperer* for you."

I will miss a comedy show called *Samantha Who?* about a woman who is recovering from a coma she was in after getting hit by a car. It is fun to watch because I totally understand what the main character Samantha is going through. She often gets flashbacks and her personality has changed drastically from her severe closed-head injury. Some of TV Samantha's problems are similar to the ones I had in recovery.

Everyone in TV Samantha's life has reacted differently to her accident. For me, old friends who I no longer hung around with anymore since junior high school, all of a sudden were hanging around as if we were always great friends. The same happened to TV Samantha.

On the show, I know they minimize how serious a traumatic brain injury is. This does not bother me, it actually makes me laugh. But the show does not make Aunt Gisele laugh, not even for a second. She feels this is sending the wrong message to the viewers about this type of injury. Maybe she is right.

It is another "strange parallel" that my new name is in their show's title, even though the show came out long after I changed my name. I could make my own show. It would be called *Doris Who?*

Part of the reason I enjoy watching it is because Christina Applegate, who plays TV Samantha, looks somewhat like Deborah. So it is therapeutic for me, in a comical way to see TV Samantha going through challenges similar to mine. Well, I have had the reminders long enough. I do not have to continue seeing her like this. It is time to move on. It is time to stop receiving cable TV. This is one thing I can control.

30
Delayed Grief

"So I will do all the paperwork with Industry Canada to become a non-profit organization," I say into the phone this evening in August 2008. "We also need to find a pianist who can perform for the music CD."

"I can contact the development office at the NAC," says Andrew. "I know Daphne Burt, from the work I did there, who is involved with artistic planning. I'll see if she can recommend someone."

"That's great. I was thinking that the non-profit's name needs to represent our mission," I say.

"I agree," he says. "Do you have any ideas?"

Andrew is now going to be the President and CEO on the Board of Directors for the non-profit. I will be the Chairman and Treasurer and Aunt Gisele will serve as Secretary. It is only a matter of paperwork before we are fully established. We work well together so far during the start-up phase.

I explain to him the name I came up with.

"It's a great idea. An Aid to Help Foundation sounds perfect, Sammy."

"Are you serious?" I ask with genuine surprise.

"Yes. I would tell you if it didn't," he says.

"Wow. Thanks, Andrew. Let's talk later."

After hanging up, I arrange some documents on my cramped desk. I wonder what work I should do next. The list of things needing to be done is growing fast. Aunt Gisele is amazed that I do not write everything down, as she would need to do. I find making lists takes too much time for me because they have to be constantly updated. But to stay aware of all tasks in my mind is the system that works best for me.

My enthusiasm to do everything to create a non-profit—from the paperwork to building a website and a music CD—surprises me. I ended up throwing in the towel on seeking charity status in Canada. I disliked the fact that the government would have monitored and controlled closely what we did as a charity. I realized that this would have reminded me too much of the surveillance I had in my life after the accident. It would not make me feel comfortable.

I also really had no interest to get monetary donations from people and to give them a receipt. There would have been nothing important to me about this transaction. I would have quickly gotten bored with the project. I like giving people a product for their donation instead. This is more meaningful to me than a tax receipt. It adds a sentimental touch to the transaction and is something I like doing.

In addition, the rules for charities made it apparent that there would be problems with me telling my story to sell the music CD. They needed me to make the charity impersonal. But this was supposed to be all about me telling my story. So I definitely have no interest in founding a charity.

For the CD, Andrew and Aunt Gisele are intrigued about my idea to have Vincent Paolucci, an artist and an old friend, create a painting for the front cover of the case. I really like his work, which even is in the collections of some famous people, including Sylvester Stallone.

My next task is to choose songs for the CD. My idea is to include a range of different types of music so the audience is not limited to one group. This will take time to research. From the work I have done so far, when I hear a song I instantly think whether I can use it or not. While listening I take note of when the piece of music changes from a slow tempo to a fast tempo. This helps me get an idea for how the slow part of the song fits into the mix I am making. I am choosing this part of songs, usually the intro, to help people effortlessly relax to while listening. This slow tempo of the song could be called the adagio. The songs are not going to be full length on the CD.

I have already chosen "Stairway to Heaven" by Led Zeppelin. The pianist will use the first two minutes of the song, then slowly end instead of carrying on to the faster part. Slowing down the whole song would destroy the original melody and I would never want to do that. To do it this way is what I think will sound best. I do not want vocals on the CD either.

I grab a CD from my desk to listen to "Here Without You" by 3 Doors Down.[24] As it plays, the music touches me, in a way I did not expect. I feel deeply sad. I wonder what is going on for me. While listening, I now want to search online for more information about the three guys who died the other week in the Muskoka drunk driving accident. My thoughts drift from the work I was doing.

As the song plays I read an article about their accident and I start to cry. I feel sorrow as I realize that those guys will not be a part of so many people's lives now. They threw their lives away. They were young, yes, but they should have known better. Deborah was twenty-one when she drove drunk and got into the accident that almost killed me. She was the same age as these young men. But Sofia was thirty-three wanting to drive drunk on the night of my party. Princess Diana's driver was forty-one.

I shove these thoughts aside. The energy in the den changes with "Here Without You" playing. I think two minutes of the song can be used as a piano arrangement in total. Suddenly, I realize that the lyrics somehow remind me of when I was Doris. I am still crying. I stop looking online.

The lyrics speak about dreaming of someone and the last time they met. It is about how a part of them could never and will never forget the other. Thoughts of when I was Doris begin to swim in my mind.

I wonder why this song makes me think of being her. The accident I was in wrecked the life I had as Doris. As her, I woke up out of a coma in a completely different body and mind than what was mine or—hers, I should say. Sadness for the young men who died fills me. The parallels between our accidents, especially the location, stand out in odd clarity.

Being injured, I could not understand truly what others went through when they saw me hurt so severely. I always tell people I changed after my injury and that I am no longer Doris. When anyone calls me by that name, I still get upset—even to this day. For some reason, to hear her name still hurts me these many years later. Most people agree I am not her anymore. I will distance myself from them if they do not agree. Sometimes I know I can be a bit headstrong about things. On this one, I know I am right. Everyone has to get over the fact that Doris is gone from my life. I wonder then why I am crying for her right now while listening to this song.

My hand reaches up to my face and I touch my scar. Suddenly I understand what is happening.

"I miss her," I say out loud, to myself. "I miss Doris."

I cry, even more now, realizing that since the accident, I have not felt this way before. I would never let myself feel the loss.

"Doris," I say with new tenderness.

I picture the last photograph I had of myself without the scars I received. It was taken the day of my accident. At one point I destroyed it. It was the one Lori used to look at while at university. The tragedy of the young men in Muskoka, along with hearing this song has unlocked another bolt on the steel door inside my mind and heart, full of memories.

"Doris had everything going for her," I tell Mya, who is lying on the chair beside me. "I miss her and always have."

Mya looks at me while not moving from her comfy spot. She knows that something is different about me right now but she does not understand what is happening. Sniffling, I grab a tissue and blow my nose. It is a pain how when I cry my nose runs constantly instead of tears.

"Why did I let Deborah hurt me?" I cry.

I hope it is it okay to be listening to this song and crying about something that happened seventeen years ago. Never before have I been tearful in this way. Sure, I was upset about immediate concerns with my struggles, especially the lack of support from my friends. But how I feel now is different somehow. It is like I am grieving for the loss of another person's life, however it is my own—the life I had as Doris. I cannot be grieving. It was so long ago. Too much time has passed since then.

Feeling tired, I turn off the computer and go to bed.

The next morning I feel a bit better. I let Mya outside and the sight of the rock and forest envelops me with its perfection. After she comes back inside, I take a deep breath of fresh air before closing the door.

I know right away what I want to hear. Since getting out of bed, it is all I have been able to think about. I go to the den and get the CD. As "Here Without You" starts to play, my heart melts. I understand now how important the work I am doing is for me and this is something I never expected. From the beginning I thought I only wanted to share my story to help others but I am learning that I need to do this project for myself as well. I had no idea this would be important for my own healing journey—at all.

I decide to call Mom. She has been supportive of my choice to re-live my story in ways in an effort to help others.

"How are you?" she asks.

"Okay," I say. "Mom, I'm sad choosing songs for the non-profit's music CD. A song I've been listening to is making me cry. It reminds me of when I was Doris."

"Really?"

"The Muskoka accident with those three guys dying is also upsetting me because of where it happened and the similarities with mine," I tell her. "Hearing the song makes me think of them dying as well."

"Oh, dear," she says.

Mom and I had already spoken about this Muskoka accident previously. It had upset her as well.

"I'm crying in a way I haven't before," I say. "I miss being Doris."

Mom stays quiet for a moment, letting me cry, then says, "You haven't cried in this way since your injury. I don't think you ever grieved for Doris and losing her life."

"You're right," I say. "This helps me understand people better. Is this why Lori said she cried at times looking at our photo taken the day of the accident? Maybe she grieved the loss of Doris and of the friendship she had with me as that person. It was sad but I no longer was her."

"We each grieved in our own way," Mom says. "You had a successful life before. Your struggles were hard for us all because we were aware you'd never be the same again."

"My name change must've been especially difficult to understand and accept," I say.

Everything suddenly appears different. My understanding and perception have changed. I can now see and feel what it must have been like for others and what they must have gone through, when they saw me hurt so badly. I had always had an idea, although I did not understand things so clearly—until now.

"In many ways, I lost you as a daughter and needed to grieve. There you still stood in front of me but so different. It was confusing," she says. "It was hard as a family to go through this."

My recovery was challenging for everyone. We should have had therapy as a family but Mom, Dad and my brother refused. They met as a group with a psychologist once and Dad was impatient. He wanted immediate tools for dealing with me. However, the neuropsychologist needed to learn more about our experience through a few sessions before offering suggestions. Dad said that this was not fast enough. They decided amongst themselves that only I would benefit from her help. I can understand their hesitation but their lack of support hurt.

My brother and I are still distant to this day. In the last twelve years, we have seen each other only once, when Omi died. He lives in Northern Alberta, over four thousand kilometres away. We talk on the phone occasionally if I am at Mom and Dad's but our conversations are always short, not more than a few minutes. We do not even have each other's phone numbers. We were closer before my head injury. I can see now that it must have also been hard on him; he lost Doris, as a sister. He struggled with my name change too.

As Doris, he used to call me Dor and was the only person in my life who did so. After I changed my name he stopped calling me anything. There were a few times he called me Dor and it really pissed me off, creating an even larger wall between us. He had a hard time embracing the new life I was trying to create.

"Is this why many old friends abandoned me like they did?" I ask Mom. "Maybe they wanted the old me back and not to help me recover as a new person. They didn't want to see me struggle. If I hadn't been injured, my friendships might not have changed the way they did."

"That is true, the hospital gave us warnings when we took you home about how a closed-head injury takes a long time to recover from and that we may see you struggle a lot," she told me. "What song were you listening to?"

"'Here Without You' by 3 Doors Down," I say.

"Oh, I don't know the song," she says.

"It's more of an alternative rock song," I tell her.

"Well, I look forward to hearing it on the CD. Are you okay now?" she asks.

"Yes, I think so. Thanks, Mom. I love you. I'll call again soon."

"Love you, too. Say hi to my granddaughter Mya from me."

The song that triggered my emotions is still playing quietly in the background. As I turn the volume up, the music resonates throughout the house and touches me deeply. Speaking with my mom made me feel better.

It is clearer to me now why my parents and brother had such trouble accepting my name change. I had abandoned the remains of my previous life as Doris, like many others did, the reason why they could not see me anymore. I cleared the slate to start a brand new life. My parents now have a new daughter in me as Samantha and my brother a new sister. I will never be Doris again.

When I was Doris, I did not want to change my name. After my injury, when I had problems being her, my solution was to forget her life had ever even existed. I see that my success in doing so was not permanent however.

My thoughts drift back again to the young men who died in Muskoka. Their families will have no opportunity to rebuild anything, like mine did. Princess Diana's family neither.

Letting the song continue on to the next, I go make breakfast. I need time to recharge from such an emotional week. My life is not usually this stressful and upsetting anymore.

It is hard because doing this work and telling my story in a way that I feel comfortable with seems like a step back. I consider myself to be an emotionally healthy woman now but here I am crying about all these memories. I usually try not to let myself get drawn into things I have no control over. I use challenges to help me change and grow as a person. I have worked hard to improve where I can and the life I have now, in my books, gets top marks. There will always be a few areas that can be worked on still or else the challenge in life disappears. So for me to cry is difficult to accept but it means something to me and I cannot ignore that.

Today I will do the laundry while I work on paperwork for the non-profit. The selection of songs can wait for another day.

31
Freedom to Feel

Sitting down at my computer this morning, for some reason I want to learn more about what happened to the young men who were killed in Muskoka earlier this summer. Their accident has remained on my mind, troubling my thoughts, stirring my emotions. Their deaths have touched me in a deep way that I am not familiar with.

An online search leads me to a website in memory of the driver, Tyler.[25] I am moved that his family created a website like this. I do not believe that he would have intentionally hurt anyone, especially his friends. How sad the group of young adults made choices that led to the end of their lives. Tyler was driving the car. His friends and girlfriend obviously got into the car with him.

Tyler's dad wrote a letter to his son that he put on this memorial website, for the public to read. Apparently the two were close friends as well as being parent and child. Tyler's dad said that he read a book about grief and learned how writing this way might help him cope. I am touched he is sharing part of his grief publicly.

Tyler's dad is trying to get the law changed in Ontario to prevent those under twenty-one from drinking at all if they are driving. I understand why he believes zero-tolerance could have helped prevent his son's accident. This however would not have stopped Deborah, who was twenty-one years old at the time of our accident in 1991. Or the many similar accidents I have learned about over the years.

If zero-tolerance laws were in place, we four girlfriends would have had trouble finding a way home that night from the bar if Stacey's sister did not come and get us. We would have needed more than the law to prevent our going to the bar, drinking alcohol and then getting back to the cottage with a drunk driver.

To learn about Tyler's dad and his efforts to change the law to help others means a lot to me. Deborah's father, as far as I know, did not do anything like this. Her parents did not even speak with my family to express their concern about me or to learn how I was doing while in the hospital. They showed little to no compassion for my family's horrible experience. They simply ignored us.

Sure I got a stuffed animal, flowers and a card from Stacey while in the hospital and the letter later from Deborah but their parents hid in the background. It bothers me that they behaved this way. Dad still says, "The Dean of McMaster University called to talk and express his concern but not one single word—ever, from the parents of the drunk driver who changed our lives forever by hurting my daughter."

I was a guest at Deborah's family's cottage. Deborah, the driver, was still living with her parents, when not at university. Her parents were shielding her from the consequences of her own behaviour. But whatever they did and why they did it, was pathetic to me.

Tyler's dad is different from Deborah's father. I see him as a role model. I believe his son would have been impressed that he is not ignoring what happened. That he has the courage and integrity to confront and deal with it. He is honest about the bad choices Tyler made and he is helping others by trying to prevent them from suffering as his family is. I feel compassion as I read him say:

"I hope that anyone who reads this will understand that we need to choose our responses to painful occurrences in our lives. We can choose to give up and have our energy and life taken away, or we can choose to allow pain and tragedy to motivate us, to compel us to use that force to make the most of ourselves in a way that can benefit others, and enrich their lives and our own."

Because I want to help others by sharing my story, I understand Tyler's dad. I continue to sympathetically look through their family's memorial website. There is a list of songs online that have been selected in his memory and can be listened to. When I see the first song my breath stops. It is "Here Without You" by 3 Doors Down. I hit play and sorrow floods my body as I cry.

I already have confirmation that I can legally reproduce a composition of the song for the CD by getting a mechanical license. Once I decide what the other songs are, I will get this and pay the necessary royalty on its use, so that I do not violate any copyright laws. I cannot believe that this is the first song on their list. I have no desire to listen to the other songs or even look at what they are. I hit play for "Here Without You" again and again. Listening to it reminds me of the night when I was deciding whether or not to use the song for the non-profit's CD and I could not stop crying as I played it. Today, I am crying again but in a different way; for Tyler, the driver of the accident in Muskoka, for his two friends who died, as well as for the life I had as Doris.

At the top of the page are dates beside Tyler's picture, his birth, April 25, 1988 and death, July 3, 2008. I always thought July 3 was only important to me because of the possibility of winning the cash prize and *The Muskoka* cottage in the lottery. Now I feel the importance of the date, as well as the name of the cottage, were for different reasons. I always knew that on that date I would learn if I would be speaking out about my accident in 1991 and of whether there was a purpose for me to share my story as a survivor. I did not realize how this information could come to me other than by winning that lottery.

An online news story, linked through the memorial website, catches my attention. The article quotes Tyler's sister as saying, on the day of her brother's funeral, "Today I may be saying goodbye to my brother Tyler but I am saying hello to a guardian angel. Tyler was my protector and he will continue to protect me. I know he will always be with me."

At his funeral apparently they sang "The King of Love my Shepherd Is". I do not know this hymn that well but the last time I heard it was when I watched Princess Diana's funeral in 1997.[26]

I am beginning to realize that maybe I survived my accident in 1991 for a reason and there is a purpose for me after all.

32
An Aid to Help Foundation

In late August 2008, I finally received documentation from Industry Canada certifying that An Aid to Help Foundation is now a non-profit organization. As a board, we decided our first meeting would be at the beginning of September.

I want the goals for the non-profit to be prevention oriented. Our mission statement is: "To provide encouragement and resources to educators, students, parents and families on ways to learn or teach others to make responsible choices in life." The non-profit's tagline is: "Learning or teaching others to make responsible choices."

The recording and production for the CD will be done well and I realize this will take time. My goal is for the organization to be able to effortlessly raise money through its sale.

The following month, I interview a few pianists. Mark Ferguson is one who lives in Ottawa and was recommended by Andrew's contact at the NAC.[27] He is a jazz pianist who sometimes performs with the NAC Orchestra. I have attended a few of Mark's performances when I was volunteering. He works as a pianist, trombonist, composer, arranger, producer and educator.

After meeting Mark I was impressed by his talent but surprisingly, I did not want or need to hear him play anything. I felt I did not need him to audition in this way considering it was the NAC referring him to me. Also since I have heard him perform some jazz before with the NAC Orchestra for the Popular Series, I did not question his ability. I simply took his word for what he said he could do for me.

He says he can arrange the pieces of music I want, by listening to the songs. He will not use sheet music, with the exception of the few classical pieces. I told him I want the classical pieces performed exactly as written. I thought that any improvisation of these would not make my aunt Gisele happy. I told him that she has classic, sophisticated taste in music. To this, Mark said confidently, "I have no problem doing this for her." I am confident he is the right person for this important position.

Mark suggested a couple of pianos we could use for the recording; one is a Steinway Concert Grand, a short drive west of Ottawa.[28] My gut feeling right away was that it would be perfect.

This is how I have been creating everything so far, by listening and watching my reaction to what life is showing me to do. It is almost like I am being led in a dance of sorts with a director who gently guides me towards what I am supposed to be doing. I have the strength and confidence to follow more gracefully in my life now, than I ever could have before.

My standards are high for the quality of this CD because professional live music is regularly a part of my life through my volunteer work at the NAC. My vision is for this music to be a gift to people that they will enjoy listening to, for helping support the cause of my non-profit.

Everything is gradually coming together. I am committed to the work that needs to be done, no matter what. I definitely needed to stop working for Sheila at the office, as well as training her and my other clients in Pilates, to be able to do this. By doing this I could focus on getting the non-profit launched. Some clients were not happy about my decision but they understood that I needed to be careful and pace myself with this work. My priorities in life have changed for the time being.

More nights than usual, I am not sleeping well due to my head injury and the sensitivity to stress that I now have. Sometimes I wake up in the middle of the night and my mind is hard to turn off. This is a problem I have had since getting hurt that I did not have before. Before the accident I could always sleep effortlessly. Now my sleep cycle is fragile.

It is important I look after myself and Mya helps me if I get busy and forget. Daily she rings a small bell inside the house near the front door. This means "walk" and the bell at the back means "bathroom".

Today she runs to the front door, rings the bell and looks over her shoulder, waiting for me to put on my shoes and her leash. We walk around the side of the house, through the backyard and enter the forest. She loves this route and takes us through the trees to the pathway in a zigzag course she randomly selects. I let her lead the way. Where we go depends on what she smells. I need to be careful not to be pulled into branches as she follows the scent of other creatures and nature.

Soon we are on the path in the woods that is canopied with trees. The leaves are starting to change colour already for the fall. Mya is sniffing everything frantically. She is in heaven amidst the abundance of sights and smells. It is unfortunate she cannot be off leash but if she gets out it is a real chase getting her back. My neighbours have all seen me running in high heels through the woods and on top of the rocks calling for her.

One time was especially difficult this past summer after it took her mere seconds to get away from me by pulling her collar off in reverse. As she did this creative manoeuvre it was almost as if the beeping of a truck backing up was all that could be heard. Once she was free she bolted away from me.

"Mya, come here," I said as I caught up with her. She took a step towards me. "Good doggie."

All of a sudden she ran across the rock further away from me.

"Come here—now. You are being a bad dog, don't behave like this. Mya, watch me," I said as I held up cooked chicken that the neighbours, who were eating dinner on their patio, gave me.

Staying a good distance away, she slowly looked at the chicken, then me and then the forest. She was thinking about her next action and Mya loves chicken. Then as if a light bulb went off in her head, she started to wag her tail. I thought she was coming for the food. But with revitalized energy she ran away from me, this time further into the wooded area.

She would not come for anything—even the chicken. I knew she was having the time of her life. Some might say it was not possible but I could see a smile on her face as she bounced around her playground that was created by nature.

She is a smart dog and this makes her a handful to look after at times because she can easily out-think me. It does not bother me however because I am determined to learn better strategies to control her if what I am doing is not working. She challenges me.

Today, the fresh air revives me. Going to the gym is part of my workout routine but this daily walk surrounded by nature is also important. This gets my mind off working on the non-profit.

For Mya, at this moment, life is good and so is mine.

33
Inner Strength

My aunt is hosting October 2008's board meeting for An Aid to Help Foundation. Before we start, Aunt Gisele, Andrew and I nibble on some appetizers. I tell them about how much easier it is for me to talk about my scar now with others. They are happy to hear this. Aunt Gisele however, expresses a desire for me to share more about my head injury to people as well. I think she focuses on this part of my injury way too much. I feel my scar was worse.

"The public needs to hear about what you went through. I believe you could really make a difference," Aunt Gisele says.

"But I recovered from my head injury. You can't tell I had one," I say.

"Yes and that is what others need to hear," she says.

Andrew agrees with her. I do not know if I feel comfortable talking about my head injury much though, I seem to be for and against it. I am going to still focus more on the external part of my injury.

We start the meeting. I show Aunt Gisele and Andrew a sample painting that Vincent Paolucci gave me for the CD's cover art. They are both interested to learn about his ideas. The quality of his work is obvious to us. As we talk about it, we realize though that as a group we are not thrilled with what he has come up with. The sketch depicts a hand and bodies. His paintings are very realistic looking and this is what I like about his work. His sketch somehow does not symbolise our non-profit's mission to help others make responsible choices in life.

Aunt Gisele loves the idea the artist had for a hand. She can tell he has talent for painting them and I value her opinion. Unanimously we all agree then that a hand should be in the painting.

I am not looking forward to breaking the news to Vincent about our decision. I have learned that he is an emotional guy. When we first became friends in Ottawa years back, he was ultra-sensitive after going through some challenges in his personal life. I noticed after I met up with him the other week that he is still under a lot of emotional stress. I do not like to upset people, especially someone I know.

I inform Aunt Gisele and Andrew that the CD creation is going well. I tell them about Mark Ferguson and how qualified he is. I also tell them that I booked the piano in Almonte and that the recording will be done this December. I then share a few of my definite song choices. I have checked already that I am able to attain the license to produce: "Wild Horses" by The Rolling Stones, "42" by Coldplay, "Every Breath You Take" by The Police, "Imagine" by John Lennon, plus more. I play them a few songs that I am still deciding on. It is surprisingly hard for me to ask for their help because I am learning day by day that this is quite a personal journey I am on. I realized this after I called Mom crying when I heard "Here Without You" and learned that I still had feelings that I never expressed before about what I went through in my life.

Aunt Gisele and Andrew know that in the end I am the only one who needs to be content with the final song selection. They can only make suggestions to help me with my creative idea. Aunt Gisele tells me that she thinks a few children's pieces need to be in the mix as well. I agree and have no problem doing this.

At home later, I pick up the phone to call Vincent to tell him his idea for the painting is not right. I am nervous that he is going to be upset. He answers the phone. I explain to him our decision at the meeting. He is quiet. Finally he says,

"My feelings are hurt. I put a lot of hard work into creating that."

"I know you did and it was really well done," I say. "We all agreed on that. But it just does not represent our mission that I told you about. We love the hand you had included in your sketch. We want that in the painting for sure. I don't know what else though."

"I understand," he says. "It can be challenging to make a decision as a group."

"Thanks for understanding. I'll decide what else will be in the painting with the hand and I'll let you know as soon as I figure it out," I say.

I am so glad I spoke with him right away about this because my anxiety has melted away.

A few days after our board meeting, I am trying to discover what else I want the painting to portray aside from just a hand. Searching through images online, I come up with no ideas. There are many hand pictures but I have no clue what else could be with it. A couple of hours go by and I am losing patience. I call Andrew.

"What about making it a hand and a barbell," he suggests, "Or a running shoe?"

He gets the stress off my shoulders with his comic ideas. It is always fun talking to him. Getting off the phone, I look back at the computer screen and sigh from discouragement. Past boyfriends have commented on how I sigh like this when I am challenged with something. I wonder what object is supposed to be painted other than a hand.

Suddenly I get an intense urge to walk around the house, confident I will find inspiration somewhere in my surroundings. I have nothing to lose by doing this. I walk around and in my living room I pick up a few books with pictures but nothing captures my interest. I return to the den and stare into space.

"Well, that was useless," I say out loud.

All of a sudden, I realize I am looking at a small crystal turtle, on the windowsill. My immediate thought is that it is a perfect image to be included in the painting with the hand. I rush over to the window and pick up the turtle. I study it closely in the palm of my hand. I am filled with certainty that it is the perfect addition to the painting. The turtle's front right foot had fallen off and I pieced it back together with sticky tape. This fix does not hold well. This is why I placed it on the windowsill, to remind myself to fix its broken foot. The turtle has a permanent flaw, like me and my scar.

An online search for images of hands and turtles gives me a few ideas on how this might look in a painting. The small turtle in the hand will perfectly represent my feelings which inspired the creation of a non-profit, to raise money for learning or teaching others to make responsible choices.

When a turtle experiences stress, it can go inside its shell to chill out. It does not text its friends, crack open a beer or light a smoke. Instead, it retreats within itself to decide what it should do next and then make a decision for itself without being influenced by others. Hopefully the decision it makes is a healthy one but at least it took the time to focus on what was going on for itself without any distraction.

To me the image of the turtle in the hand represents how the power to be strong like this, is in our own hands. We all can do it if we put in the effort to learn how. To go within to deal with stress and to find strength is a tool that anyone can develop. Many people of all ages choose negative alternatives because they do not know how to do anything else. Learning how to think independently with a calm mind can help prevent irresponsible behaviour. This might benefit everyone in the end by enabling more people to make responsible choices.

To expect parents to be the only ones teaching children about knowledge and skills in the area of emotional education is unreasonable. The job of being a parent is hard enough. Kids in most western countries attend school until a certain age. I believe that school should be the time to teach them additional skills to help them grow into capable, responsible adults. I know that effort is being put into this already but it falls short in some ways. There is a lack in consistency of what is being taught. We need to step things up a notch. Children have to learn to develop a healthy, solid relationship within themselves in whatever way possible. The most important relationship is the one you have with yourself. The key is to develop this as a well-rounded relationship that includes the needs and feelings of others as well.

I wish children did not have to go through difficulty like I did to develop emotional maturity. I understand though that this is a part of child development. I hope that to learn to build a solid inner connection with themselves first, might make them be more conscious in the future about the decisions they make, before they act. Maybe this could help them avoid destructive behaviour in their lives and choose responsible behaviour as a positive alternative. If I can only help one family, by pursuing my philanthropic dream, to be able to avoid learning the hard way, then all my work and time will still have been worth the effort.

I have seen so many people live their life on automatic pilot only, giving little thought to the possible consequences of their actions, especially where a motor vehicle is involved. The night Deborah got into the accident with me in her car she was drunk. She was not capable of thinking clearly about what she was doing at the time—just like Sofia, Tyler and Princess Diana's driver. The use of alcohol and the effects it can have on a person are complex because it may affect the brain in many ways that influence behaviour and thought.

The irresponsibility of Deborah in 1991 to get behind the wheel of a car while drunk put me and my family through an unnecessary amount of hardship. But thankfully I found the strength within myself to survive the ordeal and so have the people in my family, in their own unique ways. At eighteen years old, I had to start all over again from scratch, relearning skills I naturally had before. There was no choice for me but to learn and grow.

Children deserve access to more tools to build skills to be able to find strength and support inside themselves like I did but without the pain and trauma. For symbolic reasons the small turtle in a hand shows this meaning to me. I have decided to call Vincent's painting for the CD cover *Finding Inner Strength*.

34
Selection of Songs

It is November and the list of songs I have selected for the CD is getting longer. To help choose them, I bought a book that lists all the hits over the years. I am putting the chosen songs into categories by different style of music, popularity and historical period.

I am keeping an open mind as I do this research. My goal is for the CD to be able to attract the largest listening audience possible. Most of the songs will be shortened in length and this way I will be able to include many more than the average CD holds.

Because I want the classical pieces played exactly from the scores, it was a hunt to find ones that would work. I chose one classical piano piece called "Für Alina", written by Arvo Pärt, an Estonian composer whose work Aunt Gisele introduced me to. There is also a gentle, lyric piece I found that I definitely want to use. It is by French composer and pianist Erik Satie from 1888, called "Gymnopédie No. 1".

Aunt Gisele wants an Aboriginal song included too and that touches me. She believes Aboriginal communities need support to advance their people's education. While she worked in Alberta and lived close to the Morley reservation near Cochrane, she learned a lot about the First Nations and their struggles. I have a few Aboriginal friends so I am happy to include music of this nature. I already found a song called "Path of Beauty" by Joanne Shenandoah, an Aboriginal singer from the Oneida Nation.

I also want to use "Stuck in a Moment You Can't Get Out Of" from the album *All That You Can't Leave Behind* by U2. This song took on new meaning for me as a result of my research. I always enjoyed the lyrics but had no idea what they meant, until I learned that Bono, the lead singer of U2, wrote it about Michael Hutchence's suicide in 1997. Hutchence was an Australian musician best known as the lead singer for the band INXS. The lyrics are a fictitious conversation that Bono and Michael could have had to prevent his death. This song is meaningful for me to be included because I wanted to kill myself a few times after my head injury. It was not easy being at a point like this in my life.

Sure U2 has better slower-tempo songs I could have used but the melody of this one serves an important purpose and always will. Because the lyrics will not be a part of the piano piece, the song's meaning is what is symbolic for me. What inspired the creation of this piece of music is grief. I am learning how important creativity is to heal in this area.

I was never suicidal before the car accident—and now I definitely know what it feels like and how hard it is to go through a dark spot in life. Finding the courage to deal with challenges can come in many different ways. This music, my story and advancing education can hopefully help someone learn to manage stress better, as well as learn the skills to be able to cope with the moods, emotions and needs of anyone in life, including themselves. Children can be helped through schooling and relaxation exercises. Adults can be helped with those same relaxation exercises as well.

Many songwriters write about personal topics. Some of the popular songs I chose fit the nostalgic theme coincidentally. After selecting "Redemption Song" from the album *Uprising* by Bob Marley & the Wailers, I learned how Marley wrote it after he found out he had cancer. His wife said, "He was already secretly in a lot of pain and dealt with his own mortality, a feature that is clearly apparent in the album, particularly in this song."[29] The addition of reggae to the mix I think makes it more eclectic and diverse.

Some songs are obvious choices to me right after listening to them. For instance, "Bridge Over Troubled Water" by Simon and Garfunkel, the theme song from the movie *Chariots of Fire* and "Knockin' on Heaven's Door" by Bob Dylan, were songs I did not even have to question using.

Because this work for the non-profit has been keeping me busy, I have decided to put dance aside for now, mainly due to the fact that the studio is downtown and the drive takes up too much time. I hope to be back dancing soon.

Last week my dance instructor and I performed a rumba.[30] We did not choreograph or practice a routine and instead danced freestyle to a song. I thought we had decided upon "Fields of Gold" by Sting but he told me we were going to be dancing to a different song—a song I had not heard before—only a few minutes before we went out to perform. I was really nervous he did this. At the start when we stood together waiting for the music I was light-headed from my anxiety and I almost lost my balance. Thankfully my instructor helped me stay up. The song he chose for us to dance to was perfect. I still do not even know what the name of the song was or who it was by.

It was fun to perform. The rumba is still my favourite dance. Watching a video of my performance makes me look forward to that time when I will return to weekly dancing again. Music is and always will be an important part of my life, whether listening, watching, meditating or dancing to it. It helps me keep a balanced state of mind.

35
A Private Concert

It is December 2008 and Mark, the pianist, will be performing this week in the Almonte Old Town Hall, about fifty kilometres west from downtown Ottawa. I was surprised to learn that the inventor of basketball, James Naismith, MD, was born in this town in 1861. Naismith, as a physician, was also credited with introducing helmets to the game of football after a player he coached had suffered repetitive brain injuries. Dr. Naismith wanted to prevent further damage to this player and help stop other players from experiencing the same trauma. There is a museum for this physician a few blocks away from the town hall where we are recording and apparently it will be relocating soon.[31]

I will be there on performance day with the sound engineer to help. I met with Mark last Friday to hear him play. He wanted to stylistically be sure he was on the right track for the arrangements and he had only created a few. When he saw my look of concern after he told me this, he quickly reassured me. "Don't worry. Everything will be ready on time. Trust me."

I am not a musician. Yet, it seemed to me there was no way he could do over fifty arrangements in a few days. This did not look good. But the pieces he played sounded lovely.

"I need them simplified even more," I said.

An expression of disbelief washed over his face.

"But Samantha," he said looking back at his crumbled sheets of paper he wrote on, "this is pretty much as simple as they can get."

"I disagree," I said. "I want to hear more silence between the notes in each song."

I explained to Mark how the music is intended for relaxation; to slow the breath, heart rate and blood pressure effortlessly. For Mark, the arrangements had this effect, not for me though. This is where I see the challenge for many people that they often do not understand what it is like to relax deeply. What he put together sounded and felt too busy to induce relaxation as an end result. He usually decorates the pieces he plays with lovely jazz chords while improvising, however this was not how I want the songs to sound, even though I enjoy jazz. The reason why I am creating this CD is to help people relax deeply and I need to keep my goal in mind.

After this meeting I was nervous about whether he would be able to deliver what I needed for the recording. His notes for the arrangements also made me have doubts. I did not understand how he could possibly play anything even close to what I want from his scribbles on scrap paper.

"No one can understand these but me," he said, catching my look of confusion.

I doubt we can pull this off.

The grand piano is in the back room of the town hall. We will be recording the performance from that room today to get the best acoustics. The recording equipment is in the auditorium. The sound engineer and pianist will speak through headsets and microphones between the two rooms.

Going to the backroom the piano looks brand new and absolutely magnificent. I have only ever seen one of these from a distance on stage at the NAC. Its exterior has a flawless sheen and gives off an impressive grandeur. There is not one fingerprint on the shiny black surface. I walk over to it and press a few keys.

Suddenly there is loud noise behind me from the auditorium. Walking out of the room, my eyes and the engineers' dart to the front of the building as the noise continues. We see that a drill outside is rumbling and shaking everything. Some workers are on scaffolding, trying to restore the face of the old building.

"They can't be doing this now," I say. "Do they know there is a recording today?"

"They aren't supposed to be working today," says the engineer. "I'm sure they'll stop."

"Probably not, can you talk with them?" I ask.

The engineer leaves to go talk with the workers and when he returns, he says, "They're going to try to keep the noise down."

I stare at him, speechless. He knows that this does not mean they will and I believe I have a say in this considering I am paying for everything today.

"That's all I can do," he says, with a shrug.

Mark arrives and he immediately wants to see the piano. We go into the back room to show him where the musical instrument is. Mark touches it as if it were a fine piece of jewellery. In the music world, this is one of the best pianos to play on.

"I thought we'd have the piano on the stage for recording?" Mark asks. He seems disappointed.

"No," the engineer says. "I've recorded on this many times before and the backroom location here will give us the best sound. With the auditorium being empty there will be an echo."

We walk out of the back room as he speaks. Suddenly workers drill into the wall at the front of the building, again shattering the tranquillity inside the large room. It echoes throughout the auditorium, proving the engineer's point. Mark catches my eye to see my response and I shrug my shoulders. The engineer quickly says, "I spoke with the workers and they're going to try to not make noise while we record."

The rumbling continues and quiets down slowly.

"I need to play around a bit to warm up," Mark says.

He grabs a pile of papers from his bag and heads to the back room to warm up. The engineer goes to help him set up. I stay in the auditorium, looking at all the levers and dials of the recording equipment. Glancing over my shoulder, I try to hear if the workers are still moving around outside. The engineer comes back to sit next to me.

Mark plays some well-known jazz on the piano in the backroom to warm up. We listen and enjoy what he plays. The engineer smiles as Mark continues to play.

The engineer and I talk about the bands he has worked for. The

Guys was one of them, who he helped for quite a few years. I know some of their songs. We also talk about my non-profit's CD and fundraising plans. My ability to give a brief summary of what I am doing has improved over the past few months. I mention the driver who hurt me. I tell him how she offered no support during my recovery. And then I tell him she is on television and she haunts me. My immediate thought is that, no—I allow her to haunt me. I am surprised by my thought.

"I've seen her before on TV. I know who you are talking about," he says.

I tell him how sharing my story will help me close this chapter of my past.

Mark finishes his warm-up and returns to the auditorium with a few scrap pieces of paper in his hands.

"I want to start with the classical pieces," he says, smiling directly at me.

He has already told me that these are the ones he is most nervous about playing properly. I am not surprised that he wants to get them completed quickly. I know his insecurity is my fault because I warned him about my aunt Gisele and her passion for classical music. He knows she also plays piano and this makes him even more nervous.

The first piece he decides to play is "Gymnopédie No.1". He needs to do only a couple of takes of his performance. It sounds perfect to me. After Mark is satisfied with his performance, he asks the engineer how the recording went. When both men agree it sounded good, Mark then will come out from the backroom shuffling his papers and move on to the next song.

While recording "Für Alina", a blast of noise from the workers suddenly shoots through the room. The engineer and I look at each other, alarmed. Mark continues playing because he cannot hear the commotion. Finally he walks out while we are talking about what happened. The engineer starts to listen to the recording to see if the sound from the workers is audible.

"I'm paying for all these rentals today. That noise has to stop. They shouldn't be doing work like this on a day when a recording is taking place. You have to call someone," I say.

I decide then and there that there is no way I will let any noise ruin what I am creating.

"I can't think of who to try getting a hold of," says the engineer.

I stare at him. I am not going to repeat my request. He was the one who made the arrangements with the city for this piano; I only emailed them about where to send the cheque. The engineer senses my disapproval. He grabs his cell phone to look up a number. He dials, talks and then hangs up.

"The Town Hall office is sending someone to get them to stop working," he says.

"Thanks," I say with relief.

Mark then chooses the next song to be played and goes back to the piano. Again machinery obnoxiously rumbles outside. I want to go tell those workers to stop but it is not my job to do this. I have to speak up. If they waste more of our time today then we will need to come back for another day of recording.

"Can you please tell the workers someone from the City is getting them to stop their work?" I ask the engineer.

He looks at me for a moment. He obviously is not used to being as assertive as I am asking him to be. And because it is a small town, he might know the workers personally.

"Okay," he agrees.

Speaking into the microphone connected to the back room, he says, "Mark, hold on a second."

He then walks to the front to go outside and talk with the workers. Once back, he sits down and tells Mark to let him know when he is ready to start playing. We can hear the workers grumbling while climbing down off the scaffolding. They kick stuff along the way and make noise to show their unhappiness with not being able to work—but are soon gone.

The silence behind me brings immediate relief. The commotion was stressful. My back and neck are tense over my concern that the interference from the construction was going to continue for the whole recording session. Now my concentration can be fully on Mark's performance and our recording.

Next, Mark plays a Schumann piano arrangement called "Träumerei". His playing is flawless but I am concerned because he puts more than a few jazz chords into his performance. After he finishes and comes out onto stage, the engineer says, "I loved what you did for that piece."

"Sounded great, didn't it?" Mark asks.

The two men act like teenagers talking about how cool an old classical piece turned out to be jazzed up a bit. Listening to them, I smile to myself. I let them enjoy the moment and say nothing. I know that Aunt Gisele will have something to say about jazz being thrown into a classical piece. Sorry guys but I think I can see this one getting canned. This is only one song of many, so hopefully the rest turn out well and we will not need it.

Andrew and I often joke about how loving yet tough my aunt is. He knows about her being on my case as a teenager because I smoked. She would not accept any excuse from me as to why I was choosing to abuse my body. Thank goodness I quit and got her off my back. This is why Aunt Gisele, Andrew and I agreed it would be best for me to attend today by myself. Without intending to, we thought she might interfere with the production when only I truly knew what I wanted the non-profit's CD to sound like.

So on we go today—song after song. To see the engineer work the recording equipment fascinates me. The arrangements Mark made are exactly how I want them to sound. I am really impressed with his speed and accuracy to be able to do this. After meeting with him last week and hearing him play those few pieces, I seriously had my doubts. Today I am confident he was the best pianist to hire for this recording.

As Mark is about to play "Twinkle Twinkle Little Star", we all joke around and nickname it "Twinkle Twinkle". Mark is looking forward to playing it for us. He made the arrangement without even hearing the song. He looks happy talking about the special intro he put in and he clearly had fun working on it. He has children of his own, so I can understand why he enjoyed it. What he plays sounds lovely. He only needs to do a couple of takes of the song to get it perfect.

Coming out again from the backroom, Mark asks how long we have the piano today. After I tell him, he shuffles through his papers. He wonders whether we can complete everything and feels we may have to come back for another day. I really was hoping we could finish everything today. His best work is what I want however so I will do whatever is necessary to get it. Therefore, I will not pressure him to rush his performance for the recording. This is not a time that I want to be too assertive. I want things created, with no stress.

The morning goes by quickly and before I know it, it is time for lunch. The engineer so far, was able to record many of the songs in only one take, which amazes us all and the recording is going well. Only the classical pieces concern me. I asked the engineer to make sure, when he is back at his studio, that the construction noise cannot be detected in "Für Alina".

After lunch, when Mark plays Elton John's "Rocket Man" next, he occasionally adds soft jazz chords.

"I love what he did," the engineer says. "I like several but this is my favourite so far."

Mark comes out every time to announce what he is playing next, making it like our own private concert. When he plays Lionel Richie's "Ballerina Girl", my heart melts. The arrangement he made of the song is perfect and much better than I expected it to be.

Later in the afternoon, Mark's only challenge is with the last song, Nelly Furtado's "Say It Right". I am tired and struggling to explain what I feel is wrong with the arrangement he made. The engineer steps in to help explain to Mark what it should sound like. They are both tired as well.

"You are playing too fast," the engineer says. "There are way too many notes in your arrangement. It needs to be simplified. What you are doing sounds nothing like the rest of the songs we recorded already."

The engineer seems to understand exactly what I want. After six hours of work, Mark finishes the last of about fifty songs. We managed to do it all in one day. I needed to voice my approval of every piece before we moved on and that took a lot of concentration on everyone's part. But we did it. Mark emerges from the backroom one last time and looks at me.

"Was it what you expected?" he asks.

"It was beyond what I expected Mark. It sounded incredible," I say. "Thank you so much for your hard work. Last week, I was seriously wondering if this would work out. But your arrangements were exactly what I wanted."

Mark laughs and looks at the engineer, saying, "Don't often hear we did everything exactly right from a woman, now do we?"

They both agree with each other while laughing.

"The piano was perfect for you to perform on as well," I say.

"I really enjoyed playing it," he says, smiling.

The engineer and I say our goodbyes to Mark as he takes off to get his kids from school in downtown Ottawa. I hang around to wait for a rough copy of the recordings from the engineer. Later I want to meditate while listening to what we recorded. The whole drive home I am excited to hear the music with my full attention on every note.

At home, my concentration is solidly focused as it plays. The piano pieces sound simple and heavenly. I am at peace, in a deep cocoon of relaxation. I cannot believe that we pulled it off. This is exactly what I wanted the CD to sound like. After my meditation I call Aunt Gisele and Andrew to tell them the good news.

36
More Parallels

This Christmas 2008, I am happier than ever. Mya and I are at my parents' house for the holidays. My mom's side of the family has come over on Christmas Day. I am quiet about my new venture with the non-profit. Until I complete the piano CD for An Aid to Help Foundation, I do not want to talk about what I am doing with family other than my parents and Aunt Gisele.

As I talk to one of my cousins, I am caught off guard to overhear some of my relatives in another part of the living room talking about Deborah's father. Apparently they read something about him in the newspaper recently. Dad says the usual line of, "After the accident, the Dean of McMaster University called to express his concern but not one word from Deborah's parents—ever."

Seventeen years have passed and they still speak about my accident as if it happened yesterday. I have never heard Dad call Deborah's father by name like he did just now. It seems that my uncle and he have had conversations about her father before. I hope the work I am doing to raise money will somehow change this and help put a positive ending on an experience that hurt my family.

To spend time at home with my family is meaningful but I am glad to be going back to Ottawa, to start 2009 working on the non-profit.

Back in Ottawa, I search online for news about Deborah's father. A list of search results appears and one has an image of Deborah next to a man, who they say is her husband. Good for her, she got married. But then, I am surprised to read that the man she is married to is a member of The Guys. Seriously, I do not know what the chances are of using a sound engineer who worked for years with this band before. It is definitely a "strange parallel". I also saw them perform this year at the

NAC when I was volunteering.

I stop searching for news of Deborah's father. I do not want to learn anything about him now. Obviously this was the information I was meant to find. I quickly write an e-mail to the engineer, with the subject: "Six degrees of separation?!" explaining what happened.

"I'm assuming that you must know him," I say. "Okay, this is a bit freaking weird. I'm shaking my head at this coincidence, ahhhh!"

Our short conversation on recording day shows how everything about the performance and I were in sync. Somehow, it seems that these signs are continuously being revealed to me to let me know I am on the right path with my pursuit. Therefore, I will continue to go forward creating what I feel inspired to do.

37
Hidden Meaning

Today it is snowing heavily. I decide to spend the day setting up another office upstairs. I have a den on the main floor but the desk there is a corner armoire with no table top for paperwork. The non-profit is generating lots of documents I need to look at, so that desk has become a piled up mess.

While cleaning out the closet in the bedroom that I am converting into this office, I discover journal notes in a black binder that are written on lined loose-leaf paper.

Seeing my handwriting reminds me how it changed after the accident. I can no longer write like I did when I was Doris. I try but it does not feel normal. With time, I slowly developed a new way of writing as Samantha; however it still feels and looks odd to me. Sometimes I change it back and forth, from Doris to Samantha's style, for no real reason. As a signature I have written my last name only for many years now. I have had some people look at it confused at times because it is a man's name. I cannot put initials in front. It feels too strange.

I am surprised I kept these journal notes. I was positive that I destroyed everything I ever wrote on paper. I set the binder aside to read later. The thought of someone reading this without my permission makes me uncomfortable. I will destroy it after I look at it. With medical and legal reports being written about me for so many years, my life now is much more private.

Journal writing is helpful. If I need to write intimate stuff to myself like this, I figured out that by typing an e-mail and then saving it as a draft to delete later works best for me. Sometimes I write like this and do not even save it. Writing helps me put my feelings into words and get random thoughts off my mind. I do not have to look at it again because doing this has helped me process my feelings.

"Don't put on paper what you don't want repeated," a friend of the family once said. And I agree.

I have realized lately that speaking publicly about my past is becoming easier but this does not mean that I am not retaining my privacy. I talk about whatever feels comfortable and I know that it will always be my choice what I share.

After dinner I sit on the couch in the TV room to read my old journal. Mya joins me and jumps up on her favourite brown armchair that is covered with a blanket. She immediately scans the forest. The chair she is on is from when I was growing up as Doris. I have no idea why I chose to keep it but something will not let me part with it. I vaguely remember sitting cross-legged on it after school and watching TV. I find it cute how Mya enjoys it.

I open the binder. I wrote this during the time I lived in the condo and the PIs were following me. It was about the time when I had my lawyers get rid of the insurance company. I was not happy then. I should just throw this away. But something will not let me put the journal down. I start to flip the pages and read my last entry on February 1999:

"I'm closing my entire file with the law firm. I know this is the right thing for me to do. I feel freedom in my life, at last. The support from the insurance company was important for me to have. They helped me successfully rebuild a life. I'm relieved they understood how serious a severe closed-head injury is. Needing to share my personal life with strangers for my recovery wasn't easy. Everything about me was examined. I feel I'm meant to help others in some way from this whole ordeal—to promote change for the better in our world. I don't know how but I sense something. My intuition tells me it will be in the public eye. I'll need life to show me what to do because I want to focus solidly on a normal life now, finally. I won't go looking for anything. If it's important I do something I'll have to be shown it or else I'll just chalk everything up to experience. If there's a purpose for me, it's going to happen effortlessly."

I set the binder down in my lap. These are powerful words. My statement is like a challenge to the universe to show me what it needs me to do. Now is the perfect time for me to be working on a non-profit and doing work related to what I went through. I have healed and lived a normal life since I was hurt; I have moved on. After the accident, I would not have been capable to do this. I needed time to focus on my recovery. My family also would have been concerned to see me delving into this work at the time. They know now that I built a life beyond my accident and resulting injury.

This is my choice to confront my memories, for a higher purpose to help others. There is nothing wrong with this. It feels as if a director somewhere is navigating things for me; as if nature speaks to me on behalf of another. All I am is the observer. I wonder if this is what I have always been.

I pick the binder up again to read more of the final entry:

"What will I be doing, exactly ten years from now: what'll my life be like; where will I live; will I have a husband or children? I'm excited to see what unfolds now that this nightmare is over. A new chapter in life is starting for me. I'm no longer scared what others say or write about me. I have been walking around with my wounds open for all to see. I can now stand tall with strength as a survivor. I have my privacy back now which feels amazing."

I look at what I just read. This was the last time I ever wrote about this. It is sad to remember how I always had to show specialists that I deserved support. Their reports to the insurance and lawyers had to be in my favour or else I would not have been looked after. I never lied to them. I just had to open up to them about everything I was going through which was not easy to do.

I flip mindlessly through the other pages. Words suddenly jump off the page: *I wonder what I'll be doing exactly ten years from now.* I take a sharp breath. It is now February 2009 and it was February 1999 when I wrote this. Ten years from then is exactly now. This non-profit is something I am being shown to do. It is what I wished to happen, exactly as I wrote here; this is unbelievable.

It is almost as if something or someone was watching or hearing what I said to myself in 1999. I reread all I wrote in February 1999 with amazement and feel a renewed confidence within myself that I am following a purpose in my life. I never thought work would be important to me, at least not in the way I felt when I was Doris and wanted to become a paediatrician. My heart and soul is in this new project. To have this passion for work in common with my previous life as Doris feels good. I always missed this about her, about how she always knew exactly what she wanted to do. I am surprised to learn how healing this work is for me to do.

I look over at Mya, who is busy watching the forest. I remember something that Emile Coué, a French psychologist and pharmacist in the 1920's suggested people could use as a form of autosuggestion.[32] I have said hundreds of times over the years. *Every day, in every way, I am getting better and better.* It is like brain washing myself. But it might be working.

"Mya, I'm getting better all the time," I say.

Hearing her name, she turns to look at me. She then returns to looking into the forest. Her heart is in what she is doing. We have something in common. I get up to go destroy my old journal.

I do not understand how I did not find this before. I would not have kept it on purpose. What a coincidence to read it exactly ten years after or another "strange parallel". I asked then for life to show me what I was supposed to do with my story. This definitely has been happening.

38
Critical Eyes

I am at Aunt Gisele and Uncle Helmut's tonight for Easter dinner, 2009. This evening my uncle is cooking us a gourmet dinner. I grew up enjoying many of his delicious meals.

The menu tonight includes appetizers of chicken leek rolls, blue cheese mushroom caps, cucumber rolls, prunes wrapped in bacon with an almond inside and Finnish pea soup. The main meal is going to be lamb shanks, couscous, fried beans and peppers. We will finish with a watercress salad. For dessert Aunt Gisele has made an Austrian pastry called a Linzer torte. Uncle Helmut has also paired the dinner with some delicious wines.

"I'm so proud of Samantha for the work she started doing last year," Aunt Gisele says to the table of guests which includes her neighbours and family. "She can tell you about the non-profit she started."

I tell the guests about the accident and how serious my injuries were.

"It's surprising how badly hurt you were," says one neighbour. "I can't tell."

"Neither can I," say a few other guests in unison.

"What do you mean you can't tell?" Aunt Gisele says. "She's got scars all over her cheek." Then she touches her cheek and rubs it from top to bottom.

Oh no, I think to myself. I have no idea what she is doing. Aunt Gisele's response and gesture startles me. I do not want to be seen as a victim. We have already spoken about how I wish to present my story to others. I sit quietly. The conversation continues without my involvement. The family looks at my cheek.

"I can't see what you are talking about," someone says.

"You can see the lumpy tissue underneath called keloids," says my cousin's wife, Sherissa, who is a physician, specializing in anaesthesia.

"Yes," Aunt Gisele says, touching her cheek again to show the locations. "You can tell. Her cheeks are different."

They speak and look at me as if I am no longer in front of them as a person with feelings. I make eye contact with one couple and they sense my discomfort and appear to be uncomfortable as well. Then one young guest, who is sitting across the table from me, looks me in the eye and says, "I never could see it—seriously."

I smile softly, to thank her for the support. After I hear her concern, I decide this conversation is not helping anyone. I do not need or want everyone's sympathy. I jump in to defend myself.

"My cheeks are not drastically different," I say.

"Yes, they are," says Sherissa. "The obvious scar tissue and keloids make them different."

Aunt Gisele and Sherissa talk further about my face after the injury. I sit at the table, not knowing what to say. The conversation does not even last five minutes but the evening is ruined for me. I remain quiet, choosing not to say anything more.

Later at home, I look in the mirror and use a cotton swab to remove my eye make-up. I grab a fresh one to take off the cover-up from my scar.

I am still upset about the conversation about my scar. I examine my cheek closely and a huge weight of sadness fills up inside me. I see all the marks and lumps that make up my life's experience that is etched in my skin. I start to cry.

My aunt Gisele was portraying me as a victim, someone to feel sorry for. This is not how I want to be viewed when I share what I went through with others.

Still removing my make-up, I press the cotton into my scar as I cry. As usual no tears run down my face and today the reminder of this makes me cry more. My fingers keep the swab pressed solid against my skin. I start rubbing up and down on my cheek, harder than I have ever touched myself before. I am attempting to console myself. Soon my actions become aggressive with even more pressure as I rub my right cheek from my eye to beneath the chin. To hear and watch myself cry makes my actions speed up even more.

My thoughts are negative: I hate this mark; I don't want it anymore; I wish it would disappear; it's ugly; why did I have to get it? My anger makes my crying slow down—but my hand does not stop moving. In the mirror, in my eyes I see the depth of the hurt and sadness that I have kept buried for so long. Finally—I see it.

I continue to scrub my cheek. It feels good to try to get rid of this memory etched in my skin. This mark is like an unwanted souvenir from the worst trip in my life. I have never behaved this way with my skin before. I have always been gentle, not aggressive like this. I was confident before but now other people are teaching me to be insecure—wait a second.

I instantly stop scrubbing. My thoughts shock me, as well as my actions. I do not understand why I am looking at myself through the eyes of others. This is not good. My cheek is now bright red, especially the scar tissue. I blow my nose. After putting cream on my eyes and face, I get into my pyjamas and go to bed.

I feel better after crying. I do not understand what happened tonight. If talking about the past hurts me then maybe I should not share my story with others. I accept that this work is important in many ways for others but I am concerned about whether it is good for me as well.

As I get into bed, an incident comes to mind when someone else was critical about my scar. I am having difficulty stopping my thoughts. I know I should meditate but I am too distracted.

~

It happened in 1992, nine months after my accident, when I had to stay at the hospital. At the time I was living with a lot of anxiety because I was ordered by doctors to go to the emergency if I ever had a headache or a fever because of the possibility of contracting meningitis as a result of a CSF leak. For that stay, my neurosurgeon had admitted me for some CAT scans to locate any CSF leakage I could possibly have had. This was the leak that Dr. Rutka eventually found, four years later, in 1996.

At the hospital, while I was an in-patient, a nurse walked into the elevator. She was talking to someone and she immediately became quiet when she saw me. She stared at the marks on my face.

"What's wrong with your face?" she asked.

I said nothing.

"What's wrong with your face?" she asked me again.

I stared at her until I arrived at my floor and the elevator doors opened. I did not answer her the first time and I was not going to answer then. It was none of her business. She worked there; she should understand that what she was asking was out of line. My eyes pierced right through her as I calmly walked out of the elevator, returned to my room and started sobbing.

I cried for days. Dad was really upset about how this woman made me feel. He helped ease my pain with his support. Without his shoulder to cry on, I do not know how I would have been able to manage the rest of my stay in the hospital. Another day, students from a local high school crammed into my single room to speak with me. It was part of a program at the Toronto hospital called PARTY: Prevent Alcohol and Risk-Related Trauma in Youth. During their visit, I told the students about how severe my injuries and the accident which brought me there had been. They asked me tons of questions.

Brian was my boyfriend at the time. Many months later he told me that a friend of his from university had been one of those high school students to visit me.

"Samantha's story had a remarkable impact on me and my friends," she told him. "We spoke about it afterwards as a group about how important it is to make responsible choices in life. I'll always remember meeting her."

When Brian told me this he said, "You should do public speaking about what you went through."

"Not right now," I told him.

Tonight lying in bed, thinking about the critical comments that were said about me at dinner, I have difficulty falling asleep. As I roll onto my side, I try turning off my thoughts. I need to sleep on what happened tonight at Aunt Gisele's. Tomorrow I will feel better.

The next morning I call Mom and tell her what Aunt Gisele and Sherissa said, as well as how I scrubbed my face when I removed my make-up.

"Oh dear," she says as I start crying, "I understand they hurt your feelings. Remember, they're medical doctors. They were speaking clinically about your scar."

"Mom, many other doctors have spoken to me more kindly," I say. "That's no excuse."

"But they were speaking not as if you were a patient," she says. "They weren't using good bedside manners."

We speak for a while longer but she has a hard time cheering me up. Her support was needed though for me to share my feelings and cry.

I have to talk to Aunt Gisele about how I feel. I need to explain to her how I wish to present the story about my scar to others. There is no way I am going to ever feel the way I did last night again, when I was taking off my make-up. I must defend myself. If I do not do this, no one else will.

39
An Assertive Call

A few days after Easter 2009, I pick up the phone and slowly dial Aunt Gisele's number.

I do not know why I am I doing this. I should just let this experience go. But I know it is important I express my feelings to her and this is hard. I am nervous when she answers.

"Hi, I need to talk with you about something," I say, pausing for her response.

"Yes, what is it?"

"What you're doing to help me with the non-profit means a lot to me. I'm grateful to you for your support. Sure I want people to learn how I dealt with stuff but to speak from a place of weakness isn't how I want to present my experience because it's not true, I'm not weak—I'm strong. The other night when you mentioned my scar to your guests at dinner they immediately felt sorry for me. I felt you were portraying me as a victim and this made me uncomfortable," I say.

"Oh dear," she says. "I'm sorry, Samantha."

Aunt Gisele always likes calling me by my "new" name. She thinks it is great I changed it. She never liked the name Doris and has told me she feels Samantha suits me better.

"You didn't mean to hurt me," I say with my voice trembling slightly. "But you did, though, with your words—and deeply."

"Tell me what you want me to do," she says. "We need to talk about this."

"First off, I'm a survivor, not a victim," I explain. "The true story is how my strength got me through that whole mess. I now want to share my story to help others."

"Okay, I understand," she says.

"My scar is not something horrible like you presented it as the other night," I say. "I accept this mark as a part of me. I will never do the 'poor me' dance about getting it. Not everyone sees it the same way you do. You're educated as a doctor so you're more critical than the average person."

"Okay," she responds.

"What do you think of my mom's scar on her face?" I ask.

"I don't think anything because I never noticed it or where it is," she says, surprised.

"The scar is small on her right cheek," I tell her. "The tissue's raised a bit from keloids and scar tissue. She and her sister fell into barbed wired fence as they were trying to climb over a woodpile when they were children. She's had this mark forever. Her scar's a part of her, something you've always accepted. You could say her two cheeks are different but I know you wouldn't as you haven't even noticed it."

"You're right," she says.

"You've seen my scar from the initial injury," I say. "But it's not as obvious to everyone else. It's a part of me I accept and I won't let you change that. If others see it, I'm okay but if they don't, I'm okay as well."

"I understand."

"The dinner was uncomfortable because your guests appeared to not know why you were so critical. I'm not telling my story to get sympathy from others; I don't want or need it," I say. "I want to give people strength and hope by sharing my experience."

"I'll help you," she says.

"Thanks," I say.

As I get off the phone, I feel relief. To talk with her about my feelings was the right thing to do. It helps put the experience behind me. The other night the words used to describe me hurt and they still do. It will take a while for this to heal more. That was the hardest challenge I have had to date in dealing with the scar on my face. I hit a dark bottom that night. My scar is still sore from scrubbing it. I know that it was not what they said that hurt but it was my perception and response to what they said that hurt me the most.

On my way out the door to go to the gym I stop to look at my reflection in the mirror. I see my scar and smile. Never have I and never will I, think the scar is as bad as they do. I love myself, as I am—unconditionally.

40
The Painting's Scar

In my living room I am sitting on a black leather couch, taking a moment to rest my eyes. I am writing for the pages for the website of An Aid to Help Foundation. Thinking about what has come together so far for the non-profit, reminds me of why I am doing this work.

The critical remarks at Easter at my aunt's this year, taught me a lot. I cannot do anything to change what happened to me in 1991 and how the scars on my face look now. I am here to help others and I need to accept everything unconditionally to achieve this. Acceptance is the only way I can move forward from that initial experience.

My scar symbolizes honesty about my wounds. Everyone can see the mark if they look close enough, especially if I do not have make-up on. I think a lot of people focus too much on what is outside of them and not what is inside. We would all be like dolls, with nothing but stuffing inside, without having some heart and soul as a part of the mix of who we are as individuals.

As I look over at the non-profit's painting, *Finding Inner Strength,* above the piano, I suddenly remember something. What the artist Vincent Paolucci sent me had about six inches painted out to the left side. He had created a decorative vine-like object. He was aware that the painting was to be part of the CD case. He thought what he had created would look good around the spine of the case. But I had not asked for it and I did not like the painting with it.

The rest of the painting turned out to be exactly what I wanted. There is realism to the hand and the turtle. The colours are all natural earth tones. The quality of Vincent's work that I have seen before and loved, flourishes in this painting. It matches the décor in my house perfectly.[33]

Since this was a custom painting, I professionally had the part that he created for the CD case removed. I had an art shop resize and stretch the canvas so the framed painting now only shows the turtle and the hand. The shop asked me if I wanted the leftover canvas. I said no.

If an expert were to examine the framed painting, they might say, "We detect flaws where the left side of the canvas had cuts for re-sizing; so now this painting's not valuable." No one can tell the painting is altered just by looking at it. The experts did a perfect job re-stretching the canvas and framing it. We all thought it looks better this way. To me, the painting has more beauty with this "flaw". Part of the attractiveness of it is derived from its imperfection. I think that on the outside in ways, all people and things in life are a bit rough around the edges. This painting now symbolises that to me because of what it had to go through in its short life to become what it is today.

If you were in a room full of people and asked those who are physically perfect to stand, there would be silence as heads turned to see who stood up. If someone did, they would need to pass inspection by others. No one can ever be perfect in everyone's eyes. As they say, beauty is in the eye of the beholder.

Unconditionally accepting others is a remarkable quality. True inner beauty will always touch people most memorably; that was also the case for me when I met a princess one day.

In the children's rehabilitation hospital, when I met Princess Diana, it was not her appearance that caught my attention. None of us young patients were in a spot in life to care about this kind of superficiality. Rather, it was her heart that touched us. Empathy, concern and unconditional love, radiated from within her as soon as she walked in the room.

41
Full of Music

The summer of 2009 is unfolding. After months of work, I have finally finished the CD, naming it *Songs for Everyone*.[34] I soon realized that because Vincent's painting of the hand and the turtle speaks for itself, it was not necessary to include the title on the front of the case. With it having been done this way, anyone can stand it up now at home and they have a copy of an original piece of art, which to me, adds to the quality of the product.

Of the approximately fifty songs Mark played that day in Almonte, I ended up choosing in total forty-three of them to use.[35] Mark's arrangements and performance for the recording were faultless. After the sound engineer listened closely to "Für Alina", I was relieved to learn that the noise from the workers disrupting us that day cannot be heard. I find it is amazing how something so elegant had so much chaos behind it and no one knows but me.

I was right in guessing that the jazzed up version of "Träumerei" did not meet Aunt Gisele's approval. She still would not have minded if the piece was on the CD but I decided against it. Because this song is royalty free, due to its age, I decided to put it on the website for people to enjoy instead.[36] Out of all the pieces Mark performed that day, this one was his favourite.

There was another song Mark performed that I would have liked to include by Guns N' Roses called "November Rain". I really liked the original piece because of the full orchestral accompaniment that is with the song. The video that the band shares of this is great.[37] But unfortunately it was extremely difficult for me to get a license to use it and finally I just gave up. Mom thought this might be for the best because of the reference to guns in their name. Maybe she was right.

It was a touching experience to hold a copy of the CD in my hands for the first time. To create something like this, without words that could help in my expression of what was going on for me emotionally was therapeutic. Listening to the music relaxes me. Waking up with the soft piano melodies playing in the morning has become important to me. After the alarm goes off, I let it continue playing while I get ready. Doing this, I also no longer need to look at a clock to get ready.

Usually I take a certain amount of time to get ready, so I have noted what song is playing when this time is up. The songs are listed in alphabetical order. By listening, I can easily calculate in my head how much time is left. For example song number twenty-seven, "Path of Beauty", is at around forty-five minutes into the recording. Song number thirty-seven, "This Used to Be My Playground", marks about an hour. This alphabetical timer helps me start my day more peacefully.

While listening, I often catch myself putting on make-up, using my full concentration while breathing deeply. The music induces a therapeutic effect—at least for me.

I have already received many compliments about *Songs for Everyone*. To buy the CD for their own enjoyment is a way for someone to give to a cause they believe in. This is definitely an approach I like. A psychologist in California, who specializes in children's education, wrote:

> *"I was just putting my kids to bed with your music and wanted to thank you again for sharing it. We love it! We listen to it every night before bedtime. As soon as I turn it on, we all start relaxing… I think that other mothers will connect with the comfort of finding a good goodnight CD. Our night routine would not be the same without it."*

The website is now also complete; thanks, in large part, to the assistance of a nice man who helped me build it. Everything looks sharp, especially the layout and colours. Nalin, the web designer who is helping me, first did about half the website. Then I also taught myself how to do the rest of it. It was an enjoyable and satisfying challenge.

The web address of www.anaid.org is what I decided on. This will be easy to remember and tell others. Seeing Diana's name backwards makes me recall the time my Recovery Book was a part of my venture as I looked at it while sitting on the stairs the night of my party.

I am going to pitch Oprah and a few other talk shows to see if I can get on as a guest. I can only try my best to do this. If nobody wants to hear my story, I cannot force them; whatever will be, will be. I want to also try and sell the non-profit's CD in a few stores, maybe advertise for it as well. It is an incredible piano music mix and it would be a shame to not share it with others.

I want to speak to some charities as well to see if they would like copies of the CD to sell. By doing this, they can raise money for their own cause, as well as the advancement of education.

Other parts of my life are moving forward too, making me happier than I have ever felt before. I met a guy named Eric through an online dating website. He is moving to Ottawa from Kingston in a few months. We had thought we would wait until he moved to start to get to know each other but then he got into an accident riding his bicycle in Kingston. An SUV taking a corner hit him. He flew metres through the air, hitting hard the pavement. People came running to help him, except the woman driving the vehicle. She stood and passively watched while waiting for the police.

Eric told me about his accident in an e-mail. He sustained road rash, sprains, a chipped tooth and needed stitches in a few places. He also broke his left ankle. They had to check the swelling to make sure the blood flow did not become blocked. If that had happened, he might have had serious damage to his lower leg.

What a relief his injuries were not worse. He rides a sport motorcycle and skydives, so I guess he always lives a bit on the edge. To learn about his accident changed my feelings. He was no longer only a guy I might want to date romantically. I cared about him as a friend and wondered how he was doing following the accident. The link between his traumatic experience and mine strengthened our connection because I empathized with him.

The first time I met him in person was when I went to my parents and Dad took me to Thornhill, north of Toronto, to pick up the CDs for the non-profit. The drive into Toronto makes me nervous, so Dad had offered me a lift to the warehouse. On the way to my parent's house, I stopped in Kingston to meet Eric. You could see he was banged up from the accident. His ankle was painful, giving him a hard time getting around. He is a good-looking and friendly guy. I enjoyed spending time with him.

I learned that like me, Eric did gymnastics when he was younger. He was interested that I dance and told me he used to throw the cheerleaders around when they performed for the Toronto Argonauts. The tumbling and partner stunts interested him because of the gymnastics. He knows how to move a woman's body, so we can possibly dance together at some point.

He also told me how he volunteers at the Humane Society as a dog walker. My heart skipped a beat to learn this. I do not meet many people my age who enjoy volunteering. I too had once checked out dog-walking for the Humane Society. Then I got Mya who occupies me enough in the dog-walk department.

Eric works in management for the Canadian military. Sometimes he gets placement outside Canada for work. His last deployment before moving to Kingston was to a developing country. I am busy working on the non-profit. So if we grow closer, his going away would be fine with me. I have decided that getting to know him slowly would work best. The connection between us is worth exploring deeper.

42
Social and Emotional Learning

After extensive research, I have decided the money raised through sales of the non-profit's CD will go towards advancing education in the elementary school years. I feel it will help children learn things at an age where they can naturally practice their studies through their own life experience, while still hopefully having the guidance of their parents and teachers. Specifically, donations will be made to an educational area called Social and Emotional Learning (SEL) to help fund school programs that foster social and emotional intelligence. SEL educates children and adults in the areas of social awareness, self-management, self-awareness, responsible decision-making and relationship skills. SEL is described as being able to "improve students' positive behaviour and reduce negative behaviour".[38]

The SEL movement started in 1995 after the publication of Daniel Goleman's book *Emotional Intelligence*. My aunt and I have read the book. Aunt Gisele even once took a course on it to give her ideas how to help her patients in therapy. Emotional Intelligence (EQ) in my view means the measure of a person's skills in areas such as self-awareness, empathy and relating sensitively with all aspects of life. I feel it encompasses people, our environment and animals as well. SEL helps to enhance psychological development in children. Aunt Gisele and I believe that helping to advance this innovative advancement in education definitely meets my purpose of teaching others to make responsible choices.

More confidence and experience to talk about feelings may have prevented my accident in 1991, when nothing like SEL was taught in school. A bit more preparation through education at the start of our schooling would have helped, instead of learning the hard way like I did by taking a "crash course". I know I did not cause the accident I had been in but I wish there had been easier ways available for me to learn these valuable lessons. Having this type of knowledge in advance could have possibly saved the life I had as Doris.

43
Miracle from Nature

It is an afternoon in September 2009 and I am walking downstairs to the kitchen. Light shining on a painting catches my eye. I stop to look. Sunlight is being reflected somehow onto *Finding Inner Strength* and is directly shining on the turtle. I cannot tell where the reflection is coming from but the glow makes the turtle look like it has a light bulb inside his body. The effect is mystical and powerful. The sun has never shone on this spot, in this way. I put my original pieces of art on this side of the room on purpose, to protect them.

Up close, the painting takes on a magical haze with this light on the turtle. I can see now that somehow, sunlight is hitting the piano keys and being deflected onto the painting. I have never seen anything like this. I run to grab my camera to preserve the image as a picture.[39]

It looks incredible. With curiosity, I try to figure out which window the light is coming from. I close the blinds about three feet to the left and the painting is darkened. I step back to take a photo.[40]

As I open the blinds, the light is again shining the same way on the turtle. What a miraculous thing to happen.

I sit on my leather couch for the next seven minutes, marvelling at it all. Seeing the sunlight on the painting I recall an ancient Indian mantra that one can say to the sun. I have said it translated into English, many times. Today its meaning has taken on a strength I have not felt before. Usually I say it for myself but today I want to say it instead, for the turtle in the painting and its creation for the purpose of my CD for the non-profit.

"You—who are the source of all power," I whisper. "Whose rays illuminate the world; illuminate also An Aid to Help Foundation's heart, so that it too may do your work."

All of a sudden, in seconds, right before my eyes, the light changes where it is shining on the turtle. I am spellbound as I jump up to take more pictures. The light is now shining in a perfect arc over the turtle's shell, radiating upwards. I am speechless and watch every second. The light stays this way for about a minute before disappearing.[41]

What a truly memorable moment. I look over at another painting I have. This one is by Evelyn Klein called *Fenêtres du Passe—Windows of the Past.* It is a piece of mixed media that creatively has a collection of different things infused on its canvas. There is a small photograph as well as a quote etched on it. I know this quote well, from having read it so often.[42]

"I believe that imagination is stronger than knowledge. That myth is more potent than history. That dreams are more powerful than facts. That hope always triumphs over experience. That laughter is the only cure for grief. And I believe that love is stronger than death."

I look at *Finding Inner Strength* again but the energy of it has changed since the sunlight stopped touching it. It was almost like a "kiss" from nature. I do not want to move. I stay seated until the light show performed by the sun gradually fades from my thoughts.

44
An Important Penny

It is later in the fall of 2009 and I am on my way to volunteer in the lounge at the NAC for a concert tonight by The Guys. As the youngest volunteer there I am often put on the schedule for concerts like this. Many of the older volunteers do not enjoy the popular music and I can understand. These concerts are often deafening. I enjoy a few of their songs and I might watch a bit of the concert.

I did not ask to work this shift, nor would I have as Deborah's husband plays in this band. After I cancelled my cable TV it has been wonderful not to see her all the time. I needed her ghost-like appearance and voice in my home to stop haunting me but tonight, I realize, for some reason she is still hard to avoid.

Once I arrive at the NAC, I go to Le Café. I usually eat at this restaurant on nights I volunteer. While eating, I enjoy a glass of wine. The food is excellent. Ken, who is volunteering with me for the show, joins me at the restaurant bar. We eat our dinner and talk about things going on at the NAC.

I am nervous about being here tonight. I tell Ken about the non-profit I started and how this ties in with the band performing later. I have worked with many volunteers for years but none of them knew about the car accident, the injuries and my scar—until now.

After dinner, Ken and I go upstairs to set up the bar in the lounge. We will not be busy for a performance like this. Tonight only a few people come in to learn about the private room but no patrons visit. The Guys start performing in Southam Hall. We are in no rush to close the lounge until intermission. Walking out, I look forward to hearing a few songs. Ken is going to the restaurant again. We are about to walk in different directions when he suddenly looks down.

"Oh look, a penny," he says.

He picks up the penny and hands it to me. "Here, make a wish."

I take the coin from him. We go our separate ways until intermission. As I hold the penny, I walk to the door to see through the window to the stage where the band plays. The performance is loud and I have no desire to be inside the hall. I usually protect the hearing of my good ear at concerts like this. If I lose the hearing in that ear, I would need to wear my hearing aid daily, so I would rather be careful and make sure this does not ever happen.

My fingers play slowly with the penny I am holding. I wonder what I should wish for. The Guys start to sing an old song I know. The lyrics mean something to me so I sing along. They speak to me about how challenges are necessary in life and we must be tough enough to face and deal with our difficulties. I look at Deborah's husband on stage. My wish should include all the lessons I learned from the accident his wife got us into in our youth. I close my eyes to make my wish: *I wish to use my experience from the accident I was in, to help people receive better life skills. I believe by nurturing internal strength we can empower people to make more responsible choices for the benefit of all.*

The song ends and I tuck my special penny into a safe spot in my purse. I want to keep it.

At home, I use a gold sticker to attach the penny to the back of a *Songs for Everyone* CD case, still in plastic wrap. With pride I place it on top of my piano. Mya watches me from the chair at the front window.

"I got a lucky penny tonight," I say.

I feel more confident than ever that I am following a purpose in my life.

45
Progress

N ow I am writing to Oprah and other shows about ways I think
my story can interest their viewers. To explore my life's experience
while writing in this way has been easier than I thought it would be. I
feel Oprah's audience especially would give me a chance to reach others
of like mind to myself. To write the producers is helping me learn to say
and understand better exactly what I went through. This is different
from journal writing, which is not intended for the viewing of others.

Also not seeing Deborah on television anymore has helped me more
than I realized it would. I think that a part of me was scared to see
her so unexpectedly all the time because she had hurt me in different
ways before. I feel the accident has faded into the past for me now and
an unconscious emotional thread has been cut between myself and
that experience. I have come to realize that it was not Deborah I had
a problem with because I did and do not really know her. Instead, it
was my memory of what she did to me that was calling out for healing.

I have been delighted to see that the CD for the non-profit is selling
to all different types of people. Most have words of encouragement
when they learn what I am doing. Dreaming up more ways to promote
Songs for Everyone and increasing sales keeps me busy.

At the moment I am selling it for twenty dollars, with approximately
half of that reserved for our cause. Once I get a chance to work through
my accounting, I will know better the exact amount. The royalty,
production and distribution costs all need to be factored in. It is not
inexpensive to make, especially with so many royalties needing to be
paid out.

So far, An Aid to Help Foundation has raised close to one thousand
dollars from the sales of *Songs for Everyone* and has already donated these
funds to several charities in Canada and the United States in support

of Social and Emotional Learning programs. I am surprised to learn SEL is a new term for many in Canada. Only in British Columbia can I find a lot of such programs in schools. An organization in Chicago called CASEL—the Collaborative for Academic, Social and Emotional Learning—supports schools throughout the world and does research in this area. CASEL was co-founded by Daniel Goleman. I am still researching more areas where donations can be made.

Aside from working on the non-profit, I have been spending time with Eric. He finally moved to the city and bought a new semi-detached house close to downtown. We enjoy hanging out from time to time but in January he is set to leave for Vancouver to work at the 2010 Winter Olympics, in a few months from now.

I do not know what will happen between us. If things are meant to be more serious, I believe we will figure this out. To spend time getting to know him is what I want to do right now. I will miss him when he is gone.

46
A Proud Dad

It is Christmas 2009 and it is so nice to be at my parents' house for a few days. We had a delicious dinner tonight and are sitting around talking, when Dad says, "I'm proud of you for the CD you created. It's really well done. I enjoy when your mom plays it."

"He even whistles to some," adds Mom.

To whistle when you are happy must be genetic. I do this a lot lately. I seem happier than ever. I cannot tell if Dad is serious because I am unfamiliar with receiving this type of praise from him. His words are so heartfelt and genuine. Because I did not expect this compliment, it means the world for me to hear. The last time he praised me this way was when I wanted to study medicine. He was proud I wanted to become a doctor.

"That is incredible Dad for me to hear and it means a lot."

Mom leaves the kitchen. Soon I hear *Songs for Everyone* playing in the background. Dad and I get up from the table to join her in the living room. Mya follows us.

As I walk in, I notice the CD case sitting upright on the fireplace. The music provides an emotional backdrop to seeing the copy of the original painting of *Finding Inner Strength* and the moment becomes special. It reminds me of an experience I had with the painter.

At my condo one evening in 2001, Vincent had stopped by to visit. This was the first time he had come over because usually we always met up somewhere in downtown Ottawa. We were standing in my living room talking, when all of a sudden he became quiet while looking at the wall behind me. A tender expression appeared on his face.

I turned to see what had caught his eye. It was a painting I own by Roland Palmaerts called *The Force of Destiny*, depicting a symphony orchestra with a pianist.[43]

I was captivated by it as well, as soon as I had laid eyes on this painting, while walking past a gallery one day. Without anything to be heard I could feel the ebb and flow of music emanating from its artistry.

"It's a stunning painting," Vincent said, not taking his eyes off the canvas.

"Yes, I agree," I said. "You want to see something incredible?"

"Sure," he said.

I looked through my CDs and grabbed one. As I was doing this, I recalled a statement made by the artist who painted that painting, where he said:

"There is vibration and movement—music in other words—in everything. The mind is linked to the subject like the soul to the body, the musician to his instrument. Without such communion, the subject is no more than a still-life… All the nuances of a symphony come together in a brief moment of time—melody, lament, requiem… Each one of us possesses his own colour, his identity, and creates his own joys and sorrows, chooses his own notes, writes his own score and then performs it in the work that is his life. As an artist, I first try to make visible what is invisible. I want people to see the music and hear the paintings." [44]

In my condo, a classical Chopin piano piece began to fill the room with its melody.[45] I joined Vincent to look at the painting with the musical accompaniment.

"Unbelievable," he said. "It's almost as if the painting has come alive."

"I know," I replied.

Today as Mom, Dad and I talk, *Songs for Everyone* remains playing in the background. The music is soft and non-intrusive, going to the heart of my creative vision. I recall what I had been going through, concerning grief and its aftermath, when I was selecting the songs to be used for the piano arrangements. To hear this music now fills me with gratitude for everything that I am lucky to have in my life.

I look over at Mya who is lying on the bay window sill watching the road through the trees.[46] She is concentrating on the moment—living her life to the fullest in her own way. I can relate to that, I think, as I smile happily to myself.

47
Feedback

I t is the start of a new year—January 1, 2010 and today I am going to clean the house from top to bottom. To start the year this way gives me a feeling of satisfaction and renewal.

Last night for New Year's Eve dinner at Aunt Gisele and Uncle Helmut's I took a few notes as my uncle cooked. As an appetizer we had baked brie with figs, dried cranberries, apricot and port wine. The main meal was of beef stroganoff and noodles with carrots and then a Mediterranean lentil and couscous salad. Dessert was pound cake with lemon sauce.

Many times this past year, Uncle Helmut and I went indoor rock climbing. He is an excellent climber and has taught me a lot. Climbing is a fun challenge for me and it takes my mind off the work I am doing for the non-profit. I enjoy the feeling of pushing myself farther each time we go out. After this exercise, at his home with Aunt Gisele, we always cook and eat a delicious dinner together. It has been a surprise that these experiences have made me want to learn to become a better cook myself. I watch him prepare meals and write down details. I do not know why I am now interested in cooking for others. I have never been like this before in my life. Something has changed about who I am.

The way Uncle Helmut puts the food on the plate is interesting. The presentation of the food makes all the difference. A few of these meals I have already repeated successfully for friends and this has inspired me to learn even more.

As usual, last night on New Year's Eve, I left early. On my way home, I stopped by a friend's place near my house. They had a small party I was invited to. I enjoyed meeting some new people.

One woman I met was in her early twenties. She asked me what I did for work. As I started to tell her, my friend Heather interrupted us.

"Remember the CD we listened to on the way to Toronto the other weekend?" she said excitedly.

"Yes, we enjoyed it so much!"

"Well, she created that CD for her organization, to raise money," Heather said pointing at me.

"You did? Oh my goodness. We thought the music was great!" she said.

A few more people joined our conversation. One guy with a French accent said, "We had fun naming the songs while we listened. I was looking at the case the whole time to see who the writers of each piece were. It was really interesting. I was amazed you included a couple French pieces. We spoke about that and how nice it was to see."

I was flattered to get these compliments. What a special way to start a new year.

48
Instead of Wine

We are selling more of the non-profit's CD. Starting up An Aid to Help Foundation took many months to create. Things are turning out well. More people are sharing with me how much they enjoy listening to the music, from children to seniors and that is encouraging to hear.

Before the holidays Aunt Gisele gave a copy of *Songs for Everyone*, as a gift, to a neighbour's family who had invited her over for dinner, instead of bringing a bottle of wine. They loved listening to it so much that they bought twenty-five CDs to give away as Christmas gifts in 2009 to their friends. I thought this was a thoughtful idea. I wrote a short explanation for them of why *Songs for Everyone* was created so they could include this with the gift.

In January 2010, Aunt Gisele told me that they stopped by to share with her a letter from a woman who received a CD from them. She wrote how wonderful she found the music and how much she liked the non-profit's CD case. She enjoys listening to the songs. When the neighbour read the letter to my aunt they both had tears in his eyes.

My heart went into creating *Songs for Everyone* which is what I believe makes it stand out. My motivation has always been to help and inspire others in some way to make better decisions in life. I am grateful to all who helped me start this meaningful work. Raising money is not something I ever imagined I would do. To creatively express my emotions in this way has been one of the best therapies I ever had, to help me be able to live as happy a life possible. Despite my doubts at times, to help others find strength and happiness through my work is a rewarding aspiration. My determination for this endeavour to succeed reminds me of who I was when I was Doris. I am beginning to notice I am reminded of her a lot lately. It is surprising that I do not feel as scared to remember her as I once did.

49
A Fading Scar

In a magnified mirror at home, I look at my scar and press into the skin with my fingertips. I can see and feel a significant reduction in the lumpy scar tissue called keloid. This decrease is happening with help. But this help is not on the surface of the skin. It is something that I take internally now that is a natural mixture of systemic enzymes, called Wobenzym.

As I massage my scar, I suddenly feel a small piece of glass from the car window of the accident in 1991 that I did not realize was there before. Thick scar tissue had surrounded it; my body wanted to protect me from the initial sharp edges. Over the years, the glass edges have smoothed out so it does not hurt with the keloid tissue gone from around it, even when I press. I only had a few pieces I could feel after the injury and through massage they broke down and disappeared. I thought there were no more.

In the mirror I am studying my scar from all angles and doing the usual head tilt with the light shining on it. The marks definitely do appear flatter. I have never noticed this much of a difference in how it looks. This is hard to believe.

What I am taking was prescribed to me by an integrative medical doctor, Richard Nahas. Wobenzym is a mixture of systemic enzymes that can be bought with or without a prescription. Dr. Nahas is also helping me with the hormonal roller coaster I have been on as a result of my head injury. He prescribed bio-identical hormones, natural hormones that are identical in molecular structure to the ones my own body makes. Right now, I am using a progesterone cream that is pharmaceutically compounded from wild yam as this natural alternative. To my amazement, the problems of hormone imbalance and irregularity are disappearing.

I learned about Wobenzym on a day when I was speaking to him about the large amount of scar tissue my body forms. I showed him the lumpy scar on my cheek. He said, "You know of Wobenzym, don't you? Someone must've told you about it."

"No one ever mentioned the name," I said. "What can it do?"

He filled out an order form and prescription.

"We'll get the professional strength for you," he said. "Systemic enzymes will eat that scar tissue up for sure."

He explained a bit how systemic enzymes work. I planned on learning as much as I could about them as soon as I left his office. There are only a few people that know about my thirst for knowledge in life; Dr. Nahas is one of them. At home that day, I poured through information online.

Systemic enzymes apparently are different from digestive enzymes because they are taken without food and are meant to work on the body. When taken, they pass through the digestive track into the small intestine to do their work by helping the body in a multitude of ways to modulate, control and balance the inflammatory and oxidative processes that occur throughout the body. Wobenzym is easiest for me to purchase from my doctor's office.

Some Olympic teams use Wobenzym to reduce injury and promote recovery. There are claims of it helping some people as much as fifty percent in the prevention of injury and healing of wounds. Many others report scar minimization as an additional benefit and this explains why Dr. Nahas suggested I take them. I had not learned about these enzymes before and I believed they were worth a try.

As of now, I would say there is a twenty-five percent improvement in my scar after only taking the systemic enzymes for a short period of time. This is why I can feel more glass pieces now. The surface scar tissue, however, will be more challenging to notice a difference.

After the episode at Aunt Gisele's about my scar, I finally took full responsibility for my feelings concerning this mark. I figured out how to cope with being upset, which resulted in a deeper shift happening inside me. The change did not happen overnight, it evolved over time, stemming back to how I dealt with that whole experience at the Easter dinner. Since then, I no longer have a need to hide from others when I am not wearing make-up—at all. I even sometimes go for a walk with Mya and open the door for delivery without any cover-up on, something that would never have happened before. I am genuinely less self-conscious now about how I look because I know my scar does not define who I truly am as a person.

At a Christmas party the other month, someone commented on how good my scar looked.

"Your scar is much flatter," she said. "I can hardly see it anymore."

I thanked her for the compliment and told her what I was taking. Others overheard our conversation and jumped in to say they could also see the difference as well. I had already had conversations with these people before about my scar so their opinions matter to me. A few of them work in dermatology.

One month of taking a professional-strength dose of the enzymes so far is all I did to achieve this result and that is impressive.

By March, almost no keloid tissue is left below the surface scar on my cheek. Those few little glass pieces I felt dissolved into nothing. I guess the scar tissue was holding the old stuff together.

Dr. Nahas already noticed the improvement. At a recent appointment he mentioned right away how he saw the enzymes have changed my scar, making it less visible. He expects further improvement.

Systemic enzymes have decreased in my body as I have gotten older, as they naturally do in everyone's. To give my body a boost will apparently help me in other ways as well. Dr. Nahas wanted to know if I noticed anything else was being helped by taking them.

I told him my shoulder usually gives me problems. I got this from the arm hold in Latin and ballroom dance, as well from walking Mya. She occasionally pulled hard on the leash and I dislocated my shoulder a couple of times. I could not lift my arm over my head without severe pain. While taking the enzymes, I have noticed I no longer experience any pain—at all and my range of motion appears to be normal again.

The ringing in my ear has decreased as well and this I did not expect. It is more constant at an even sound and with a lower tone, whereas before it would fluctuate with sound and increase or decrease in volume as well. I am happy if this change is permanent. It was an annoying and stressful problem to have before but now, this is—okay.

Meanwhile, Eric hurt himself skiing in Whistler during time-off from working at the Olympics. He is an advanced skier but he took a hard fall. His shoulder and ribs were painfully damaged. Nothing was helping, even physiotherapy, so I sent him a sample package of Wobenzym. Because they are also available non-prescription, I saw no problem for me doing this. He took them and the next time we spoke through e-mail he said, "My problems got better within a few days. I can go skiing on runs at Whistler before going home."

I do not expect a miracle from these enzymes. I accept my scar now, so removing the entire mark and memory would not be my wish—ever, which is an unexpected surprise. It is hard to believe but I have had this scar on my cheek for over half of my life now. How fast time has passed by. My scar is unique. It is my body's own creation as a result of healing and nobody can ever copy it. It is as if an artist etched the marks on my face and gave me a piece of art that is a one-of-a-kind reflection of who I am today as a result of all I have been through in my life.

The timing is perfect for reducing my scar now though because I am moving forward in life with the work I am doing, closing the doors on my emotional past. This is making me feel fulfilled in ways I have never experienced before.

50
Time Away

My friend Ben and I are enjoying breakfast in a restaurant at a
hotel in Vail, Colorado, during a ski trip in March 2010. We
have been friends since 2006 when we met at a social gathering. He is a
friendly guy who lives near my house and is originally from the Toronto
area as well. We are only staying here for the one night at the hotel and
then a home on the mountain side for the rest of the week.

Ben suddenly looks up from his plate. I am reading the *New York
Times*.

"Believe me. This never happens." He pauses, waiting for me to
look up at him from my newspaper. "I'm getting a strong message I am
supposed to tell you something. I keep on trying to brush it off but I
can't. Do you want to know what it is? I feel I need to ask you this first."

"Of course I do, what's up?" I say, setting the newspaper down.

"It's weird," he says, looking to the side. "This message is loud and
clear to me. I've never experienced anything this way before. I'm not a
psychic kind of guy."

I can see he really feels awkward about this. I hope it is nothing
bad. I wish he would just spit it out however because I want to get back
to reading.

"Well, what is it?" I ask.

Looking me straight in the eye, he says, "You are going to write a
book."

"Oh—I don't think so." I say.

What a crazy idea he has, I am not going to write a book. I ask
laughing, "Does the 'voice' tell you what I will write about?"

"No. I don't understand how the message is coming to me," says
Ben. "It's out of nowhere but I feel it is important to tell you. This is so
strange." He looks off to the side again, as if he is worried that someone

is listening.

I am surprised this is bothering him so much. He felt inspired to share with me an idea and I can tell him it is not going to happen—end of story.

"That's why I created a music CD for the non-profit to raise money. I didn't want to write a book. The people who I think need to learn from my story don't read books. From the start, my aunt Gisele and I agreed on this," I say.

I think to myself about how I would not want to tell the whole story of what happened to me anyway. The story would be boring and stressful to write. I could not do that to myself.

"Never before has anything like this ever happened to me," he says.

"Well, great idea but it's not going to happen. I've nothing to write about. I don't remember my accident or the time leading up to getting hurt. So I would have to make it up. A non-fiction book I could easily write with my aunt, since she's a doctor, however that would not interest me. So there is no story to tell. Hey—you might want to get those voices in your head checked out," I joke.

With a smile on my face, I get up to go grab more breakfast from the delicious buffet, leaving Ben sitting at the table alone. I have no idea what that was all about and I do not really care either. This vacation has turned out to be a wonderful, much-needed break. After starting the non-profit in 2008 I have not taken any time off.

Much to my surprise, Vail reminds me of Omi, who passed away in 2005. Part of the reason was because we had spread her ashes in a small ceremony in the Rocky Mountains, outside Calgary. We chose the spot because my grandmother loved the mountains. For her funeral we played a piece of music she loved called "Dance of the Blessed Spirits" from the Gluck opera *Orfeo ed Euridice*.[47] She would have been pleased we did this for her farewell. It was what she wanted. Driving to Vail from Toronto made me start to think of her. While driving through the Colorado Mountains with Ben, we were listening to classical music on satellite radio when I felt her presence around me. We had not listened to any classical music the whole trip. With the winding roads going through the mountains, I had wanted to listen to music to help me relax and concentrate, so it needed to be of a slower tempo. Omi loved classical music.

Another reminder of Omi is that Ben's parents are German, like she was. When we met in Toronto for the trip I tried speaking a bit of German to Ben's mom and dad. I would need lots of practice to get better. Since both my grandmothers passed away, my motivation to speak the language is gone. My parents surprisingly did not speak German at home, even though they were both born and raised for part of their childhood in Germany.

After the long drive, yesterday I needed to relax. I drove the entire trip myself. Ben was amazed at my ability to drive the whole trip by myself. My concentration was solidly on the road. He said he could not have done it. We got here earlier than expected and needed to grab some rooms for the night and this was why we stayed here last night. Of all the hotels in Vail, we coincidentally chose the most German looking one to stay at. Amidst the picturesque, snow-covered mountains, it seems almost as if we are in Germany.

Once we checked in, I went right away for a massage at the spa. My birthday was the other day when we started driving so I gave this to myself as a late gift after the long drive. The therapist who gave me a fantastic massage was from Germany. Omi worked as a massage therapist until she was in her mid-eighties. I have had many massages over the years with different therapists but few before were ever as good as hers. The therapist I had here definitely came close with her precision at being able to loosen my muscles. It made me both sad and nostalgic to remember my grandmother while getting this massage.

When Omi moved to Canada she worked for Elizabeth Arden at the Simpson's department store in downtown Toronto. She then wanted to work for herself and became a private registered massage therapist. I remember meeting a few of her clients. One lived in a big country home with fish in a pond.

After the accident in 1991, Omi massaged me while I was in the hospital and afterwards as well and this is how I know she was good. I read about this in Aunt Gisele's medical notes. She was a nice grandmother. It felt wonderful to be cared for by her in a therapeutic way. I also received Reiki and Therapeutic Touch from Mom and Aunt Gisele. I needed regular therapy in this way to cope and receiving it from people who loved me was special.

Well I believe Ben gave me a message today from Omi that she wants me to write a book. I do not think I will write one, however, I cannot wait for my next trip back to Vail in memory of her.

The rest of the trip to Vail was enjoyable. It was the boss of Ben's friend, whose big house we stayed at. I kept to myself by driving around Vail while Ben hung out with his friends.

Although I know how, I did not have a good feeling about downhill skiing on this trip, so I did not go on the slopes. I think this mainly was because I did not want to wear a helmet. Last year, Natasha Richardson, a forty-five-year-old British actress, died from a head injury after a fall while skiing on a beginner's hill at Mont Tremblant in Quebec. It is becoming more familiar to see people with helmets on while skiing. Natasha had no helmet on.

On this trip I decided to start skate skiing instead. I only needed to go on some of the cross country hills to practice. The leg motion is more like skating and is a good workout. This gave me no stress about falling and hitting my head, which made it more fun for me than going downhill skiing would have been.

I also would have felt weird wearing a helmet on the slopes. I wish someone would invent something different to protect the head. The way I look at it is that, I do not need to drive my car with a helmet on. So I believe there has to be other creative ways to protect a person's skull. There are some ways that I have read about before.[48]

Ben's friends were from Toronto and Ottawa, as well as Florida and other states. The first night I was not drinking. We were downstairs hanging around the pool table when the guys decided to take out the ATVs parked in the garage. It did not even occur to them that they should not drink and then drive these recreational vehicles.

A few started drinking beers with breakfast and their tendency toward irresponsible behaviour quickly became apparent. The last night there, everyone went to a bar. I was going to go but the guy who would have been driving had been drinking moderately the whole day from what I saw, so I decided to stay behind and read. I had the companionship of the dog that came on the trip from Florida with his owner. Sure I could have walked the short distance to the bar and back alone but I was content to be dog-sitter. Part of the reason I did this as well was because I missed Mya. I was homesick and ready to go back to see her at this point.

Also social drinking really has lost its allure for me over the years. I will not preach to others how they should behave; all I can do is look after myself.

Since coming home from Vail, surprisingly, my life is now full of signs urging me to write and tell my story surrounding An Aid to Help Foundation. One day, while sitting with Mya, watching the forest, I realized that I can write about my present life and share what little I remember of the accident, in 1991.

After this deep acknowledgement, many creative ideas sprang to life in my thoughts. What makes me happy is that to have my story written as a memoir will help sell the *Songs for Everyone* CD and raise money. To raise money through the music will always be my goal. My memoir will have a soundtrack and this is kind of unique.

As Andrew told me when I was starting up the non-profit—it works best to tell things as a story. This was probably the best advice he gave me and now that wisdom guides my writing. All those talk shows I wrote to in 2009 and 2010, from which I never received a response, prepared me to write a memoir. I probably approached over a hundred shows with different story ideas. I responded to the show's ideas or offered producers different ways how my story might help others and be of interest to learn about. I tried my hardest to come up with as many different ideas as possible for my story, which helped dissolve my guards to talk openly about the ordeal I went through. It is interesting because now that I know this was why I was approaching the shows, I have lost all desire to write to a show producer.

Prior to me writing them, I would not have mentioned having a lawyer or how private investigators followed me or how lonely I was from the lack of support from so-called friends. To talk about the consequences of my severe closed-head injury would have been minimized. That would be an inaccurate portrayal of what my family and I went through as a result of my getting hurt so severely.

It has always been hard for me to admit to anyone I had this type of injury at all. As I read in the news more about head injuries and the challenges people have coping afterwards, I understand now that I can help others by sharing what happened to me. Most people think receiving brain damage means you must show obvious signs immediately and forever after as well. Many of the problems I experienced were hidden and continue to remain that way.

Before now, I would have been shy to talk about my scar. But I can speak about it now, freely and openly as a result of the work I have been doing. I used to only be able to tell half the story, now I can tell all of it. I needed practice expressing in writing what I went through. With every submission to a talk show I would explain to them how my story could be told. To have to empathise with others as I figured out how to help meet various producers' needs was a huge learning experience. My focus now is just to write my memoir and really, this looks like it was my unconscious goal all along.

Life gave me an experience I could write about, something I did not understand until now. My work of creating the non-profit over the past few years has prepared me to write. Everything I went through was on the pathway towards this goal. I found that the majority of the support I needed to get this far was inside myself. My life challenged me to take apart the armour I had encased all my hurtful memories in, so that I could share my experience. Once I took down my guard, looked at my feelings and let myself acknowledge them, I became stronger than ever. Through this experience, I am learning that anger, when expressed appropriately is surprisingly not as scary an emotion as I thought it was.

There was a hidden part of me I was ignoring that was still hurt. As I stop ignoring this, the memory and weight of my suppressed emotions has been continuously emerging and naturally dissolving. To be injured so badly was a huge learning experience for me. By taking the time to heal the hurt of my heart and soul, I am more accepting than ever of my internal and external scars. I do not even look for the shadows of my scar in the mirror anymore like I used to. It has smoothed out a lot. Of course, if I look closely enough, in certain light, it is still there, as both a mark and a memory. All that I am doing is helping me to become even stronger to live as full a life possible and move on to the next chapter in my life.

The memoir is coming along. I sometimes write at Starbucks, a restaurant at Brookstreet Hotel or a tapas restaurant near my home. The manager at one restaurant worked in the United Kingdom before coming to Canada. He says J.K. Rowling used to come with her child to write in his old café. I guess creativity needs good food.

My favourite spot to write, though, is at the kitchen table or in the TV room. I look out back with Mya. We watch the forest together. I find nature, as well as the companionship of my dog, inspiring.

51
A Bike Ride

It is now April 2010 and Eric has returned from working at the Olympics. I hosted a dinner party last week with him and a few friends and cooked a meal from Uncle Helmut's recipes, something everyone enjoyed. Afterwards, we had fun playing pool.

I will entertain more now with smaller gatherings. I never thought I would feel this way again about hosting something. I have been insecure about hosting any type of get together since my party in 2008 when drunken Sofia wanted to punch me in the head. I often say to friends that I might host something and then when I am alone afterwards I always talk myself out of it. At least I have warmed up once again to have something. To have a big party will not make me feel comfortable ever again. It places too much responsibility on me for the behaviour of other people as the host. To be threatened by Sofia did not leave a good memory.

Today, Eric and I went for a lengthy bike ride along the Ottawa River, down the Rideau Canal, then through the Experimental Farm back to his house. The Experimental Farm is situated on 1250 acres of land where Agriculture Canada grows experimental crops. I have not ridden a bike since before my head injury. To challenge myself to get back on one has paid off. I cannot believe how much I missed cycling. There are enough off road trails around this city to be able to not have to ride on the road.

We are at Eric's house, sitting on the couch playing a card game he taught me. He shuffles the deck.

"How is your ski injury now after taking those enzymes?" I ask.

"Much better," he says.

"They really helped me as well," I say as I point at my scar. "Can you see the difference?"

"I can't pay any attention to your scar," he replies coldly. "I never wanted to. So I don't."

"What do you mean you can't? It's on my face," I say.

"I pretend the scar is not there. I only look at your eyes," he says, looking straight at me.

There is no warmth in his voice or expression. His peripheral vision cannot hide the scar on my face.

"It has improved," I say, trying to help him feel comfortable. "You'll be able to tell. I don't mind if you look."

I am a person who is passionate about a lot in life and these enzymes are amazing me at the moment. I want his opinion.

"No," he says. "I can't and I won't."

He shakes his head, as if almost in disgust. With his last comment, he means the conversation is over. I am quiet as I look at the floor. My thoughts consume me. I did not realize that he lacked compassion to this degree. He has a heart defensively buried—somewhere. He has shown me both sides at different times before. I wonder what his work in the military and his life experience have done to him. He seems desensitised.

From the first time I met Eric, I cared about him. His bicycle accident and what he was going through opened my heart. But my feelings cannot be turned on and off like a switch, as he seems able to do. He has shared with me his confusion about the reason why, a few of his past relationships ended. I do not want to have a deep psychological conversation with him but it is obvious, from how he is treating me, that part of the problem is his emotional distance. I wonder why I did not realize how uncomfortable my scar makes him. I question now why I am with him.

I tried to not let his comments bother me and we went to bed after playing cards. On an emotional level I had lost interest. This part of intimacy is huge for me. To know that he could not look at my scar made me uncomfortable.

Usually men do not have a problem accepting the mark on my face. Most show sympathy for what I went through but Eric appears to be different. This surprises me considering his line of work. I know he works more in the military's office but I thought he might be more familiar with the effect of injury on the human body. With his lack of sensitivity for my feelings with what he said about my scar, maybe I should rethink this relationship. He is going away again this summer. I get the feeling we will drift apart.

52
Empathy

Today I feel sad. I am going to a funeral of a relative through marriage. Krista Ritchie died at forty-four years old last week on the night of Canada Day, July 1, 2010. Her death shocked everyone because she had no health problems before and the cause of death remains unknown. She woke in the middle of the night with chest pain. After being rushed to the hospital, she could not be resuscitated.

Over the past few years, Canada Day has been significant. I remember sitting with Andrew and Aunt Gisele at the NAC two years ago. It was like a celebration beyond a national day for our country. Later I learned July 1 was also Princess Diana's birthday—what a "strange parallel", as my Uncle Dieter would say.

Krista's death made me grateful for my own life because I know that my cards in life are going to be up someday, like hers. I definitely came close before.

Before leaving for the funeral, I go online to donate four hundred dollars raised by An Aid to Help Foundation to a registered charity called Roots of Empathy.[49] As always, I am proud of being able to make a donation.

My discovery of Roots of Empathy came about due to a book called *Born for Love: Why Empathy Is Essential and Endangered,* by Maia Szalavitz and Bruce D. Perry, MD, PhD. I found the book in a bookstore I had not been in before. It was on a day while driving down Elgin Street that I suddenly had the impulse to stop. I looked over, saw the bookstore, walked in and asked if they had a book, one waitress at Al's Steakhouse had told me about.

The store is close to the NAC where I was going to volunteer that night for a performance of *Avenue Q,* the Broadway musical. I thought the musical might be sad because Gary Coleman, an actor portrayed in the musical, had just died from an intra-cranial haemorrhage following a head injury received in a fall at his home. He was forty-two years old. I did not yet know if I would watch the musical or not, which is why I wanted a book to fill the time.

Learning of someone dying from head injury always affects me. Aunt Gisele realised this when I called her crying last year after lightly hitting my head on a cupboard door. This had upset me—way more than necessary. This happened right around the time Natasha Richardson died from the skiing accident.

When I called Aunt Gisele crying, she was comforting. She first checked to be sure I had not actually hurt myself and then we spoke about the British actress. Learning about Natasha's death made me realize once again how lucky I am to be alive but even getting lightly hit caused me to have emotional and physical flashbacks. I cannot stop this from happening; a subconscious part of me will always remember what extreme pain feels like.

This was why learning of Gary Coleman's death was hard for me. I was already scheduled to volunteer for this evening before he died, so there was no reason to back out of helping the NAC this night. I am a reliable volunteer. So instead of seeing the performance, I wanted to stay in the lounge and read.

In the bookstore, they did not have the book I was looking for. I then walked straight to the middle of the room and looked directly down at a book on a shelf. I do not even know what section of the store I was in but *Born for Love* was the only title I saw. My gut feeling was to immediately buy the hard copy. I read it quickly.

Born for Love begins by describing the success of a Toronto charity that is teaching children Social and Emotional Learning skills, fostering positive childhood development in the area of Emotional Intelligence.[50] Roots of Empathy's mission is to build caring, peaceful and civil societies through the development of empathy in children and adults.

The founder of Roots of Empathy, Mary Gordon, has put their program into classes of kindergarten up to Grade 8. She also created another program called Seeds of Empathy aimed at pre-schoolers. Through evaluations of the program they are finding that there are notable reductions in negative behaviour and increases in positive behaviour from these children.

With Roots of Empathy, a parent of a newborn child from the school's immediate area brings their baby to the school throughout the year to visit the class. On the day that the baby will visit, a green blanket is set on the floor where the small guest and parent will sit in the centre. All the children from the class will take a seat in a circle, around them.

What happens during this visit is that the children will talk about and get to experience how the baby cannot communicate with words. They learn that in order to understand what the baby wants or needs, they have to empathise with him or her, like the parent does. They learn that as the baby develops with time, many changes will happen. After each visit there are weekly exercises that the children will work on until the next visit.

The Roots of Empathy charity is expanding beyond Canada to the world at large. To help put this advancement in education into schools worldwide would make me feel great. Twenty schools in Ottawa included it in their curriculum in 2009–2010. I want this charity to be the focus of An Aid to Help Foundation's fundraising. I believe the Roots of Empathy mission and program fulfils my personal quest to help learn or teach others to make responsible choices in life and to be more caring individuals.

As I am about to donate to Roots of Empathy in memory of the late Princess Diana, I pause. I get the feeling that somehow, this charity is close to where I met her in Toronto. It turns out the charity's office is about four kilometres away from the children's rehab centre where I met the princess in 1991. It is interesting how the spot in Toronto where I met her is where my tale returns to as a tribute to her. I live almost five hours away from Toronto. It is another "strange parallel" that my story literally, has come full circle.

As I finish making the donation to Roots of Empathy, I look at the time and realize I am going to be late for Krista's funeral. I quickly grab my purse and car keys. As usual, Mya gets in position at the window to wait for my return.

53
Unexpressed Emotion

I inspect the piece of mixed media in front of me, sitting on a table full of art and craft supplies. It is April 2011 and we are in the attic of an old log cabin, in a village west of Ottawa that my friend Christina uses as her studio. I enjoy Christina's art work and have one piece of mixed media hanging in my home called *the key is gratitude*.[51]

A woman and I are learning about different mixed media techniques we can do on top of a canvased photograph. For this, I chose a picture I took the other year of the chimes in my backyard. They are the ones hanging on the tree that keeps its leaves throughout the winter. Since looking at those chimes in 2008 was what really inspired me in ways to create *Songs for Everyone*, I thought this photo would be fitting for the cover of my memoir. I am going to try and create something I can use. I wonder what I am going to do first as I grab a paint brush.

"We can use paint in different ways on our painting," Christina says. "If you take your paint brush on an angle and do not smooth out the paint with the brush, you will have a bit of a textured effect."

I look at my paint, then my brush and then the canvased photograph. I notice that the picture suddenly arouses negative feelings. I wonder why. I take my brush and start to copy Christina, as any cooperative student would. But all of a sudden, my attention is drawn fiercely to the photograph; my eyes are glued to its image.

I remember the anger I felt towards Sofia as I walked past her the night of my party to get the piece of my Recovery Book. For some reason I wanted to hold it as a result of the irresponsible behaviour she was about to do. I had never held Princess Diana's signature this way before. After that night I did not express my feelings of anger to Sofia. I only ever assertively spoke to her on behalf of others, to protect them. There was little of Doris' emotion in this conversation. In many ways I was deeply upset when she threatened to hit me in the head.

I do not even look up at my teacher anymore as I dip the brush in the paint. I keep on going back to the painting, smearing the beige coloured paint everywhere I can, with unbridled intensity, sparing only some of the leaves and the chime. I would not call my technique, painting. My feelings have turned it into something else altogether. I move the brush around aggressively.

I look up to see what we are going to do next. Christina is smiling at me. I do not return her smile.

"That looks like you got a lot done," she says, holding back laughter.

"Yes, what can I do next?" I ask impatiently.

"Anything you like. I will help with this painting here but if you need my help, let me know," she says.

Looking at the table of supplies I try to decide what I want to use next. My heart is pounding in my chest. A mischievous smile comes to my face. I embrace the emotional heat I am feeling, not totally sure of its origin. My fingers seem to pulse with a need to get these feelings out. I wonder what I am up to.

I look at my mixed media as it dries, recalling further my anxiety about the possibility of winning the lottery and *The Muskoka* cottage as I gazed at the chimes outside with Mya that warm day. Then I recall I had the idea to do something to try to stop irresponsible behaviour like Sofia wanting to drive drunk. How I then wanted to go on a talk show to tell my story.

At the moment I feel like Mya must when I tell her not to bark at something outside the house. She has emotions that she wants to express, even though I told her to be quiet, so she taught herself to stuff the fabric door mat into her mouth and throw it around side to side, up and down while grumbling and pawing at the door to help her express them without barking. My eyes narrow as I gaze at my piece of art.

My memoir now is telling the story about what happened to me. I am interested what else I can do here to help express myself—without words. I pick up a metal tool, whose sharp edge glints in the spring light and start to scrape off some of the half-dry paint. I am doing whatever

I feel like doing, following my impulse, letting pure feeling take over. Visually, I could care less how it turns out in the end. In spots, I cut through to the wood frame below. Accidentally I cut myself but I push on, not bothered by the emerging drops of blood.

Christina sees I hurt myself and asks, "Do you need a band aid?"

"No," I say flatly.

With my finger, I smear my blood onto the painting in different spots. My cut stops bleeding. I hold my mixed media. My fingers anxiously tap the back of the painting as everything dries. I wonder what I should do next.

I survey the mixed media that the woman taking the class with me is creating. It is a nature piece with sky. There is no emotion in hers. I look back at mine which crackles with pure, raw emotional energy. I want to express more of my feelings. I have no clue what I can do. I look at the blood that is drying. The thought of burning it comes to mind. Excitement about this idea springs up inside me. I cannot do that here though.

Taking another metal tool with a flat edge, I start to dig into parts of my painting, leaving deep grooves and slices. I feel Christina's eyes on me and I look up at her to see if she wants to say something. She looks amused, saying nothing.

"I wish I could burn parts of this," I declare.

"Go for it," she says.

Out of her tools she pulls a small torch and hands it to me.

"There you go," she says smiling.

I can tell that she has done something like this before. I grow excited as I turn on the flame and the fire springs to life. My anger burns too—almost as if it is the fuel for the fire itself. I hold the mixed media upright with my left hand. Carefully, I touch different parts of the painting with the flame. Making sure not to burn too much, I trace the flame around the border of the mixed media, pleased with the appearance of the burn marks.

The paint and the photograph bubble from the heat in different parts. Smoke rises from the canvas. I pass the flame over the marks left by my blood, now already dried. As I stop and turn off the flame, I know my piece of art is finished. Sitting back I hold my mixed media and take in all the detail.

It looks perfect and was fun to create. I definitely know it will not be on the cover of the book. I would feel uncomfortable using something which is an expression of my negative feelings in more of a dark way. I did not expect my anger would surface so passionately. It was a surprise to express my feelings without words. It felt like both Doris and Samantha were a part of this creative session. I sign the painting with my last name, Michael and call my piece of art—*My Anger.*[52]

54
Parent as Teacher

I am staying with my parents at their house for the Easter holidays. I am telling Mom about how good it felt to create my mixed media art piece. I just explained how I cut myself, put my blood on the canvas and then burned it.

"Oh my goodness Samantha," she says. "I don't want to hear about this."

"It was great," I say, ignoring her. "It gave a voice to my feelings—deeper than words. They were negative feelings that I wanted to express—angry ones. I felt better after. I hung it on my wall at home. A couple of friends think it is cool."

"Okay," she says.

She sounds confused and obviously does not want to hear what I am saying.

"Oh, I remember I have a picture of it attached to an email I sent to Andrew. He loved it. I can show you," I say.

I walk into their office and sit down at the computer. I open up my webmail to find the attachment with the picture.

"See," I say smiling proudly at the monitor.

Mom quietly looks at the image, seemingly at a loss for words.

"You—did that?" she asks.

She cannot take her eyes off the picture of my mixed media.

"Yes. I am proud of myself when I see it at home. It reminds me how I worked through something important," I say.

"That came from inside you?" she says turning to look at me with wide eyes. "Oh my goodness—I can't even look at it. I don't like it. It doesn't make me feel comfortable. Where did you have those emotions stored in you? Why couldn't you do a pretty piece of art like the cover of *Songs for Everyone*?" she asks.

"But it's an expression of my feelings. It should not scare you to see this. You are not being helpful," I say.

I am showing more disappointment in my voice than I actually feel. I know her and it is fun to torment her with this.

"I can't look at it anymore," she says turning away.

"This is constructive what I did," I say. "You should be a supportive parent. I called it *My Anger.*"

Mom quickly walks out of the room attempting to plug her ears so she no longer has to hear me talk about a topic that makes her feel uncomfortable. I look back at the picture of my art work and smile proudly as I close the image.

Mom knows that I am trying to push her buttons. Normally I have her support. The topic of anger and my expression of this emotion in a creative way is not something she is familiar with. I am sure other parents would also not be supportive if their child were to creatively express their emotions in unfamiliar ways.

As I get off the computer, I want to go talk with Mom further about my emotional painting. Her discomfort sparked my curiosity to understand her better. I wonder why my creative expression bothered her so much. I know that she will not change but I just have to see the expression of discomfort on her face again in an attempt to figure her out. A part of me feels like Doris wanting to perform a science experiment.

And Mom thought our conversation was over with. I smile to myself as I get up to go look for her.

55
Michael's Non-Profit

This year, 2011, I brought Aunt Gisele again to the NAC for Canada Day with the private patron's dinner and viewing of the fireworks. With focusing on writing my memoir the year had passed quickly since the last time we attended. That evening I received an unexpected gift from Aunt Gisele. When I picked her up, she handed me a certified cheque. This was a small inheritance for me from the estate of Uncle Dieter who passed away in early May.

This money came to me on July 1, the day my idea for the non-profit and music CD started to take shape three years prior. I stopped all other work at the time to focus on the non-profit. The amount I received from Uncle Dieter was exactly how much I would have made over those three years from the previous work I was doing part-time. This is yet another "strange parallel".

Receiving money from Uncle Dieter which is really money passed along from Omi finally gave me the ability to pay Andrew something for helping me the past three years. He did not ask for one cent ever for all he had done. He was always there to help me in whatever way he could. He is a great guy.

While at The Rideau Club one time, the President and CEO of the NAC said to me when Andrew was in another room, "You could not have found a better person to help you with your non-profit than Andrew. He will help you succeed. I wish you the best of luck."

Andrew and I spoke and he is stepping aside from direct involvement in the foundation. He helped me get everything up and going but he understands I want my mom and dad to help now. To have my parents support me this way feels special. Andrew will still do work for me as an advisor to the board and I will pay him properly for his time and commitment.

The Board of Directors now includes Aunt Gisele, whose maiden name is Michael, Dad, Mom and I. Mya is also on the board as our advisor and mascot. After learning from my neighbour what Mya means in his native language of Punjabi, I knew this was Mya's purpose for us. Apparently her name means—money. Now, whenever I see my neighbour when we are out for a walk, he cheerfully greets her. "Come here Money. Good Money. I love you Money." So I think it is perfect that Mya is a good luck charm for my family's non-profit to help raise money for the advancement of education. Children adore her.

Now An Aid to Help Foundation is officially Michael's non-profit. My family's support to help in raising money for learning or teaching others to make responsible choices means the world to me. Dad will only help with the paperwork of the organization. He says, "I won't read your book. I can't relive that time in our lives."

I understand his feelings and would not even think about forcing him to read it. His comment does not bother me in the least. I have learned in life that I cannot directly change other people; we are each on our own journey. I know that I can influence people to change and grow, simply by being an example for them to learn from. So who knows about Dad, maybe one day he will read my memoir. His support, in whatever way he is capable of, is what I need from him. And he has always done an excellent job in this area.

When talking with Dad one day about my memoir, he relaxed when I told him about the memories I am sharing that include him. That I remember these experiences well surprises him. He is amazed that our ride in the Corvette that day in 1991 was nothing dramatic for him like it was for me—he thought we simply took a company car for a drive—hello?

56
A New Princess

Looking at the computer screen, I cannot take my eyes off a news video. The sound is muted to have avoided distraction while I was on the phone.

It is July 2011 and the newlyweds William and Kate, the Duke and Duchess of Cambridge, have arrived at the Calgary airport.[53] Will and Kate got married this April but, surprisingly to many, I did not watch their wedding. I am still on my no-TV break and enjoying it.

After getting off the plane, a six-year-old cancer patient in a pink dress rushes up to Kate with a gift and flowers. Kate bends down and they hug.

Her name, I learn, is Diamond. Diamond lost her mom to cancer in addition to struggling with the disease herself. One day from her bed at the Alberta Children's Hospital she wrote a letter to Kate, who is a "real life princess". Diamond apparently told Kate she had been named after William's mom Diana. She wrote on to say that now her mom was with Diana in heaven as well.

For Diamond's dad to read how much this woman meant to his daughter inspired him to write to the Children's Wish Foundation describing his daughters dream. He told them how much she loves princesses. He also told them how she had been through a lot losing her mom and that now she is sick with cancer herself as well.

Thanks to her dad's heartfelt efforts, her dream to meet a princess is now coming true.

Kate speaks with Diamond's dad and stepmom while still attentive to the girl. It is obvious she cares about Diamond and wants to include her in the conversation.

After Kate stands up, I am touched to see Will kneel down to talk with the little girl as well. Diamond's stepmom holds her and she listens shyly with her head turned to the side as he speaks. Prince William just keeps on speaking sweetly to her, trying to help her feel comfortable.

Seeing him reminds me of meeting his mom, Diana, when I was in the children's rehabilitation hospital. I see similarities in their mannerisms as he speaks with Diamond and how his mom had spoken with us that day.

Recently, I read that the late Diana had once said of her sons, "I want my boys to have an understanding of people's emotions, their insecurities, people's distress and their hopes and dreams." Seeing Prince William talking to Diamond, I would say Diana did a good job as a parent.

While online I look at the schedule for dance classes. Getting back to my regular lifestyle as my writing is almost complete, I started dancing again. I find the exercise stimulating and enjoyable. I really missed it the past few years. My favourite dances at the moment are cha cha[54], merengue[55] and foxtrot.[56] I took some videos of my private lessons which are helpful for me to look at.

This year I decided that I want dancing to be even more a part of my life. I decided to have a few renovations done to my basement and put in a dance floor, along with my Pilates studio. I want to have friends over to dance. Finally I feel I can host another party after I had that bad experience with Sofia years back. I seriously did not think that I would ever want to again but I was amazed one day when I thought about having a party and I did not talk myself out of it.

I also put in a five foot tall cedar hot tub that is over six feet wide in the basement that I can use to exercise in the water with Pilates, dance barre exercises, Yin Yoga and aquatic fitness like movements. This has motivated me to start to train people again in Pilates once my memoir is published. My first client is going to be Aunt Gisele. I cannot pay her, like I did Andrew for all the help and support that she has given me over the years to create An Aid to Help Foundation because I know that she would not accept money. But offering lessons to her as a thank you is something she welcomes and I will have fun doing this.

57
Peer Support

I t is later in the summer of 2011 and I am reading an autobiography called *The Man Without Boundaries* by Spencer Miller.

Spencer and I were in the rehabilitation hospital at the same time in 1991. He was almost seven years old and was there in another part of the Centre. The children's rehabilitation hospital chose Spencer to be the Ambassador on behalf of the students and patients. Spencer had started to become a young motivational speaker only a few years before. He lived with his parents but was brought to the school on weekdays. He would speak locally and across Canada to help raise money for the Centre, something he accomplished with great success. In his book, he talks about the challenges he has had dealing with his Cerebral Palsy.

I remember briefly hearing about him when I was staying at the hospital. At that point in my recovery my memory was really bad. Because of our age difference and area of handicap, Spencer and I were in need of different types of care, so I do not remember ever directly speaking with him. Learning about his experience reminds me of my own in the children's rehab but in a different way.

In his book he recounts the time when Princess Diana came to the hospital. Spencer was asked to give her flowers. He says he refused to give her the flowers until she listened to what he had to say—and she did.

"There was an instant connection between us," he writes. "She was one of the first people in my life who actually looked at me as a person and didn't see the wheelchair."[57]

I definitely felt the exact same way in her response to my scar, facial paralysis and head injury at the time.

While serving as the Ambassador for the rehabilitation centre, Spencer learned about empathy through his own experience, as well as being taught privately through informal social and emotional learning. His family and staff would praise him when he would speak well about the needs of others.

I was one of those children with special needs he spoke out on behalf of to raise money. To learn to live with learning disabilities and brain damage was challenging. But the skills I learned to help myself are priceless gifts.

After reading that another patient at the children's rehabilitation hospital still remembers Princess Diana visiting us, I am reminded of the song I chose for the non-profit's CD as my personal tribute to her. It is the theme song from the movie *Titanic*, "My Heart Will Go On" by Céline Dion. As I can see here from reading Spencer's book, I am not the only person who felt loved by the late Princess, in a special way.

My wish is that the kind of emotional intelligence Princess Diana shared with us in 1991, touches others through An Aid to Help Foundation. Because I am doing my work as a tribute to Princess Diana, I am honoured I can let her heart still touch other children and families through money raised from telling my story. Princess Diana was a kindergarten teacher before she got married. A part of me feels that she would be happy to still help children even though she is no longer alive.

Setting my reading aside, I look over at Princess Diana's framed signature on my desk and pick it up. It has been here beside me for many months now. I no longer want to hide it. As I hold this piece of my past it feels even more important to me than ever. I look down at her signature, as I did on the stairs that one night a few years ago. I will always be grateful for her visit and the time she took to write in my Recovery Book. I would be touched if a child I visited during my volunteer work would pay tribute to me later on in life; I hope she felt the same.

58
My Illusion

The treadmill whirs around on its belt, giving off its familiar, rhythmic sound in the gym at Brookstreet Hotel. I raise the incline while watching the small television screen attached to it. I do not have earphones. Flipping channels, I immediately stop as I recognize the station Deborah works for.

I have not seen her on TV since I cut off my cable years ago. A part of me still does not want to see her. I look over at the clock; she will be on any minute if her schedule is still the same.

I do not have to put myself through this torture anymore. I still have time to switch the channel. I surprisingly do not want to. I hold my breath as I walk and close my eyes a bit, dreading the sight of her. Finally Deborah comes on screen and I slowly open my eyes to look fully at her. My immediate thought is that she has a new haircut. I am surprised however that I do not feel anything.

I take a moment and hunt around within to see if there are negative emotions hiding somewhere. But the familiar unpleasant feelings that used to be stirred up by the sight of her on television are gone. At last, I feel closure surrounding our experience together—what a relief. But I do not think the battle was ever between her and me anyway—it was between me and myself. It was within my power only to help myself in the way I have. No one else could have fixed my wounds for me.

As I continue walking, I note how the image I see of her on the screen is not real, it is an illusion. And this is like any other memory that I keep as well. I know now that challenges will happen in my life. But the perception I hold of what happened is my choice.

Goodbye Deborah—and with this thought, right before my eyes, her image changes into something completely different. This time, I am confident I did the work necessary to move on.

59
Hope and Remembrance

I t is the early morning of September 11, 2011. Aunt Gisele and I are walking onto the outdoor terrace at the NAC. The weather is perfect with clear skies. Off to the left is a stage set for the Symphony Orchestra to perform *9/11 Hope and Remembrance.*

Reading the *Ottawa Citizen* the other day, I was touched by "9/11: Ten Years Later". In the article Natasha Gauthier wrote about the significance of today's concert and all who helped in its creation. The NAC Orchestra's manager of artistic planning spoke about what motivated her to help plan this event.

"Daphne Burt was busy packing a few final boxes in her Milwaukee apartment, getting ready to move to her new job in Ottawa, when the news came over the radio: a plane had hit the World Trade Center in New York," the article explained. After hearing this tragic news, Daphne continued to get ready for the long drive to Ottawa. A few days into the trip in northern Ontario, a story on CBC radio caught her attention. The Canadian Prime Minister was calling for three minutes of silence as a tribute to the lives lost and the tragedy of September 11.

Seeing many other cars pull over to the side of the road, Daphne was surprised when she realized that this moment of silence, for an event that happened in the United States, was important to all these people. She said she would always remember this profound experience as her first introduction to Canada.

Daphne has worked with the NAC's orchestra conductor and the guest conductor of the concert, Peter Oundjian, who is the music director of the Toronto Symphony Orchestra, to create today's program. The interesting thing about Daphne is that she was the NAC contact that Andrew knew and approached to find Mark Ferguson as the pianist we used for *Songs for Everyone.* Andrew had explained to her a bit about what our non-profit was doing. She recommended Mark and also wished us good luck.

The free performance today is set to start at exactly 8:46 a.m., in memory of when the first aircraft struck the World Trade Centre. I was surprised to learn how many of the orchestral musicians are American and have chosen to be here for the performance today. Because this year, September 11, is on a Sunday, it normally would have been their day off.

Daphne said she "hope[s] [*9/11 Hope and Remembrance*] gets people to acknowledge that it doesn't matter what nationality you are, or what religion, or what your politics are. We're all human." The pieces of music "will move everyone in a different way. Music helps you to express what can't be said in words."

Her statement about the power of music is very in sync with me. Mark helped me put my feelings into music. To create *Songs for Everyone* helped me find closure. I hope this performance today does the same for others.

Aunt Gisele and I look around the audience to find two empty seats together. We are half an hour early but many people are already seated. We sit close to the middle of the audience. My legs get cool and wet from the morning dew on the chair. I tried to dress warmly in a long-sleeve dress; it may not have been warm enough however. Aunt Gisele realizes my discomfort.

"I'm okay," I quietly say.

While we wait for the performance, I close my eyes to meditate. With my eyes shut I am attuned to all the commotion around me—the man sniffling beside me, a baby crying in the background and the greetings of a nearby camera crew. I am totally in the moment as my breath and heart rate slow down. My body settles effortlessly into relaxation. I feel at peace.

Opening my eyes, I am delighted as the performance begins. Listening to the live music on the open terrace is lovely. I recognize some of the pieces that were chosen for the concert. I especially enjoy the moving, sublime pieces by Mozart and American composer Samuel Barber.

As the performance continues, I rest my eyes downward, so that I do not strain them. My weakened eye muscles can impact me when I am tired or relaxed as well. As I listen, I am looking at my shadow on the back of the man in front of me.

For the final Brahms piece, my eyes are eagerly drawn back to the stage. I am captivated by the conductor and cannot recall ever seeing him conduct before. His arms and body speak to the orchestra without words, communicating what he wants each musician to do with minute precision. His passion for music is obvious.[58] It is incredible.

In an email to reporters, the Toronto Symphony's conductor spoke about the feeling behind the pieces they chose and the sequence in which they will be performed. He said that listening to Brahms' work, "We deal with the ominous feelings of fear, threat, and grief, which, in the end, are overpowered by nobility and the faith in mankind's capacity to overcome adversity."

I have seen many conducted performances over the last decade but this one is different. I feel and see an unusual depth of emotion in everyone. During this concert, our hearts are open to memories of this tragedy. From my own experiences I know that to open up to life and feel appropriately all the emotions we are capable of, is important for being able to heal and move on.

60
A Need for Change

The leaves in the forest this fall 2011 are rich and radiant with colour. I take a sip of my coffee as I look outside at Mya in the backyard. Eric, has dropped by to visit and we are sitting in my TV room.

"It is great to see you," I say.

"I was posted this summer for three months overseas while you were writing," he says, as if there is no comparison between our two jobs.

"Writing has been a huge challenge for me. I never thought it would affect me the way it has. I realize now I am supposed to speak out on behalf of head injured people," I say, noting how I always feel I have to prove myself to him.

"Yeah," he says, his voice ice cold, "but you recovered completely from yours."

"I will have problems for the rest of my life from the brain damage," I say. "I never would talk about this before because it was so embarrassing."

"What brain damage? You recovered," he says. "You are fine, like me."

This is why I did not speak to him much before about my injuries. He does not understand or care to understand what happened to me. I knew this about him all along. I am so turned off by his lack of compassion. My heart starts to pound in my chest.

"There has been a lot of attention recently in the media on head injury. Some sport players are committing suicide and having it linked back to their brain injuries and it concerns many," I say.

"Come on, that was maybe one of a huge number of reasons why they killed themselves though," he says. "They have a lot of other stuff going on in their lives. That is a pretty lame excuse to use."

I am quiet for a moment thinking about how to respond because

I know that a lot of that "other stuff" may be a part of their lives as a result of their head injuries as well. Why does he not understand this? Suddenly I am reminded of writing my memoir.

"Part of my book talks about the time when I became suicidal," I say, looking straight at him.

I do not sense an ounce of concern in return.

"Yeah, but you didn't," he says. "You only had one head injury, those hockey players had many. You healed from yours. So you can't get off using that as an excuse."

He looks away.

"I had a severe closed-head injury—not a concussion," I say assertively, trying to not let his callousness get to me. "I was in a coma for weeks. With a CAT scan a doctor can still detect brain damage to this day. A person does not just regrow brain tissue. I am doing well now because I learned to manage and recover as best I could. I had to re-educate my mind how to work effectively in many areas. I will always have challenges. I could not work a regular full-time job now. I manage well on a schedule I can set for myself," I say.

"Give me a break," he says, rolling his eyes. "You can work full-time as I can. Look at all you are doing now, writing the book, the non-profit and so on."

He just rolled his eyes at me. He is so unsupportive. I know I should stop our conversation but a part of me wants to discuss this further with him. His attitude is enlightening in an odd way. He is a perfect example of the ignorance that many people display about what it really means to have received a head injury. Everyone always expected me to be back to normal right away. I do not know why I did not clue in to how shallow this man is before today. We are incompatible, even as friends.

"No, I cannot work full-time," I say. "This is why I got help financially for future income loss. I would not be where I am right now in life without this support."

Eric knew nothing about this part of my life before now.

He laughs. Then without even looking at me says, "You had good lawyers, plain and simple."

"So I lied about needing financial support?" I say. "I don't think so." I cannot believe him. He is quiet.

"It depends on what part of your brain was damaged as to what problems you might experience," I say. "No two head injuries are exactly alike. My dad could tell you how seriously hurt I was. He cried after I was injured and through my recovery when he became aware of all the struggles I was going through. He doesn't cry ever. I completely changed my personality afterwards. He did not know how to deal with the huge impact this had on our entire family."

"You had good lawyers," he says again, staring hard at me before looking away.

My thoughts consume me. What is his problem? How can he be so cold, to learn about the struggles that someone has gone through in their life? His attitude is pissing me off.

"My case did not have to go to court. It was obvious to everyone how hurt I was," I say quietly.

"Again," he says with a smile, nod of his head and show of his hand, "you had good lawyers."

My thoughts are consumed with what else I can say to him. This guy is an asshole. Our conversation is going nowhere.

"Those sports players who killed themselves had money. I guess head injury is part of their job?" I say sarcastically.

"Yes."

I know I should stop this conversation but I do not want to.

"Imagine the hard drive of your computer," I press on. "You take it and throw it against the wall, then turn it on and it still works. But for how long will it work and at what level in comparison to before? There has to be damage you cannot see. The problems it will have may surface now or later."

"But we all have small problems," he says.

I have heard this so many times and I am sick of it, I think to myself.

"And difficulty with bladder control after I was hurt at eighteen is a small problem?" I say, as I start to cry.

I am letting him hurt me by opening up and talking about my

injury. I know this does not make it any easier to confront his lack of support.

"I will need to work on physical therapy in certain areas—forever," I say.

"Well," he says. "Maybe you were hurt more than I realize but you still had good lawyers."

Never and I mean never, do I want to get romantically involved with this guy again. He is such a loser. I do not even want to be his friend. There would be no reason to tell him this however in an assertive way. I will walk around this problem. He can be whoever he wants to be.

"So one severe closed-head injury compared to a concussion is not even comparable," I say. "I guess I will shut up then."

"Yup," he says.

He thinks he is such a know-it-all. He needs to grow up. I now sit quiet. An awkward silence hangs over the room. It is time for the visit to end. Walking to my front door, we say goodbye. As I close the door behind him, I start to cry. I always knew this guy was capable of hurting me like this and today, I allowed it on purpose. I do not know why I did this.

Compassion floods my body. Suddenly, I realize with a new sense of clarity that my mission for the non-profit is evolving as I am healing and growing stronger. I am gaining confidence that my mission is definitely to be an advocate for head injury. Eric is not the only ignorant person out there. To share my story from strength to help others who have and who will incur similar injuries as I received is important—they need to know that they are not alone. My Aunt Gisele always thought this was my purpose and I finally agree with her.

When I met Princess Diana, I was not in the children's rehabilitation hospital for a cut on my cheek; I was there because of a traumatic brain injury. It took a lot of hard work to rebuild my life—and others who suffer from head injuries of all different levels of severity should learn that they can become stronger too.

61
Speaking Out

The room is busy with people being seated on this early Saturday morning, a few weeks before Christmas 2011. I am surprised how many people are attending the seminar on concussions being put on by the Ottawa District Hockey association. I sit along the side wall near the back. I do not feel comfortable sitting as a part of the audience but am content to observe everything.

For the first half of the seminar the specialists talk about concussions and recovery. There are some medical specialists, in the area of concussions on the panel, as well as the Chief Medical Officer from Hockey Canada.

I find them to be so vague in what they are saying. I know the brain does not heal as a broken bone does, especially if a person has had more than one concussion. This was a waste of time for me to come. I want to go home but I cannot because Aunt Gisele will ask me about today. I have to stay. I am bored and tired. I stayed out too late last night. I need sleep.

Mid-morning a neurosurgeon from the children's hospital speaks. He is director of a non-profit called Think First, whose mission is to prevent brain and spinal cord injuries through education aimed at healthy behaviours in children and youth. He immediately captures my attention, saying things about head injuries that I know all too well. I hear compassion in his voice as he speaks about how difficult it can be to recover from this kind of injury.

Then a physician who studied medicine at Harvard and founded a concussion clinic in the west end of Ottawa speaks.[59] I feel he also understands the depth of the struggles one can experience from a closed-head injury—often referred to today as simply "a concussion".

I am interested especially in the last few speakers. It is now the end of the morning and they have set aside twenty minutes for questions to the panel. There are two microphones set up. I do not want to ask anything.

I start to speak with a woman sitting beside me about the seminar. She coaches boy's hockey. While we talk, I am listening in the background to see what kinds of questions are being asked, so that I can tell Aunt Gisele. Out of the corner of my eye, I see a man step up to the microphone.

I start to tell the woman about how vague I thought a few of the presenters on the panel were. All of a sudden I hear the man who is asking the questions to the panel say something which causes me to stop my conversation mid-sentence.

I just heard him say he had multiple concussions while playing in the NHL when he was younger and he accredits his success in recovery to meditation. Seriously, he did not just say that. Instantly I jump from my seat, apologizing to the woman I was speaking with and rush closer to the front of the room to hear what he says next. Without realizing it, I find myself in line to ask a question at the second microphone. There is a man ahead of me.

I do not know why I am up here. I should go back and sit down but I will look like an idiot walking away. I cannot believe what I heard that man say. I agree with everything he was saying about what helped his recovery. I have not met another person who is on the same page as I am with how I coped with stuff. He sounded strong. Like a survivor—like me.

It is now my turn to speak. I take a step forward and my legs feel like butter. I am staring at a panel of medical specialists. Strangely, it also feels as if I have done this before. Oh no—I have—when I was in the children's rehabilitation hospital! There was that line of specialists I had to speak to. Maybe it is not too late to run away. I slowly take another step towards the microphone.

"First, I want to make a comment about something the former NHL hockey player said and then I will ask a question," I say. "What I want to comment on is what he said about meditation helping him to recover."

I briefly tell the panel about my severe closed-head injury and how I have kept it a secret from many people for the last twenty years. I point out my scar. I tell them how hard I found it for others to understand the depths of my struggles. I tell them through hard work I was able to rebuild a life for myself and how meditation was essential for my success.

"I agree with what a few of you specialists said, that if someone was successful in school prior to receiving a head injury, this would help them recover," I say. "This definitely was an advantage I had."

I tell them briefly about An Aid to Help Foundation and my memoir.

"I'm starting to speak out now," I say. "I'm here today for this seminar but I don't have a child in hockey."

The Hockey Canada physician thanks me for telling my story. He says it helps them to hear about survivors succeeding by using meditation as a recovery tool.

"My question then is about the emotional consequences of a head injury," I say. "I have heard a lot today about the anxiety and depression that can be experienced as a result of this type of injury. What about anger and emotional control? I'm concerned when I hear about or see the fighting that occurs on ice."

The Hockey Canada physician quickly jumps in to answer my question. I was hoping the neurosurgeon from the children's hospital or the specialist from the concussion clinic would. The doctor tells me that at this point there is no conclusive evidence that a player's loss of emotional control is a result of head injury.

I know if my dad were here right now, he would disagree with what was just said. He would have something to say about the anger I felt after my injury. So I completely disagree, based on what I had experienced from my head injury as well as what I learned through my own research.

The physician's answer is short and vague. I do not want to get into a debate with him. I have no reason to. So I do not challenge his response. I listen politely and bite my lip. I feel he is minimizing the emotional consequences that can result from a concussion. A neuropsychologist would have added more insight to this panel. They have more knowledge about the behavioural challenges from a head injury. But even they do not know everything,

I finish at the microphone and people start clapping. I do not understand why they are clapping because they did not clap for anyone else. As I walk away, people rush up to me. A woman starts to talk a mile a minute, while an older gentleman approaches too. My heart is still pounding from having spoken so it takes me a second to understand why they are approaching me.

The woman is a mother of a young woman who received a head injury. She thinks I can help her daughter. I am not a therapist but despite the cost, I feel her daughter definitely needs to see one. I do not want to suggest something that helps but she cannot afford. I do not really know what to say. She is catching me off guard.

The woman speaks to me trying to explain what has been happening since the injury. I can tell, in ways, she is desperate for help. It reminds me of my own family's struggles dealing with my closed-head injury. I encourage the woman to get her daughter to practice meditation. This only needs to be done for five to ten minutes a day in order to reap some benefits, I explain, adding that there are a lot of books she could read on the subject.

I then see the other person who had approached me and walk over to speak with him. We introduce ourselves. He is from the Brain Injury Association of Canada.[60] He has met Aunt Gisele before, who had told him that I would be coming to the concussion seminar today. I share with him how I felt the first few speakers today were minimizing the consequences of a concussion. He agrees and we discuss this further.

As I leave the seminar I definitely know that there was a reason for me to be here today that I did not expect. After hearing the hockey player confirm my experience with meditation being an essential recovery tool it was obvious to me why I had come.

This was not easy, to speak out publicly. I was nervous and scared to talk about my injury. I do not feel this way to speak about other things. It was the topic today that made me self-conscious. I am proud, though, for literally, jumping at the chance to speak out for—the first time.

62
Brain Training

As I look at my calendar for the coming week, I see a few notes I made for the concussion seminar I went to yesterday. For me to speak out was a step in the direction I believe I was meant to go in all along. I would not have guessed I would want to be an advocate about head injury specifically. Drunk driving, my scar, severe injuries yes but head injury—no.

Aunt Gisele always emphasized how the public needs to become more aware of the serious challenges presented by a head injury. I believe that whatever the cause of brain damage, we need to respect how fragile this part of our body really is. There are many ways a person can get a head injury. At some point, we all may go through challenges in life in one way or another.

Since the mom at the seminar asked me for help with her daughter, I have been thinking about what else I might have said to her. I really was not prepared for being asked to help this way. I realize that she is not the only one who will ever want my advice—so I need to have a better response than I did. I wish at the time I could have said I had suggestions online or elsewhere.

I recommended meditation but I realize this may not be helpful for all. I also know not everyone can afford to pay to learn how to do this effectively. I spent thousands of dollars on different courses and material to learn things. I learned as much as I could about meditation so that I could create my own way to focus and relax. I know not everyone is as motivated or passionate to learn as I am.

Meditation is really plain and simple, concentration practice. There are no secret words and routines to know in order to reap its benefit. What I do is easy to learn and I want to share it with others. I am going to put together simple audio recordings to help people practice strengthening their concentration on a regular basis. I feel that a variety of words and/or thoughts will work the best. I want to make it as therapeutic as possible to those who practice regularly. The five minute recordings will be of my voice. By listening it will remind them of what they are doing. Eventually they will be able to practice without my help. I will sell this by mp3 for An Aid to Help Foundation to be able to raise even more money. I will create enough for people of all ages to be able to choose hopefully at least one that they would like to practice with. I think I will call them *An Aid to Help Concentration.*[61]

But there is more needed for people recovering from a head injury. I remember a website called Lumosity.com. I had tried out some cognitive training games and exercise on this site years ago and always wanted to get a membership but it was not on the top of my priority list. Now, I will check it out again to see if this could help others recover from a head injury.

I am impressed reading about Lumos Labs. It was founded in 2005 and has used neuroscience to create games and exercises to help people strengthen their memory, concentration, flexibility, speed and problem solving. They call their brain fitness program Lumosity.[62] It is being developed by many neuroscientists throughout the world. They believe that anyone, regardless of their age can have a healthy mind and increase their intelligence.

I register for a trial membership with a user name of MyaHappy and a picture of Mya for my profile. I decide to start a game called Word Bubbles which helps strengthen verbal fluency. I become enraptured in the game, enough to sign up for a full membership and eager to explore these fun creative ways of developing cognitive skills. Looking around the Lumosity website, I also see they have program arrangements set up for Traumatic Brain Injury (TBI) as well as Attention Deficit Hyperactivity Disorder (ADHD).

It would benefit any person to challenge their mind and brain to play these. No pills needed—only time and attention. This is definitely a great way to help build inner strength. It is a source of support for people.

This definitely can help me excel even more at dealing with the challenges from the "cognitive deficit crap" I received from my head injury. This is an unexpected source of help for me. I am grateful for finding this.

Lumos Labs program can also be helpful to parents as a way to feel more confident that their children are prepared for the falls and injuries that can and will happen in life. Wearing a helmet definitely helps to prevent some head injuries but not all. I have one picture of when I was Doris, at four years old on my parents' driveway and I was riding a tricycle backwards with no helmet on. It looks like an accident waiting to happen.[63]

As I continue exploring their website, I am surprised to read a recommendation for meditation. They say, "Periodically calming and focusing the mind has been shown to help with attention, processing speed, and response time." After using their program to see where my strengths were, I would agree. My dedication to meditation to strengthen my concentration and attention shows definite results on Lumosity.

I know from first-hand experience that my brain works as a muscle does and the more I strengthen it in different ways, the better everything functions. After my head injury I did not regrow the brain tissue that had been damaged, rather I re-educated my brain to work in new ways to do the same thing it was doing before. There is research being done in this area called neuroplasticity. I have a book about it by Norman Doidge called *The Brain That Changes Itself.* My aunt Gisele has borrowed this book twice from me because she finds it so interesting to read. Lumos Labs does research in the area of neuroplasticity as well.

To succeed further in these areas through training my brain is definitely a challenge I will take on without complaint. Now that I have used this program, I feel more confident to recommend it to help others. Without Aunt Gisele's encouragement all along, I still would have kept my challenges hidden as I had already been doing for many years. That I could benefit as well from cognitive training like this is wonderful.

My desire now is to have other people understand what brain

damage is, whether from a concussion, head injury or due to natural atrophy with age. Each case will always be different for the head injured person and how it affects their lives. This is where I hope that the money An Aid to Help Foundation raises can go to help educate people to be more understanding and supportive to others in their lives, no matter what the challenge is. I believe that Roots of Empathy's program in schools from kindergarten to grade 8 is a great start.

This makes me remember one of the last times I saw Omi in Calgary before she died, while Aunt Gisele was at work. I delighted that day in playing Scrabble with my grandmother and uncle all day.

"She can't play by the rules anymore," Aunt Gisele said, surprised I had enjoyed myself. "She makes up words. It's not fun to play with her now."

"But she is slowing down mentally," I said. "She doesn't know the difference anymore. I wanted one of the last few times that I see her to be one where she was happy. So we played Scrabble for eight hours. You are right about her word choice. It seems as if she's mixing German and English together. Hey, remember me after my head injury, I thought it was 1942. The woman is in her 90's, you have to give her a break. We all could be old and challenged in the mind like her someday."

I gave Aunt Gisele examples of the challenges Omi was having at the time, such as avoiding group gatherings. I explained to Aunt Gisele that I thought her multi-tasking skills were slowing down. I saw evidence of it during the day we spent together.

I had compassion for her because of what I had experienced after I was injured in 1991 with challenges in my focus, memory and problem solving. I empathized with her and the struggles she had.

As the weeks go by, more opportunities to support others in my life are presenting themselves. One time was when a good friend of mine was injured after falling on a bathroom floor as she was getting out of the shower. She hit the back of her head really hard on the edge of the bathtub and sustained a moderate closed-head injury. I have been hearing from her the struggles she has been having with migraines and memory problems and I am a valuable source of support for her.

The other opportunity was one day when I had lunch with my cousin and his friend. His friend is recovering from a closed-head injury she received last year when she was at a bar and a heavy painting fell off the wall and struck her in the head. She is still struggling now in many ways. Her children say she is a different person as a result of the injury. They gave me many examples, such as when they walk into a mall or public place, she will burst into tears for no reason. They say she was never this emotional before. I explained to them how she will still get better with time.

I wish there had been someone close in my life who could have expressed the same to me and my family at the time I was hurt. Sure there were some sympathetic survivors who approached me but there was no one I ever felt who was on the same page with me or could understand how to help me get better. I was a solo trooper in many ways and still am. I now have no problem helping these people, which truly surprises me. I did not think I would want to venture into the unpredictable rehabilitation of the brain again, in any way.

At lunch that day, we all spoke about the importance of protecting your head from injury as much as possible. Shockingly, my cousin's friend said, "I still don't have a helmet yet for when I ride a bike."

Oh my goodness.

63
An Aid to Help

It is evening and I am sitting at the vanity table in my bedroom. Looking in the mirror I notice how much the scar on my cheek has disappeared even more over the past few years. I am still taking the systemic enzymes and at the same time in the evening I will gently massage the marks with depth, by using the rounded end of a makeup brush. My reasoning for doing this is that to cause a bit of inflammation in the tissue will attract the enzymes to this area more urgently. Aunt Gisele cannot believe the difference this has made to the scar tissue. She said it is tremendously less noticeable. I still remember how critical she was at that dinner the other year so this compliment means a lot to me. Tonight, I remove the makeup from my scar with a cotton swab slowly.

Suddenly I remember being in pain. I quickly tell myself to forget about it. I look to the side, trying to follow my orders to stop my thoughts but my eyes are quickly drawn back to the mirror, to my scar. I know that what I read online a few minutes ago has upset me. Something will not let me stop touching my scar. It feels like a heavy weight is expanding in my chest. I start to cry.

I just read about Sheila Nabb, a thirty-seven-year-old woman from Alberta who was on vacation with her husband in Mexico when she was found unconscious on the floor of the resort elevator with her face completely smashed. She remains in a coma. But it was when I read how her facial bones were severely broken that I felt strong twinges of the memory of pain inside me.

Learning what happened to her has triggered a flashback from my own accident—now the memory of my injury and the pain I felt are troublesome as they become vivid. My skull begins to throb. My eye sockets, the bridge of my nose, my cheekbones.

I do not understand why I read the news before going to bed. That woman in Mexico must be in agony right now. That is how I must have felt when the bones of my head were severely broken and shattered. The agony I must have been in. I have never thought of or felt before the excruciating pain that I must have endured, while I was in a coma. I always say that I was lucky I was in a coma so that I did not have to experience the pain. My heart is beating faster. I strain to breathe. My breath is shallow and rapid.

"What a horrible thing to happen," I say, as I continue to cry.

I do not understand why this bothers me so much. She is in a coma now. She will not remember afterwards. I need to calm down. I am really crying as I finish removing my make-up. I start to tidy up, trying to distract my thoughts. I cannot slow my breath down as I ready myself to go to bed. The level of empathy I feel for Sheila is immense. I am crying for a woman I have not met before but also for me and what my family and friends must have gone through to see me hurt, so many years ago.

A stranger did this to Sheila. I do not understand how a person could do such a thing to another. I do not understand what is wrong with people.

"It is time for this heartless behaviour to stop!" I say out loud.

I look at myself in the mirror before grabbing a tissue to blow my nose. As I start to organize things again, my breath is still rapid. I begin to hum a melody to help calm myself down. I move stuff, cry and then move more stuff, still humming to myself. To do this is making me take longer, slower breaths.

Then I realize what melody it is that I am humming. I stop abruptly and look open-mouthed at myself in the mirror. It is "Ballerina Girl" by Lionel Richie, one of the songs on *Songs for Everyone*.

It is hard to believe that I am comforting myself with music that I had created to help others. This has always been my favourite song from the CD. I still listen to the music to meditate or sometimes I just relax with it playing in the background. A friend has even stretched with me while we listen. We hold a stretch for the length of one song and then when the next song comes on we change stretches. The songs are not too long, so the CD works perfectly for this. It feels like meditative stretching. For me, it is a form of concentration practice. In Pilates some stretches are held for a length of time on the equipment but there also is a form of yoga called Yin Yoga that is similar to what we are doing. I am actually going to take a teachers certification in this so that I can train others.

I go back to tidying up and anxiously humming, thinking about Sheila again. I do not understand how a person could do that to her. I wonder how would they feel to have been hurt, as they had hurt her and be in the pain she is in right now. This motivates me even more to want to make a difference by telling my story. I am determined to have an impact on others through An Aid to Help Foundation. One of the melodies from the CD I have created helped me tonight, what a surprise.

Going to bed, I decide to meditate to calm myself down further. Under the covers I lay on my back with my knees bent. As I begin to breathe deeply, my thoughts slow down and relaxation floods my body. As I breathe "in", I say to myself, I love you. I breathe "out". As I breathe "in", I'm sorry. I breathe "out". As I breathe "in", please forgive me. I breathe "out". As I breathe "in", thank you.

I continue repeating this ancient Hawaiian mantra to myself. Ho'oponopono is about taking 100% responsibility for what I experience in my life. So I am saying this to heal whatever is going on in my life that may have needed me to learn about this woman getting hurt in order to take the next step on my journey forward. By looking at things in this way and taking complete responsibility, everything that happens in my life can be used as an opportunity for my own personal growth and development. I believe that we are all interconnected on some level in our world and to have an attitude about life that embraces this is what would work best.

This mantra was used by Dr. Hew Len at one time to treat mentally ill criminals at Hawaii State Hospital without him ever having met them. He simply took patient's files into his office and repeated this mantra as he studied them in-depth to heal himself. To the amazement of everyone, gradually the prisoners healed and were able to be released.

Even the staff became happier in the work environment with less sick days being taken by them. The few inmates that remained were able to be relocated elsewhere and the clinic eventually was closed.

I love you. I'm sorry. Please forgive me. Thank you. I say it for Sheila, for her family and friends as well as for the man who hurt her. I love you. I'm sorry. Please forgive me. Thank you. But the most important person I am saying it for is myself, as both—Samantha and Doris.

My body relaxes and sinks deeper into the mattress as I continue my meditation. My breath has slowed down. My circulation is better and I feel warmer as a result. I am at peace and relieved knowing I am helping myself.

As I straighten my legs and turn on my side, I start to drift off to sleep. The mantra continues automatically in my mind. I love you. I'm sorry. Please forgive me. Thank you.

64
An Old Friend

I t is a sunny spring day in 2012 and I am listening to *Songs for Everyone* while working in my office upstairs. Mya is lying on a mat on the floor beside me. This upstairs office has become my own personal spot. Hanging on one wall is the picture I took of Princess Diana before I met her, as well as her framed signature. I have decided that until the non-profit is no longer something I want to work on, these items will stay there for me to see. It motivates me to look at them. I do not feel like I need to hide her signature anymore.

Also, on a bulletin board there is an old LP album cover for the soundtrack of the movie *Flashdance*. This movie is a favourite of mine in both parts of my life—as Doris and as Samantha. Mom gave me the cover a few months ago, after she found it in a closet at home. She had a hard time throwing out something that belonged to me when I was Doris. Seeing the picture on the cover triggered memories about my enjoyment of the movie and my enthusiasm for dance.

Even though I would not consciously allow myself, as Samantha, to like the same things as I did when I was Doris, there is no way I could have ever been able to extinguish the passion I have always had for dance. I remember the scene in the movie where "What a Feeling" by Irene Cara was used by her as the song for her audition routine.[64] Her dance was totally freestyle and full of life. It is interesting how the lyrics and that part of the movie about feeling, passion, dreams and dance apply to my life today.

To see this, as well as the part of My Recovery book that Princess Diana signed, continues to fuel my motivation to do something as a tribute to both her lost life and the life I had as Doris getting severely damaged beyond recognition.

Another picture on my office wall is a puzzle of flying pigs I put together. The puzzle had no borders and this made it really hard to do. I bought this before my lawyers mediated closure with the insurance company in the 90's. I thought this would be fun to complete. The task of putting it together was extremely challenging, so I decided I definitely would not want to do it again. I framed the completed puzzle and I used to say, "When pigs can fly my legal work is going to close."[65]

Well, they did finally fly in that area of my life. Looking back at it now, it reminds me that big dreams are often attainable, even if they seem impossible.

Last is a small framed picture of three birds on branches of a tree. This was a birthday present from my mom's mom, my grandmother that in my family we called Oma, who passed away in the 80's. The back is signed and dated, 1981 from Oma and Opa. As Doris, I would have been turning eight years old. This is another reminder of myself as Doris. I love seeing this on the wall when I sit and work at the desk. This gift from my grandparents represents what I learned: that my family stands behind me, each in their own way. Their support and encouragement strengthen me.[66]

Oma and Opa used to take us grandchildren up to their cottage to enjoy nature and this taught me that fresh air is important. My parents did this as well by raising my brother and me in the country. I learned that nature always seemed to want to help support my recovery from the accident I was in. It showed me in quiet, gentle ways the route I should take to succeed and conquer my struggles. Through meditation and looking after myself, my relationship with nature grew stronger.

The picture of the birds also reminds me of kindergarten, when Mom taught my classmates about the birds while we all piled up into the kitchen. Seeing it, reminds me of what I learned from that experience when I was young. So this motivates me to want to work my hardest to help Roots of Empathy get into as many schools as possible in our world.

These memories are from the life I had as Doris, which surprisingly I accept and embrace once again as a part of me. There were a few potholes and detours in the road on my journey forward in life as Doris. But the important thing I have learned is that—I am still her. Sure a more evolved version but I am still Doris. I feel as though I have regained a large part of my lost identity back. This is great news. All those years I was not being my true self, sadly can never be returned to me just because this has happened. My life as Doris was buried for a long time.

It was a shock for me one night when I looked in the mirror in the bathroom to see myself, as Doris, looking back at me. I noticed a new sparkle in my eyes—for the first time. A subtle twinkle like the one I always had, before, as her—that was almost extinguished forever on that summer night in 1991. Excited, I told Mom and Dad.

"I just got used to calling you Samantha," Mom said. "Please don't change back!"

I understand she was scared because I might make the family call me Doris again. She needs to calm down however, since Samantha is who I am now. But Doris is still my middle name and unlike before, I would not mind if anyone called me by it. The other day when I was introducing myself to someone, I said my name was Samantha but in my mind I thought Doris. This had not ever happened before and that is another surprise.

How I feel now when I remind myself that I am still Doris is unbelievable. I cannot even describe what it feels like, other than to say that I immediately feel complete. If I ever need cheering up, this reminder instantly lifts my spirits. I walked around without letting her be a part of my life for too long. Doris was, sadly, forced to sit in the shadows of the new life I had created for myself as Samantha. This was a result of the injury I received as well as an unconscious choice I made trying my best to cope with what had happened to me. My life did not feel entirely real without all parts of who I am included. And this would not have changed if I did not do the work I have to help myself, by creating something which, at first, I thought was only to help others.

When I met Princess Diana, I asked her to write in my Recovery Book, plain and simple. The purpose of having this book was to help me get better. What she wrote that day and how meaningful it turned out to be, is profound. Her help was the essential ingredient necessary for me to heal from my injuries as well as possible. Princess Diana helped me that day, more than she would ever have realized and I am so grateful to her.

I now better understand the loneliness I experienced over the years. I thought new friends could fill this void but they never could. I struggled, not realizing I missed being my old self. Knowing this makes understanding everything else easier. Life joined up with my creative wisdom to give me an opportunity to reconnect with Doris. This part of who I am as a woman is probably one of the dearest friends I will ever have. The Doris part of me witnessed and experienced the ups and downs of my life after the accident as well. Even to witness a severe closed-head injury would have been one heck of an experience.

One change from the past is that my social life has regained its fullness, like in ways when I was Doris. Friends, old and new, are a more welcome part of my life. I feel much less insecure than I was for over half of my life because of the results of the head injury I had.

The recovery from the life-changing accident was lengthy and stressful, sometimes agonizing. Professionals told this to everyone in my life after I was hurt. To have lived through the experience, I would say I agree. To cope, I abandoned Doris, who is innately a part of me. Her life was giving me difficulty, so it was much easier for me to walk away and start anew than to dig through the rubble that remained.

This was a strange process. If, as Doris, I liked something previously, I, as Samantha, often did the opposite only to prove I was no longer her. As Doris I liked green apples. As Samantha, I hated them and would only eat red ones. As Doris I enjoyed contemporary furnishings. As Samantha, I liked every other style. As Doris I was a smoker. As Samantha I am not. And when I did still smoke I did not let myself smoke Doris's favourite brand. So even though as Samantha I welcome Doris as a part of who I am now, I will never inhale a smoke again, sorry Doris.

Fast-forward to a time when the Doris side of me, that I thought was long dead in the shadows, comes to life again. To witness this part of myself emerge as I created everything for my family's non-profit was unexpected. As these two parts of my identity were and still are being fused together as one part of my life, I finally feel whole again as a person.

I recall a poem a guest, visiting from New York and I in the 90's wrote in a guestbook I keep.[67] We just handed the book back and forth writing as we spoke about other things while other friends played a game of pool. Now it means more to me than ever to read:

The 10th Floor

Brings new life
What will hatch from this spiritual
nest manifested
    is a celebration.
an incarnation of yesterday's energy
    building a paradise on Earth
I question the jubilation, longingly of course
    To learn to grow beyond pain
    is the sweetest gift of all
this is your mantra, your response.
My question is what butterfly is forming here?
    A damn happy one.
Caterpillars spin silk.

Reconnecting with Doris through the work that I have been doing was important and crucial even. I always would have been a bit lost in life had I not allowed myself to embrace again the part of me that was still her. To celebrate her as a part of the woman I am today feels like a gift. I am so grateful that I took the time and energy to achieve this reunion within my heart and soul.

A lot of people close to me say they can feel and see a positive change in me—Aunt Gisele and my parents especially. I realize now how the purpose of everything I have done over the past few years was to tell my story and continue to heal. Had I started out with this as my goal I would have definitely not been as passionate to help myself in this way. Copying the silence that had already surrounded my closed-head injury was easy to do and I would have stayed on the same route. But now I hope I can touch and inspire others by sharing my experience.

This is why in the end I did not really need to speak with Deborah again to resolve anything. She did what she did and she will have to deal with things in her own way. I can only take responsibility for my own health and well-being, which was exactly what I did by working on finding closure for myself.

I will no longer waste my energy being angry at anyone. It is not worth my time. Life is too short. I gave my anger a voice in many unique, creative ways. I released as much as possible any emotional issues I still had that were surrounding my experience. I know I do not like Deborah as a person. However not liking someone and being angry at them are two different things. And this will not change. She apologised to me after the accident but it was not enough. I needed more to move on, to truly forgive her and others, as I feel I have been able to do now. I know I will never forget what happened to me and that is okay. I love my life though and everything about it. And my challenges, successes and struggles are what got me to where I am today.

While I was at the gym last year, seeing Deborah on television was an unexpected surprise but the confidence I felt afterwards made me understand that everything I have done for myself and others was right on target. I know that my journey of healing the wounds I had with her is complete. I realize now that seeing Deborah all the time unexpectedly in my personal life on TV made me protect myself. She hurt me as Doris once before and a part of me was scared she would hurt me again. I had to defend myself. She still felt like a threat to me. Therefore, my unconscious choice was to not allow Doris to see the light of day. I built layer upon layer of defences to prevent this. It was not until I got rid of my cable TV and could no longer see Deborah in my home that a part of me finally opened up to feel the loss of the life I had as Doris and to grieve for her. I finally felt safe to do this because I no longer was seeing the person who hurt me.

If Deborah had apologized to me better, as I needed, I might have been able to move on effortlessly. Actions mean more than words.

Saying sorry is sometimes enough but not in all cases. For me, hearing, "I'm sorry. How can I make it up to you?" would have been more meaningful. Everyone has and will make mistakes in life. To use an experience to benefit others transforms it into—a gift.

I believe everything happened to me so that I could have a career working for the benefit of children. As Doris, I wanted to work with children as a paediatrician; as Samantha Doris, I work as someone who inspires creativity for healing and raises money for the advancement of education. Deborah hurting me was only the first step of my journey.

I will no longer let myself be haunted by memories from the past. By taking the time to look at the dark, hurtful experiences in my life more closely, I discovered that things were not as bad as I thought they were—they after all could have been a lot worse. What I created as a result of a near death experience and two decades of intensive recovery was—definitely worth my time and effort. Welcome back, Doris.

Epilogue

You use a glass mirror to see your face;
you use works of art to see your soul.

—George Bernard Shaw (1856-1950)

O ver the last few years, the anniversary of my accident passed unnoticed, something that was definitely never the case before. I would always cry on that anniversary day. Even my mom commented how the date passes by for me with no sad memories.

Through my experience since 2008, I have truly learned about the power of creativity and healing. To create An Aid to Help Foundation and *Songs for Everyone* has been therapeutic for me. The music touched me at a depth no words could ever reach. Today, when I play "Here Without You", I no longer cry but have feelings of internal strength and empowerment. To allow my body to naturally express itself in creative ways has had a long-term positive effect on how I dealt with what happened to me.

Now, writing my story is giving me another method for healing; my creative intelligence has been restorative and rejuvenating. I allowed nature to guide me in gentle ways to show me how I might be able to do this. I was the student; life was my teacher. Mya is part of this nature and deserves credit. She taught me that observation is never boring. Life has inspired me during quiet time.

Deborah's wish for me in her letter in 1991—that my internal and external injuries heal and that I can get on with my life—is finally reality. I would say my recovery from the facial trauma and severe closed-head injury is now complete. I am free. I cannot ever change what happened to me but I faced my mistake and the mistakes of others, learned from them and moved forward. If Deborah and her family had been available for me in some way after, I do not think I ever would have needed to heal as I have. Since I did not have their support, I created and found my own.

At the depth of who I truly am is an unyielding desire to be healthy and happy. This part guided me to find the inner strength to achieve it. It did not happen overnight. It followed along the lines of the story of the turtle and the hare in which the slow turtle won. I guess that my choice for Vincent to paint the turtle in the hand for the CD case had more meaning to me than I previously realized. I used to be fast at everything; I was speeding through life before I was hurt.

I decided after taking a Yin Yoga course that I will be privately training clients more to do this, along with Pilates. I want to also approach corporations in the Ottawa area to offer meditative stretch classes to them. It will be fun helping others learn to relax. I may call my classes *An Aid to Help Stretch and Relax*. I have the music from *Songs for Everyone* to use and this could help people learn to relax upon hearing it. Part of what I earn from this work, without a doubt, will go to An Aid to Help Foundation. This is another way for donations to be made to a good cause that is beyond just receiving a tax receipt. It will be a symbiotic relationship between me and the people I help. This is something I think we need more of in our world.

As well from my involvement in this work with the non-profit, I now wish to continue my university studies part-time to finish my degree and apply for graduate studies. I learned first-hand of the healing power of creativity. To allow myself to speak with and without words was a delight to witness and I want to learn how to impart this same wisdom to others. Both parts of me as Samantha and Doris are passionate about this idea. Finally my motivation for school is back. I have no problem being a student for life.

I am going to look for graduate studies which incorporate the creative human element such as music, art, writing and healing. I have already found a Master of Art Therapy program through distance education, at Athabasca University in Alberta and I am eager to learn more about it. Having a goal in mind as I finish my Bachelor of Arts will make the effort I put into my studies worthwhile. I have a purpose now for wanting to complete a degree and this is something I never had since I was hurt in the accident in 1991.

I am honoured to have been the Artistic Director of the creation of *Songs for Everyone, Finding Inner Strength,* as well as www.anaid.org, An Aid to Help Foundation and now *The Beauty of My Shadow.* And despite my mom's objection, *My Anger* should be included in this list as well. But the list does not end here! To my total surprise, I wrote two more books that will also help raise money. One will have the *Songs for Everyone* CD as a soundtrack as well and this will be available digitally as well as in hard copy. One book is called *The Princess in Pink: A True Tale* and in the other, I am the ghostwriter for Mya. The title of her memoir is *The Butterflies Above My Bed.* In both story's I try to narrate my and Mya's emotional tale in language and themes that any child can understand. These books will be made available through An Aid to Help Foundation as well as other online venues.[68]

To be able to heal deeply through this work was a life-changing experience, one which I will always remember. Moving beyond an experience in my life that I thought would haunt me forever was worth the effort.

Afterword

The impact of head injury on patients and families is tremendous and much more information and assistance are available now than there was for my family in 1991.

The Brain Injury Association of Canada (BIAC), established in 2003, provides information, support, education, research and more. Traumatic brain injury (TBI) is considered a silent epidemic. It is more common than breast cancer, spinal cord injury, HIV/AIDS and multiple sclerosis combined. TBI is a leading cause of death and disability for individuals under age forty-four. Brain injury is suffered by someone in America, usually a young person, every fifteen seconds.

The Ontario Neurotrauma Foundation (ONF) states that neurotrauma (acquired brain and spinal cord injury) is devastating and costly and is largely predictable and preventable. It creates a significant burden for individuals, families and communities in addition to a phenomenal cost to healthcare and long-term care.

Chronic Traumatic Encephalopathy (CTE) has been in the news recently. While once thought to primarily affect old, retired boxers, recent evidence of autopsies of footballs players contradicts this finding. The condition that carries with it significant neurological and psychological signs and symptoms is found as well in younger athletes who have had repetitive head injuries. Most recently, although Derek Boogaard, a former NHL enforcer, died at age twenty-eight of a drug overdose, his brain showed changes in keeping with CTE.

To this day, I have great admiration for the neurologist at University of Toronto, who successfully stopped boxing as a university sport in the 60's because he maintained that every knock-out was a concussion. He supported his cause by showing us medical students a row of abnormal electro-encephalograms, brain wave tests of boxers. MRI, CAT scans and other investigative neurological procedures were not invented at the time.

More ongoing awareness and effective preventive strategies are necessary to combat traumatic brain injury—the silent epidemic.

Dr. Gisele Microys,
a.k.a. Aunt Gisele

Acknowledgements

I am grateful to many people for helping me and most have already been mentioned in my memoir. I could never have created all that I have without their support. There were some people not spoken about. First were the editors that helped me with my writing. There are too many to list, so I will not name them all here but I could not have completed my book without them. A special thank you goes out to three of them who were very helpful. One was my cousin, as well as an editor from First Editing and then the editor of Global Writing and Editing Services.

My cousin, Caroline Nolan's, supportive encouragement to tell my story was paramount. Before she got her hands on my manuscript I was still quite closed in ways to speak about the severe closed-head injury I had and the special needs that this type of injury entails. To have one more family member on my team, along with my aunt Gisele, as I shared what I went through was tremendously helpful.

David Ferris was another editor who helped me with multiple edits of the manuscript from his office in Berlin, Germany. He inspired me to open up more in my expressions and better articulate to readers the reality of my life experience that I was sharing with them. I found that as we worked together I felt more confident about my writing. As a result, my story was able to become even richer in depth, much like a piece of art.

Danielle Stoia, PhD was the final editor who was the most helpful of all. She showed me how to put the final touches on my story, to make it sparkle in my eyes. Because of this, I finally feel I can say that I love my story both in the written form and in memory. I have a great life now, challenges and all. What happened to me has the power now to help others.

The last person who I would like to thank that helped me was Jeff G. Saikaley, LL.B. from the Caza Saikaley law firm. His counsel was very important to me. He was only going to read parts of my story but he enjoyed reading it in full and generously even gave some of his time, without charge, as a contribution to my goal to help raise money for others.

Therefore, I will be forever grateful to all of the people who supported and inspired me on this journey, each in their own unique ways, which enabled *The Beauty of My Shadow* to come to life.

Purchase *Songs for Everyone*

www.anaid.org

S tylishly arranged and performed on a beautiful Steinway Grand piano by Mark Ferguson are songs and parts of songs that set the tone for slowing down the pace of life. Enjoy listening to music that was originally performed by many popular singers and musicians throughout music's history. Some of these performers are Coldplay, Lionel Richie, Leona Lewis, The Police, Bryan Adams, Erik Satie, Usher, Mariah Carey, Nickelback, John Lennon, Avril Lavigne, Bob Dylan, Celine Dion, Bob Marley, Elton John, Nelly Furtado, Led Zeppelin, U2, Rhianna, Bette Midler, Madonna, Nat King Cole, Louis Armstrong and The Rolling Stones, plus more. Hopefully everyone from young to old will find a song they like with over 70 minutes of music!

1. 42
2. A New Door
3. Ballerina Girl
4. Bleeding Love
5. Brahm's Lullaby
6. Bridge Over Troubled Water
7. Chariots of Fire
8. Do You Know Where You're Going To
9. Drops of Jupiter
10. Every Breath You Take
11. (Everything I Do) I Do it For You
12. Frère Jacques
13. Für Alina
14. Gymnopédie No. 1
15. Here I Stand
16. Here Without You
17. Hero
18. If Everyone Cared
19. Imagine
20. Innocence
21. Into the West
22. Knockin' on Heavens Door
23. Look Around
24. Love Me Tender
25. My Heart Will Go On
26. Nobody Knows
27. Path of Beauty
28. Redemption Song

29. Rocket Man (I Think it's Gonna Be a Long Long Time)
30. Sailing
31. Say it Right
32. Stairway to Heaven
33. Stuck in a Moment You Can't Get Out Of
34. Superman (It's Not Easy)
35. Take a Bow
36. The Rose
37. This Used to Be My Playground
38. Try a Little Tenderness
39. Twinkle Twinkle Little Star
40. Unforgettable
41. What a Wonderful World
42. When You Wish Upon a Star
43. Wild Horses

Proceeds received from the sale of *Songs for Everyone* will be given back to communities based on the objectives of An Aid to Help Foundation's mission to provide encouragement and resources to educators, students, parents and families on ways to learn or teach others to make responsible choices in life.

You may listen to samples and purchase a copy of the CD at www.anaid.org. The CD will be available as well in mp3 format and links to where it can be purchased are on the website. Or you may also purchase a copy of the CD by Mail. Send a cheque or money order of $20 in Canadian or US dollars to the address below. Please make cheques payable to An Aid to Help Foundation. Do not send cash or gifts. Thank you for your support.

An Aid to Help Foundation
5-499 Terry Fox Drive
P.O. Box 91017
Kanata, Ontario
K2T 1H7 CANADA
info@anaid.org

Notes

Please go to http://www.anaid.org/notes
and click on active links for this page.

[1] *Songs for Everyone*, performed by Mark Ferguson, http://www.anaid.org/listen-buy-now/

[2] Picture of Samantha Doris' Recovery Book, http://www.anaid.org/notes

[3] Picture of Mya, http://www.anaid.org/notes

[4] Picture of Samantha Doris' backyard, http://www.anaid.org/notes

[5] Mya on Facebook, http://www.facebook.com/mya.happy.michael

[6] Picture of Samantha Doris when she was a young girl, http://www.anaid.org/notes

[7] Picture of Samantha Doris' scar on her right cheek, http://www.anaid.org/notes

[8] Video of Samantha Doris dancing waltz, http://www.anaid.org/waltzVideo.html

[9] Picture from Gisele's medical notes, http://www.anaid.org/notes

[10] Samantha Doris' graduation picture, http://www.anaid.org/notes

[11] Picture of Princess Diana at rehab hospital in 1991, http://www.anaid.org/notes

[12] Picture of Princess Diana and Samantha Doris, http://www.anaid.org/notes

[13] Shakespeare, *Hamlet*, act 1, sc. 2. O, that this too too solid flesh would melt.

[14] Picture of Samantha Doris' parents country road, http://www.anaid.org/notes

[15] Picture of Samantha Doris' parents bridge in winter, http://www.anaid.org/notes

[16] Pictures of Samantha Doris' Thought Book, http://www.anaid.org/notes

[17] Picture of tree with chimes in Samantha Doris' backyard, http://www.anaid.org/notes

[18] Picture of Samantha Doris' atrium window in the fall, http://www.anaid.org/notes

[19] Picture of Samantha Doris' atrium window in the winter, http://www.anaid.org/notes

[20] Picture of painting *Always Happy*, http://www.anaid.org/notes

[21] "About pinhole glasses", http://www.en.wikipedia.org/wiki/Pinhole_glasses

[22] Picture of Mya wearing pinhole glasses, http://www.anaid.org/notes

[23] Video of Mya watching the forest, http://www.anaid.org/myaVideo.html

[24] "Here Without You" by 3 Doors Down, www.youtube.com/watch?v=kPBzTxZQG5Q

[25] Memorial website for Tyler, http://www.tylermulcahy.com/

[26] Video from Princess Diana's funeral in 1997, www.youtube.com/watch?v=iu83WQdQ7-Y

[27] Pianist Mark Ferguson's website, www.markferguson.ca/

[28] Grand Piano in Almonte, www.almonteinconcert.com/

[29] "About Redemption Song", http://en.wikipedia.org/wiki/Redemption_Song, December 2012.

[30] Video of Samantha Doris dancing rumba, http://www.anaid.org/rumbaVideo.html

[31] Museum for Dr. Naismith, http://www.naismithmuseum.com/

[32] Emile Coué, *Self Mastery Through Conscious Autosuggestion* (New York: Malkan Publishing, 1912) http://archive.org/stream/selfmasterythro00amergoog#page/n4/mode/2up

[33] Picture of painting *Finding Inner Strength,* http://www.anaid.org/notes

[34] Music CD *Songs for Everyone,* http://www.anaid.org/listen-buy-now/

[35] Samples of *Songs for Everyone,* http://www.anaid.org/CDSongSamples.html

[36] Song "Träumerei" performed by Mark Ferguson, http://www.anaid.org/Traumerei.html

[37] Video of "November Rain", http://www.gunsnroses.com/media/videos/19832/27902

[38] CASEL Collaborative for Academic, Social and Emotional Learning, http://casel.org/why-it-matters/benefits-of-sel/, December 2012.

[39] Picture of sunlight on painting *Finding Inner Strength,* http://www.anaid.org/notes

40 Picture of painting *Finding Inner Strength* with no sunlight, http://www.anaid.org/notes

41 Another picture of sunlight on painting *Finding Inner Strength*, http://www.anaid.org/notes

42 Picture of painting *Fenêtres du Passe—Windows of the Past*, http://www.anaid.org/notes

43 Picture of painting *The Force of Destiny*, http://www.anaid.org/notes

44 La collection, *Roland Palmaerts* (St-Lambert, Quebec: multi Art, 2000)

45 Listen to a Chopin music piece, http://www.anaid.org/chopinMusic.html

46 Picture of Samantha Doris' parents bridge in summer, http://www.anaid.org/notes

47 Video of "Dance of the Blessed Spirits" from the Gluck opera *Orfeo ed Euridice*, www.youtube.com/watch?v=xTZgMQ7TVes

48 Alternative way to protect the skull, www.hovding.com/en/

49 Roots of Empathy Charity, www.rootsofempathy.org/

50 Bruce D. Perry and Maia Szalavitz, *Born for Love: Why Empathy is Essential—and Endangered* (United States: William Morrow an imprint of Harper Collins Publishing, 2010)

51 Picture of painting *the key is gratitude*, http://www.anaid.org/notes

52 Picture of painting *My Anger*, http://www.anaid.org/notes

53 News video, July 2011 at Calgary Airport, www.youtube.com/watch?v=MeAc1zE3hKk

54 Video of Samantha Doris dancing cha cha, http://www.anaid.org/chaChaVideo.html

55 Video of Samantha Doris dancing merengue, http://www.anaid.org/merengueVideo.html

56 Video of Samantha Doris dancing foxtrot, http://www.anaid.org/foxtrotVideo.html

57 Spencer Miller, *Man Without Boundaries*, Pdf Edition.

58 Video of NAC Orchestra performing on September 11th, 2011, www.ustream.tv/recorded/17206205

59 Paediatric Sports Medical Clinic of Ottawa, www.concussioncentre.com/home

60 Brain Injury Association of Canada, www.biac-aclc.ca/

61 *An Aid to Help Concentration*, http://www.anaid.org/concentration.html

62 Lumosity, www.lumosity.com/

63 Picture of Samantha Doris riding a tricycle, http://www.anaid.org/notes

64 Video of "What a Feeling" by Irene Cara, www.youtube.com/watch?v=ILWSp0m9G2U

65 Picture of puzzle with flying pigs, http://www.anaid.org/notes

66 Picture of painting of three birds, http://www.anaid.org/notes

67 Picture of poem *The 10th Floor*, http://www.anaid.org/notes

68 Books by Samantha Michael, http://www.anaid.org/books

About the Author

First-time author Samantha Michael was born in Ajax, Ontario. A bright, ambitious student on the verge of beginning university, her life was unexpectedly and permanently altered when in 1991, she suffered near-fatal injuries as the passenger in a single-car accident cause by a drunk driver.

That moment marked the beginning of a long and difficult recovery process starting with a month-long hospitalization. Despite the severe physical and emotional trauma she sustained, Samantha willed herself to push on and reconstruct her life—an experience that has inspired her to passionately pursue a range of activities, including Pilates, meditation, music therapy, art therapy, volunteerism, philanthropy and dance.

Today, Samantha serves on the board of the Ontario-based non-profit An Aid to Help Foundation, which she founded to help raise money for charitable causes in Canada and beyond. She has also assisted the National Arts Centre since 1999 as a volunteer. She lives with her beloved, ever-loyal canine companion Mya, in a home overlooking a vibrant forest, where the gentle sway of the wind chimes helps remind her of the beauty and tranquillity of life.